THE CHANGING FACE OF BRITAIN & ITS EMPIRE

PAUL TURNER

United Kingdom: Folens Publishers, Waterslade House, Thame Road, Haddenham, Buckinghamshire HP17 8NT.

Email: folens@folens.com

Ireland: Folens Publishers, Greenhills Road, Tallaght, Dublin 24.

Email: info@folens.ie

Editor: Dr Sarah Ryan

Page design and layout: Redmoor Design, Tavistock, Devon

Illustrations: Ian Heard, Nick Hawken

Cover design: Jump 2

Cover image: Jump 2

First published 2009 by Folens Limited.

British Library Cataloguing in Publication Data. A catalogue record for this publication is available from the British Library.

ISBN 978-1-85008-355-9

The Changing Face of Britain and its Empire

Contents

Time Terms

Week: 7 days.

Month: 28 days during February (or 29 days in a leap year). 30 or 31 days in the remaining months.

Year: 365 days, or 366 days in a leap year.

Decade: 10 years.

Century: 100 years.

Millennium: 1000 years.

Centuries

Time is an interesting concept. It is only because we have clocks that we can see it passing by. Many people find it difficult to remember dates and to understand some of the terms used when discussing time. If this is a good description of you, perhaps this page will help.

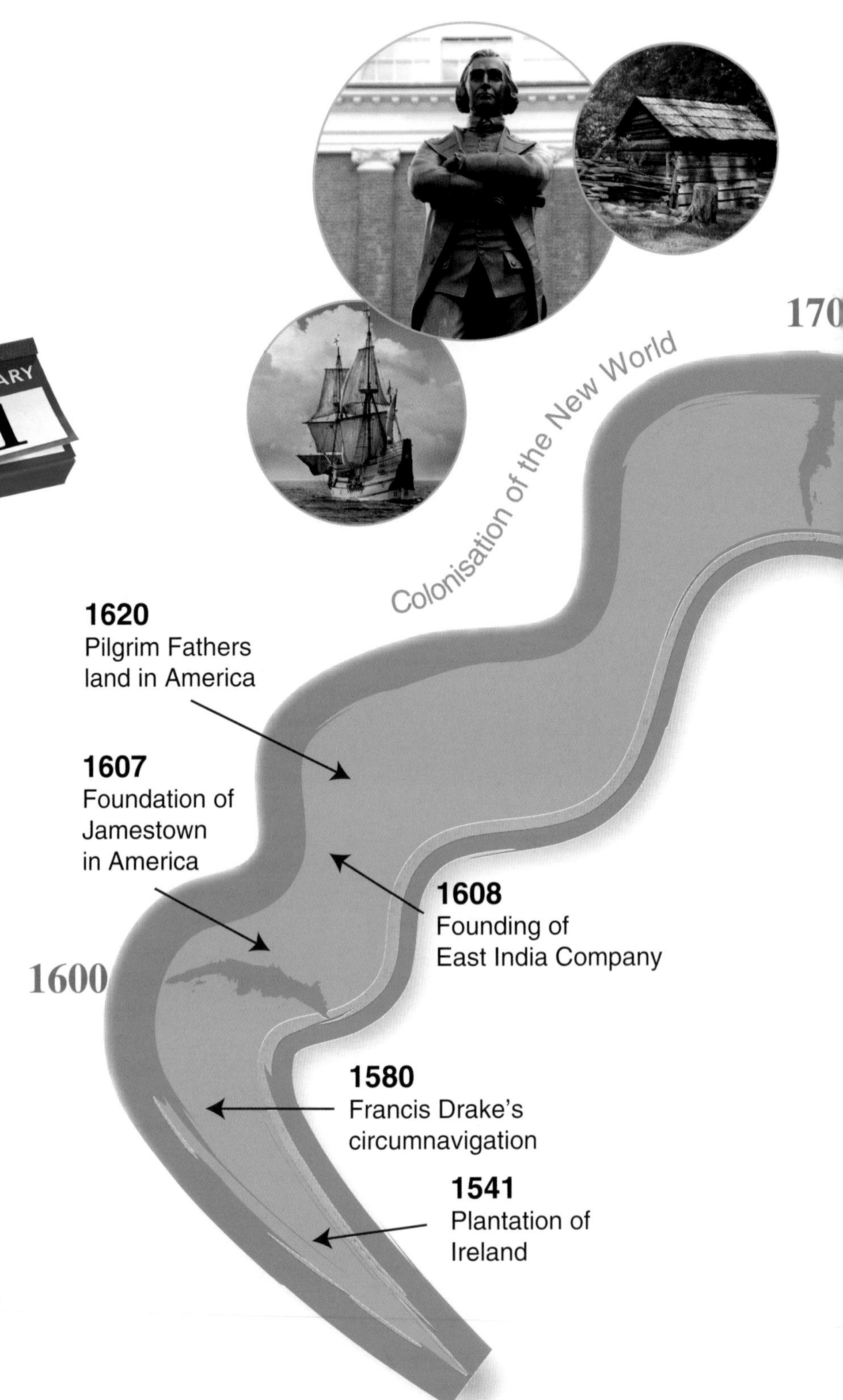

Chapter 1

Empires and empire building

Introduction

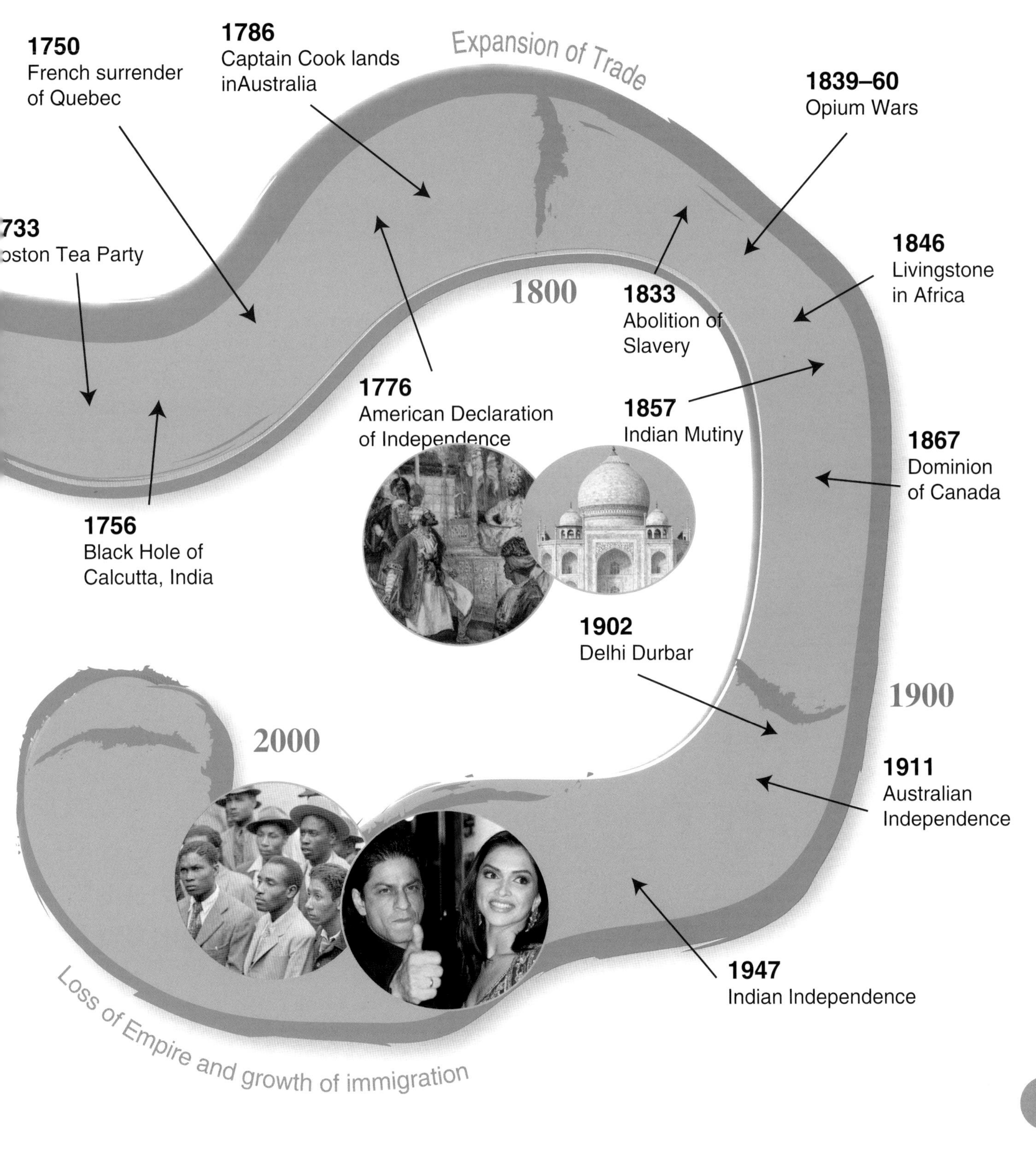

1.1 What is left of the British Empire?

This unit looks at what remains of the British Empire. You may be able to answer:

- What is an Empire?
- What remnants of the British Empire still impact on our lives today?

What do you know about the British Empire?

"This royal throne of Kings,
This sceptred isle,
This earth of majesty, this seat of Mars,
This other Eden, demi-paradise,
This fortress built by Nature for herself
Against infection and the hand of war,
This happy breed of men, this little world,
This precious stone set in the silver sea,
Which serves it in the office of a wall,
Or as a moat defensive to a house,
Against the envy of less happier lands."

William Shakespeare

This small 'happy' island, as described by Shakespeare, came to control a huge empire. The British Empire is a part of our British history that has in recent years been either 'glossed over' or seen by some as 'shameful'. This is because the British Empire has been widely criticised for many of its actions around the globe. In particular: the treatment of **indigenous** people who lived in the countries that were colonised, and the Empire's part in the worldwide slave trade.

However you will find out that the British Empire also had a positive impact in many ways as well, which will be explored later in this book. Some people have even wondered if this period of British history is worth celebrating or not, and whether it should be taught in schools at all. Think of your own views on this question as you study the topics in this book.

What makes telling the tale of the British Empire so appealing is that there is so much interesting information available: each stage of the colonisation of individual nations around the world is so different. The subject matter is wide and varied, and contains information gathered from a number of groups and perspectives.

This book may help you make up your own mind, or at least give you the opportunity to judge the information provided on its own merits and to decide whether you would be proud or ashamed of the British Empire.

Areas marked in red show the extent of the British Empire at its height.

Are we still aware of the British Empire in our lives today?

Even though the British Empire no longer exists, it still has an indirect impact on all our lives today. The next few pages show some examples of how you may have made reference to, or thought about, the Empire without even knowing it.

Land of Hope and Glory

You may have sung or heard a patriotic song that makes reference to the British Empire. One of the most famous is 'Land of Hope and Glory'.

'Land of Hope and Glory' is enthusiastically sung every year on the final evening of a series of concerts called The Proms, held in London. 'The Last Night of the Proms' is quite a famous event and the singing of this song is thought by many people to be extremely patriotic, and very British. Strangely, however, this was never supposed to be the case; the words were not originally written to accompany the music, but were added by a man called A.C Benson to accompany the separate music by Edward Elgar called 'Pomp and Circumstance March No 1'. In fact Elgar was not too happy that the words had been added at all!

Source A

Some of the words to 'Land of Hope and Glory'

"Land of Hope and Glory, Mother of the Free,
How shall we extol thee, who are born of thee;
Wider still and wider shall thy bounds be set;
God who made thee mighty; make thee mightier yet."

Flag-waving and patriotism? 'The Last Night of the Proms'.

The words added by Benson praised Britain as a free nation which was constantly expanding its boundaries and its power. As 'Land of Hope and Glory' states, the British Empire truly was mighty and had expanded its influence on the nations of the world tremendously. Such a small nation had managed to multiply its potential power through expansion, colonisation and trade. So is 'Land of Hope and Glory' a fitting title for Britain? What do you think?

Britannia on our coins

Look at a selection of 50p pieces, and you may see a symbol that has been associated with Britain for nearly 2000 years – the figure of 'Britannia'. The name Britain comes from the Roman name for our island nation – Britanniae – and the figure of Britannia, first seen on Roman coins, has long been a symbol of Britain.

Lately, however, it has been the subject of controversy. Some people see her as being representative of the might and **oppression** of the British Empire and therefore the oppression of other nations and cultures. Modern politicians have even gone as far as to suggest that the figure of Britannia should have no place on our national coinage because of the controversial history of the Empire. Again, what do you think?

The Commonwealth Games

The remnants of what was the British Empire now exist in the 'Commonwealth'. Most of you will have heard of this through the 'Commonwealth Games'. Although the countries that take part are governed independently, a part of their history which is to the British Empire and the British Commonwealth.

Source B

Members of the Commonwealth

Anguilla
Antigua & Barbuda
Australia
The Bahamas
Bangladesh
Barbados
Belize
Botswana
Brunei
Cameroon
Canada
Cyprus
Dominica
Fiji (suspended)
The Gambia
Ghana
Grenada
Guyana
India
Jamaica
Kenya
Kiribati
Lesotho
Malawi
Malaysia
Maldives
Malta
Mauritius
Mozambique
Namibia
Nauru
New Zealand
Nigeria
Pakistan
Papua New Guinea
Seychelles
Samoa
Sierra Leone
Singapore
Solomon Islands
South Africa
Sri Lanka
St Kitts & Nevis
St Lucia
St Vincent
Swaziland
Tanzania
Tonga
Trinidad
Tuvalu
Uganda
United Kingdom
Vanuatu
Zambia

To do task 2

Create it!

Design a poster including the Britannia symbol, that celebrates Britain and the Commonwealth. What information do you think the poster should include?

Countries that drive on the left-hand side of the road

In Britain we drive on the left-hand side of the road. Why this is the case is not really important to the book, but why other nations also drive on the left is, because it shows a link to the British Empire. This link is usually through colonisation. Therefore some of the laws that were imposed upon Britain have also been imposed upon these countries, such as which side of the road people drive on.

Source C

A list of countries that drive on the left-hand side of the road, as in Britain.

Australia
Bahamas
Bangladesh
Barbados
Bermuda
Bhutan
Bophuthatswana
Botswana
British Virgin Islands
Brunei
Cayman Islands
Channel Islands
Ciskei
Cyprus
Dominica
Falkland Islands
Fiji
Grenada
Guyana
Hong Kong
India
Indonesia
Ireland
Jamaica
Japan
Kenya
Lesotho
Macau
Malawi
Malaysia
Malta
Mauritius
Montserrat
Mozambique
Namibia
Nepal
New Zealand
Pakistan
Papua New Guinea
St. Vincent & Grenadines
Seychelles
Sikkim
Singapore
Solomon Islands
Somalia
South Africa
Sri Lanka
St Kitts & Nevis
St. Helena
St. Lucia
Surinam
Swaziland
Tanzania
Thailand
Tonga
Trinidad & Tobago
Uganda
United Kingdom
US Virgin Islands
Venda
Zambia
Zimbabwe

The English language abroad

More than a billion people worldwide speak English. Many of these nations have a link to the British Empire. Such was the size and influence of the Empire that English was imposed on many cultures and also became the language of trade, industry and commerce. Despite the decline of the geographical Empire, the growth of the English language continues. Current predictions are that by the middle of the 21st century almost one third of the global population will be speaking English. Although European languages are growing in popularity, English maintains the prime spot among them all. This is a clear byproduct of British Imperialism because you wouldn't usually expect the language of such a small island to be spoken in so many places across the globe.

To do task 3

Conclusions

1. Read Source A on page 7. What do the words of 'Land of Hope and Glory' suggest about Britain? What does the song tell you?
2. write four bullet points to summarise the impact of the British Empire on the world today.

British overseas territories

Some aspects of the Empire still linger, such as a few countries called the 'British Overseas Territories'. These are places that are often far away from Britain, but are technically still part of Britain.

You may have visited some of them.

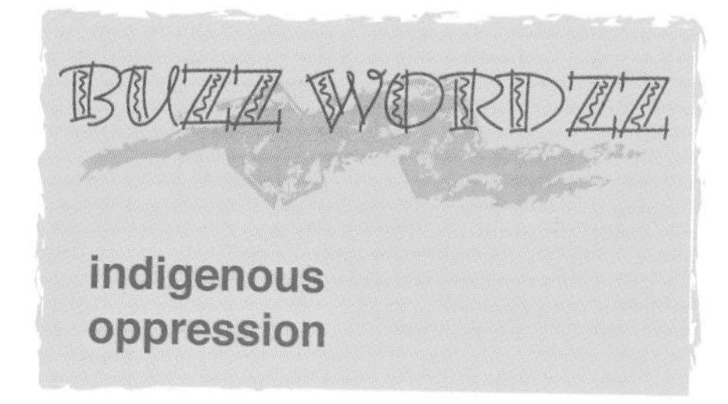

Source D

Countries that make up the British Overseas Territories

Anguilla, Bermuda, British Antarctic Territory, British Indian Ocean Territory, British Virgin Islands, Cayman Islands, Falkland Islands, Gibraltar, Montserrat, Pitcairn Islands, St Helena and Dependencies, South Georgia and the South Sandwich Islands, the Sovereign Base Areas of Akrotiri and Dhekelia in Cyprus, and the Turks and Caicos Islands.

1.2 Famous world empires

Now that you know a bit more about the British Empire, it's time to learn about some other empires that existed. Do you know:

- What other empires have existed before, or alongside the British Empire?
- Were they as powerful, or more powerful than the British Empire?

Building an empire

The process of empire building, no matter what country is involved in it, is known as 'Imperialism'. There are a number of different definitions of what it means to be imperialistic.

Source A

A dictionary definition of imperialism

"The practice of one country extending its control over the territory, political system, or economic life of another country."

This definition describes the nature of a quest for Empire quite clearly and highlights the characteristics of the British Empire and its constant search for territory and trade. However, it was not only Britain that followed imperialism to gain control over a vast empire, and to impose its character upon it.

To do task 1

Comprehension

1. What is an Empire – in your own words
2. Which empire rivalled Britain's?
3. Can you name any other countries with large empires?

Great empires in history

Many empires have left behind a powerful and lasting legacy. Listed below are just a few of them:

Egyptian

Greek

Chinese

Roman

British

Spanish

French

Images from great empires throughout history: which empires can you identify?

Let's look at one from the list…

Perhaps even more famous than the British Empire was the Roman Empire. Although the Romans are not the focus of this book, it's probable that you will have heard of the Roman Empire. You may even know more about it than you know about the British Empire.

Throughout history many rulers have dreamed of an empire as large and successful as the Roman Empire. None have ever achieved it. As with the British Empire, slavery was a vital part of the Roman Empire and its conquest of nations. Also similarly again, the Romans imposed their culture on the nations that were gathered up along the way, and it oppressed the native people who lived there.

Unlike the Romans, the British Empire never controlled its territories very successfully from home. Although Britain controlled large areas of land by using its armies and navy, it was simply not on the same successful scale as the Roman model. The actual geographical areas may appear larger, but the success in controlling that area and over a long period of time, was less.

A modern re-enactment of a Roman soldier

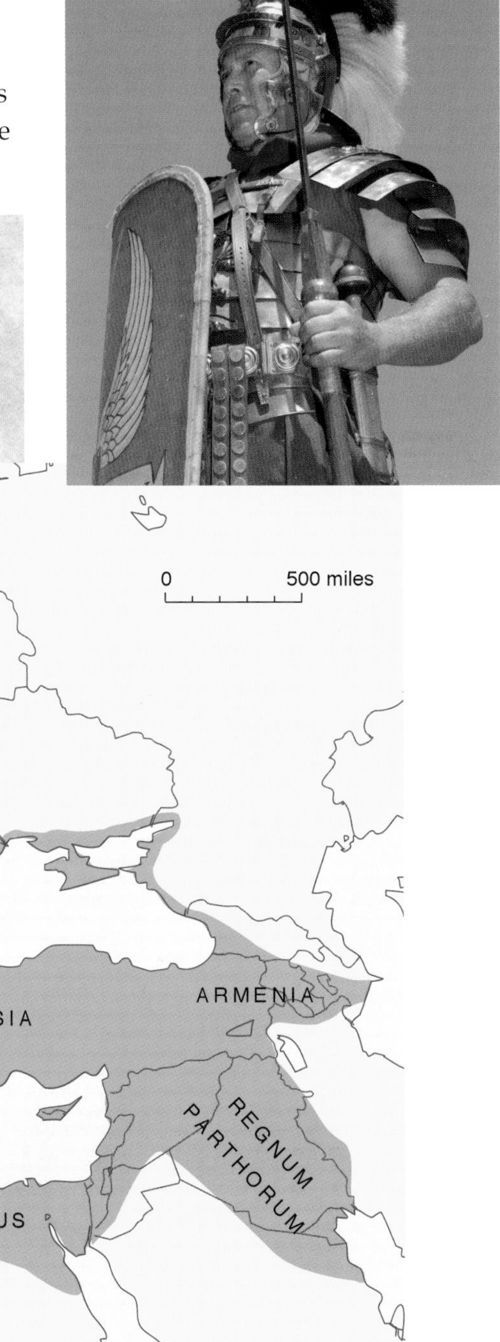

Source B Extent of territories successfully controlled at the height of the Roman Empire

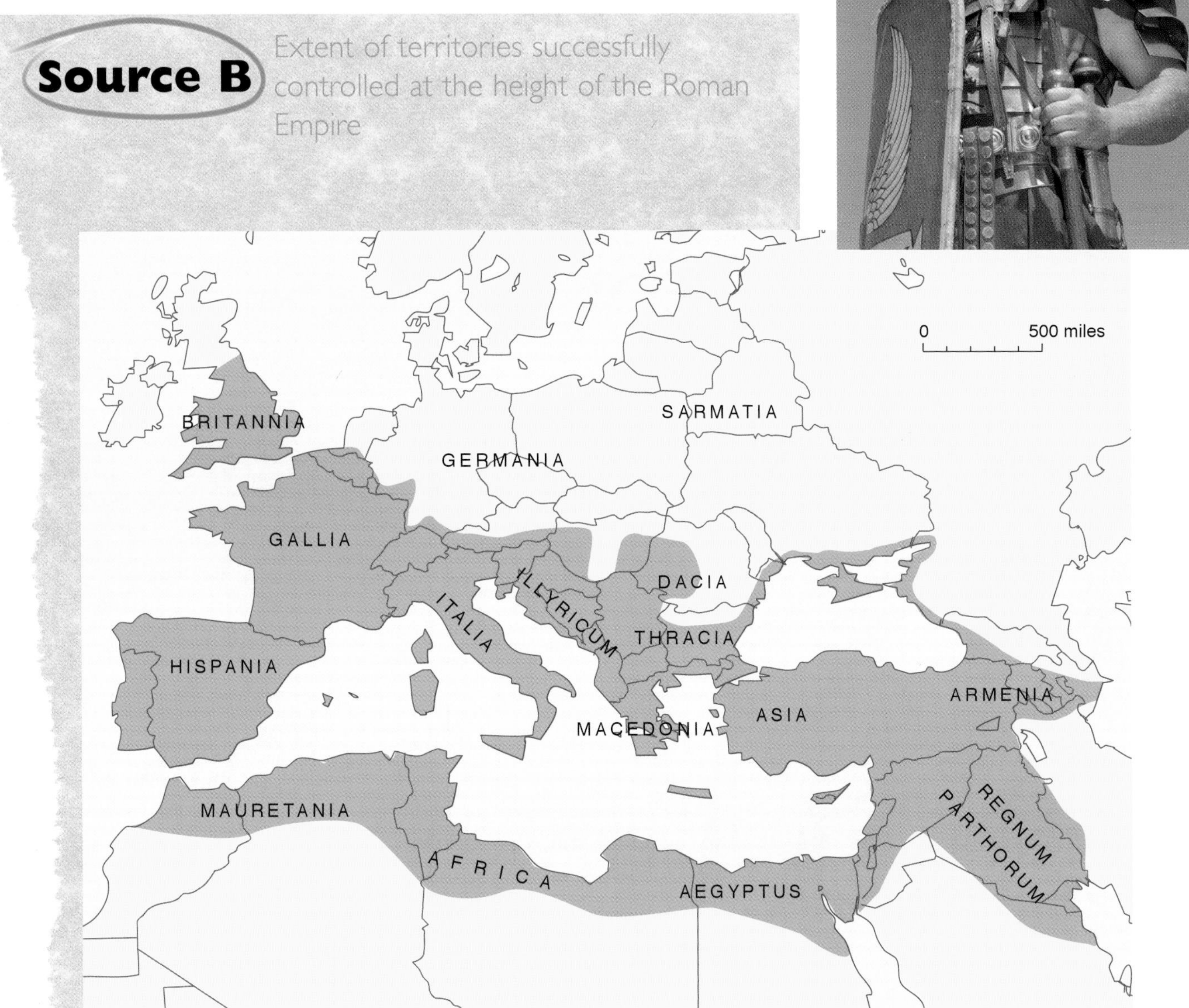

To do task 2

Study it!

Study sources B and C carefully.

1. How different/similar were the two empires?
2. What common features are there?
3. How do you explain the differences?

NB

In the pink!

Many maps of the British Empire look as if they are printed with the Empire coloured pink!

Actually this was not the case, it is because of the pigments used in old printing ink.

This mosaic was found in the ruins of a Roman villa, and is a useful source for historians studying the Roman Empire.

Source C

Land areas controlled by Britain at the height of its empire

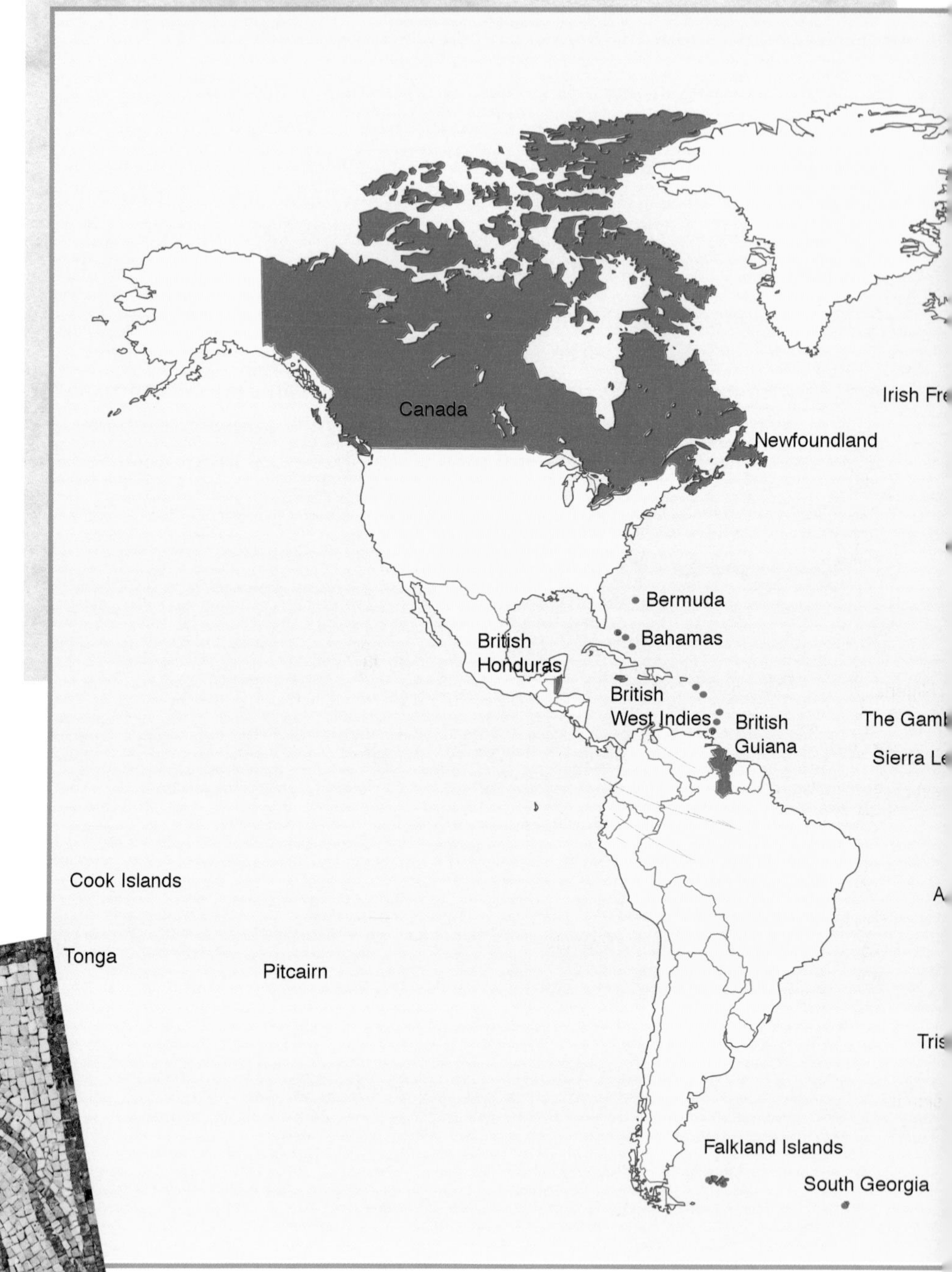

If the Romans had been able to get to the regions that were colonised by the British, how long do you think it would have taken them to overcome nations like Australia and America? After all, they had little or no problem at all overcoming Britain and other nations who had powerful armies. However, they did not have much success with Scotland and Ireland: why do you think this was the case?

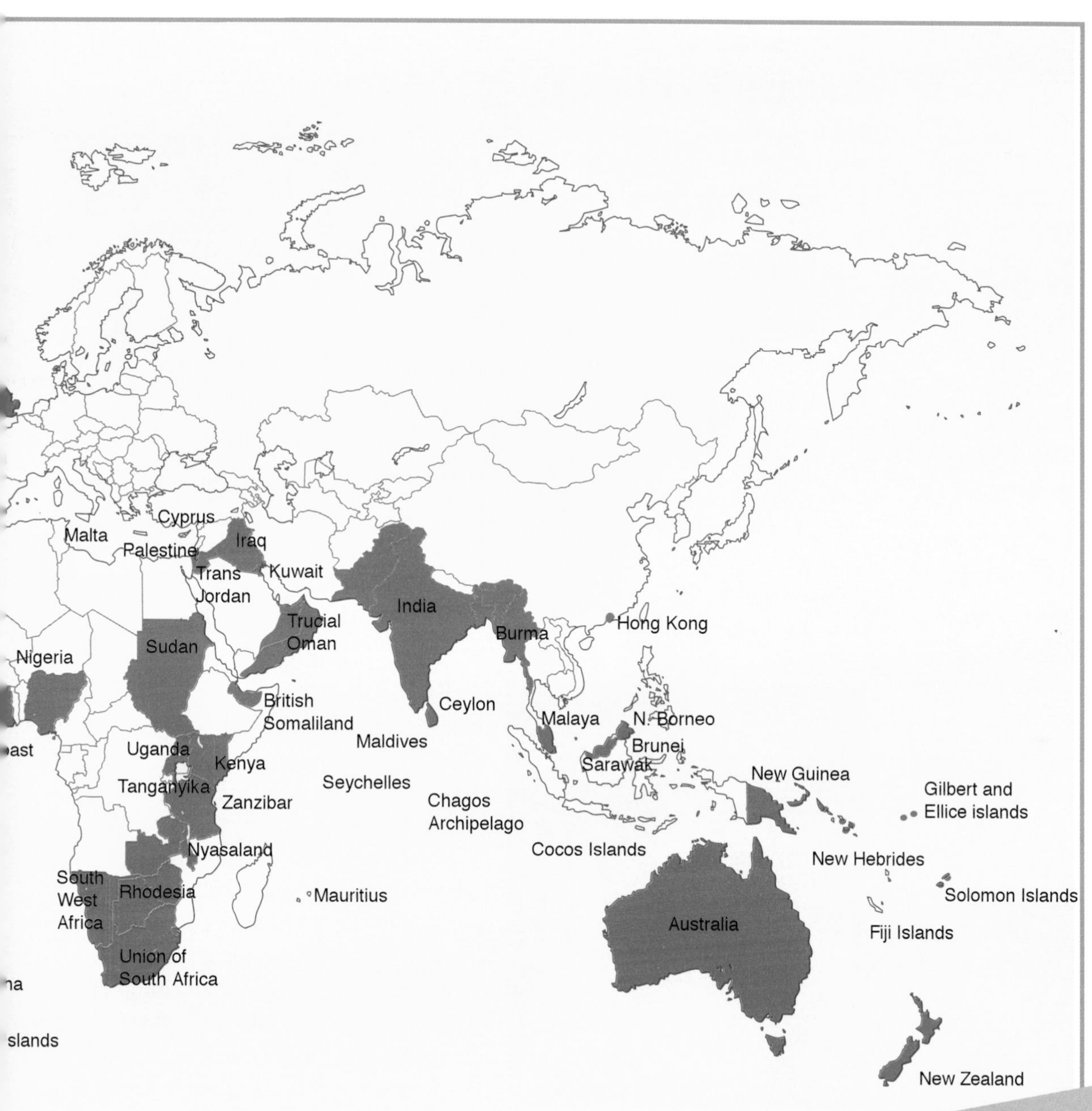

Discussion POINT

Choose one aspect of the Roman Empire and research it in detail.
For instance: What were the countries that the Romans conquered like? What was life like in the Empire?

These are the ruins of a Roman amphitheatre, showing the passages and rooms below floor level.

1.3 Early explorers: The founders of empire?

The increased knowledge of the world and the colonisation of new areas have as much to do with the individual efforts of brave explorers as to the power of huge empires. This topic details how:

- Many nations followed imperialism, sending out expeditions to the four corners of the earth.
- Individual explorers charted, discovered and also often plundered the areas that they had found.
- Individual efforts showed the way for colonial expansion later on.

To do task 1

Comprehension

1. Do you know what Sir Francis Drake is most famous for?
2. Where was John Cabot born?
3. What star did sailors navigate by?

What do you know about the British Empire?

British explorers

Many of you will have heard of some of the famous British explorers mentioned here, but you may not have heard of them all.

Sir Francis Drake

Possibly the most famous of all English sailors and explorers is Sir Francis Drake. By the time Elizabeth I was Queen in 1558, Drake was well known for his attacks on Spanish treasure ships. He gained enormous wealth from robbing the ships of their gold, as well as giving much of the treasure to Elizabeth herself. One of his greatest achievements was sailing around the world between 1577 and 1580 in his ship the 'Golden Hind'.

John Cabot

John Cabot was actually called Giovanni Caboto and was born in Italy in 1450. However he spent much of his life in England and it was for this nation, not his native Italy, that he did his exploring. Cabot set out to discover a route to Asia on his ship the 'Matthew' and in so doing he is credited with actually finding and exploring the coastline of North America and Newfoundland. His fate is wrapped in mystery as he disappeared on his last voyage in 1498.

Sir Humphrey Gilbert

Sir Humphrey Gilbert (1539-1583) is the half-brother of the famous explorer Sir Walter Raleigh. He is well known for his search for a 'northwest passage' to the Orient (Asia) and for claiming part of Newfoundland – St John's – for England. He also founded an English colony in Ireland, called Munster.

Other British explorers like John Davis, Sir Hugh Willoughby, Richard Chancellor, Sir Martin Frobisher and Sir John Hawkins also made an impact.

Famous European explorers

The awareness that we have of our world today is also down to men from other nations. Men like Jacques Cartier, Samuel de Champlain, Christopher Columbus, Sebastian Cabot, Ferdinand Magellan, Marco Polo, Hernando Cortes, Bartholomeu Dias and Vasco de Gama, as well as many more, had a major impact on the discovery, exploration and settlement of the modern world. You may not have heard of all these explorers but they were just as important as the major British names.

The tools of exploration

These explorers were all brave, but they weren't stupid – they set out with aids to navigation that allowed them to know where they were going and how to get back to where they had come from. All the explorers named on these pages needed relatively sophisticated devices to help them navigate around the globe.

Navigating by the stars

Without modern day GPS, a compass or detailed charts, sailors navigating from place to place relied on the stars to indicate both location and direction. The most important star for navigation is the Pole Star – 'Polaris'. The position of the Pole Star in relation to the horizon will allow the trained eye to calculate the approximate location of the vessel.

Using a sextant

Two mirrors are positioned on the sextant to allow you to measure the angle between a star, a planet or the sun, and the horizon. Look through the eye piece at the heavenly body in question and adjust the arm, so that it appears to touch the horizon. This will allow you to read the angle on the scale at the base. This also has to be done at an exact time as the time factors into the complex series of calculations that allow you to determine where to draw a line on your map or chart.

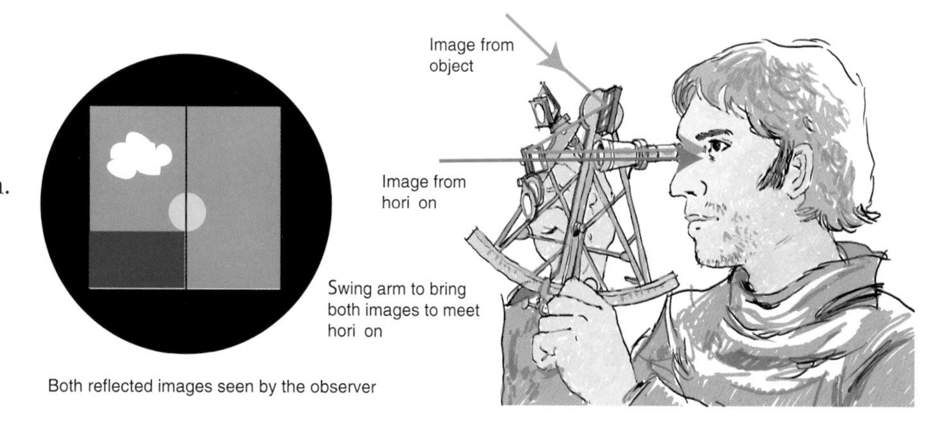

Both reflected images seen by the observer

Source A

From the website www.thesurvivalexpert.com

"Remember that the sun always rises in the east and sets in the west. When it reaches its highest point at noon, its direction will be true south in the northern hemisphere. The North Star determines a northerly direction in the northern hemisphere and although it's not the brightest star, it's important because unlike the rest of the stars in the night sky, its position remains fixed so if you follow it, you know that you are heading north."

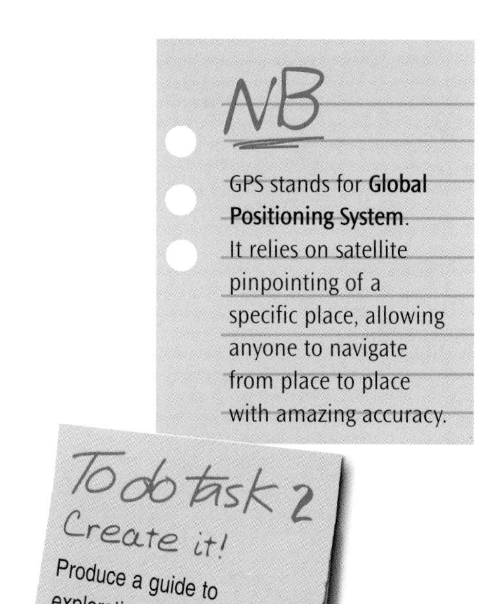

Cartography

As map-making – cartography – improved, so did the accuracy of navigation. Without detailed, accurate maps it is very difficult to plot direction or location. Explorers had a real need for quality maps. The more that the globe was explored the easier it became to create accurate maps. However, because the maps were for use only at sea, only the coastlines and little else were charted initially. The interiors of the countries were not charted very well at all.

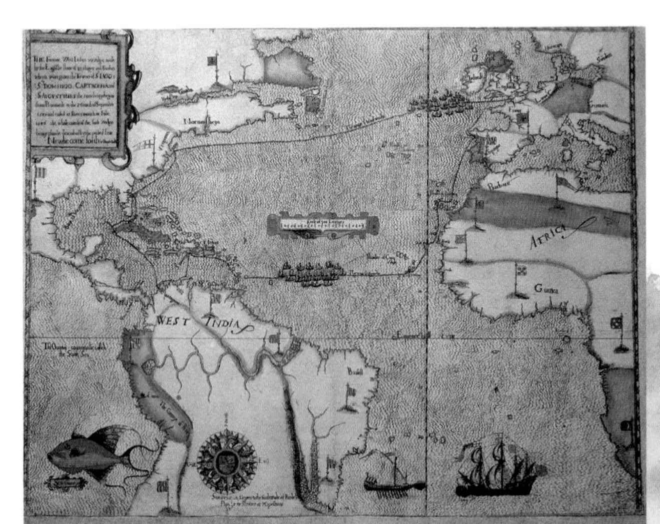

Early maps did not give a totally accurate representation of the shape of a country, and as you can see here the interior of countries were largely uncharted. This is a map showing Drake's voyage to the West Indies

English galleon of the early 16th century with a 'lateen' sail at the back, helping to keep the ship sailing into the wind.

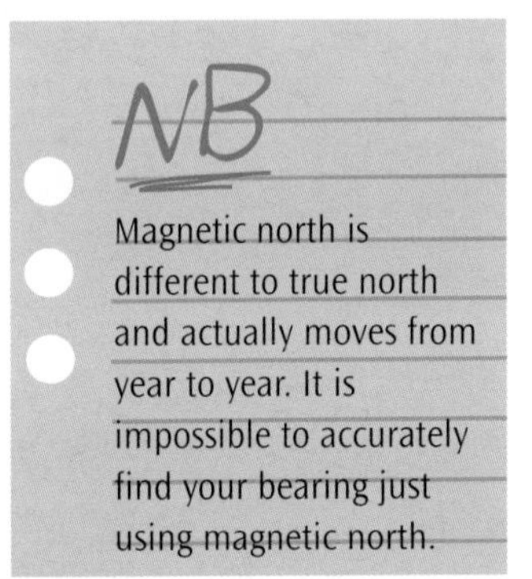

NB

Magnetic north is different to true north and actually moves from year to year. It is impossible to accurately find your bearing just using magnetic north.

Ship design

Travelling long distances requires a good boat and advances in boat design made this a reality. The old, cumbersome ships with square-rigged sails were no good for travelling long distances quickly, especially if the prevailing wind would not fill their large sails. By reducing the size of the ships, especially the height of the sides, and exchanging the square sails for triangular ones, ship design advanced tremendously in a relatively short time period. They could move faster and over longer distances.

Compasses and magnetic compasses

The ability to plot direction was improved by the introduction of the compass and the magnetic compass, which would enable the sailors to proceed in the correct direction without having to use the stars.

Initially, when using magnetic compasses, sailors failed to understand that magnetic north is different from genuine north. The result was they sometimes got lost because they were deceived by the variations shown in magnetic north depending on where the boat was at that time. The compass also allowed them to plot their direction and route against the more accurate maps.

The astrolabe

Source B

From the BBC website www.bbc.co.uk

"An astrolabe is both an observing tool – it has a moveable rule at the back with sights that you can use to find the height of stars, the Sun or even a building above the horizon – and a calculating tool. At its simplest it can be used to calculate the time from the height of the Sun or a star, and to find their rising and setting times."

To do task 3

Evaluation

You have been asked to review the piece of maritime technology or invention that had the greatest impact on marine navigation. Choose one and explain your choice in no more than 150 words

The cross-staff

Source C

From The Science Museum website www.sciencemuseum.org.uk

"The cross-staff was used at sea from the beginning of the 16th century until the first half of the 18th century. It was used to measure the sun's altitude, especially at the meridian passage. With the knowledge of the sun's declination, the mariner could then obtain his latitude."

NB

Altitude – a measure of distance vertically.

Meridian Passage – the movement of the sun along an imaginary curve that connects the North pole to the South Pole.

The telescope

As a navigational tool the telescope has little use, but for observing far off land masses it is vital, even if it just prevents the boat from sailing past its destination. It is believed that it was first invented in 1608 by the Dutch, with many variations on the design making an appearance over the following centuries.

Many more devices and instruments helped the early explorers to reach their destinations. Those that are mentioned in this book are just examples. Without all of them however, the ability to find and reach far-flung destinations would have been severely reduced.

An early telescope from the time of exploration.

1.4 The European Empires

In the 15th and 16th centuries, most major European nations sought expansion of their individual empires.

Take time to think about:

- Why did they do this?
- How might this expansion have affected the British Empire?

Empire building in Europe

The Dutch Empire

The Dutch favoured expansion across the North Atlantic and later by charting a route to the 'East', taking a route that became known as the north-westerly passage. Their empire covered land in India, South Africa (around Cape Town), America (around New Amsterdam which is now New York), South America and the Caribbean (around Guyana.)

The Spanish and Portugese Empires

The Spanish Empire was truly mighty. It was even described as 'el imperio en el que nunca se pone el sol' by King Charles I of Spain. Translated this means the 'Empire on which the sun never sets', although this phrase has become linked to the British Empire as well.

The Spanish had actually claimed the 'New World'– the Americas – for themselves, but under the Treaty of Tordesillas in 1494 they divided it with Portugal. Spain would have control of the uncharted land in the west, and Portugal control of the uncharted land in the east.

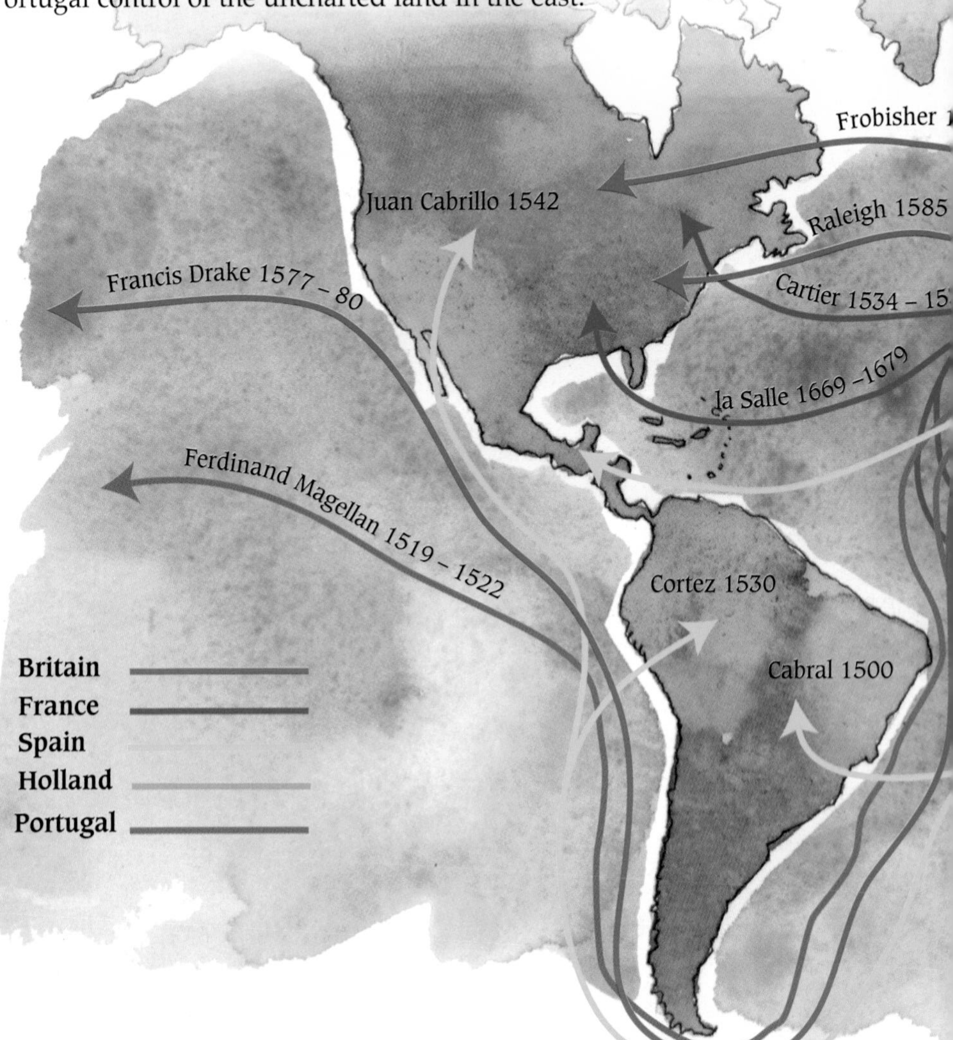

Source A

Empire – How Britain made the modern world

Niall Ferguson

"Christopher Columbus had laid the foundations of Spain's American empire. That empire was the envy of the world, stretching as it did from Madrid to Manila and encompassing Peru and Mexico, the wealthiest and most populous territories on the American continent. Even more extensive and no less profitable was Portugal's empire, which spread outwards from the Atlantic islands of Madeira and Sao Tome to include the vast territory of Brazil and numerous trading outposts in West Africa, Indonesia, India and even China.'

Spanish explorers attempted to navigate their way to the 'East' by sailing in westerly and south-westerly directions. Their Empire took in places such as Hispaniola, Cuba, Puerto Rico, Central America, Mexico and Peru amongst others.

After the Treaty of Tordesillas, the Portuguese were able to sail to the 'East' in an easterly and south-easterly direction in their own attempt to find a trade route to the 'East'. The Portugese explored Africa, the Mediterranean, India, the East Indies and China.

The French Empire

The French Empire was a serious rival to the British Empire, particularly in North America with land around the St Lawrence River. This area was initially called 'New France'. They also colonised land around the Hudson Bay area in America as well as Newfoundland, India, the Caribbean and Africa.

Rivalry

You may have noticed that the European nations had similar ideas about what areas it would be profitable to colonise. This led to fierce competition over the rights to certain areas of land and trading rights within those lands. Whatever nation came out as victorious would only do so if they could overcome all the other Empires AND indigenous peoples in each new territory.

Britain, of course, was also involved in this power struggle.

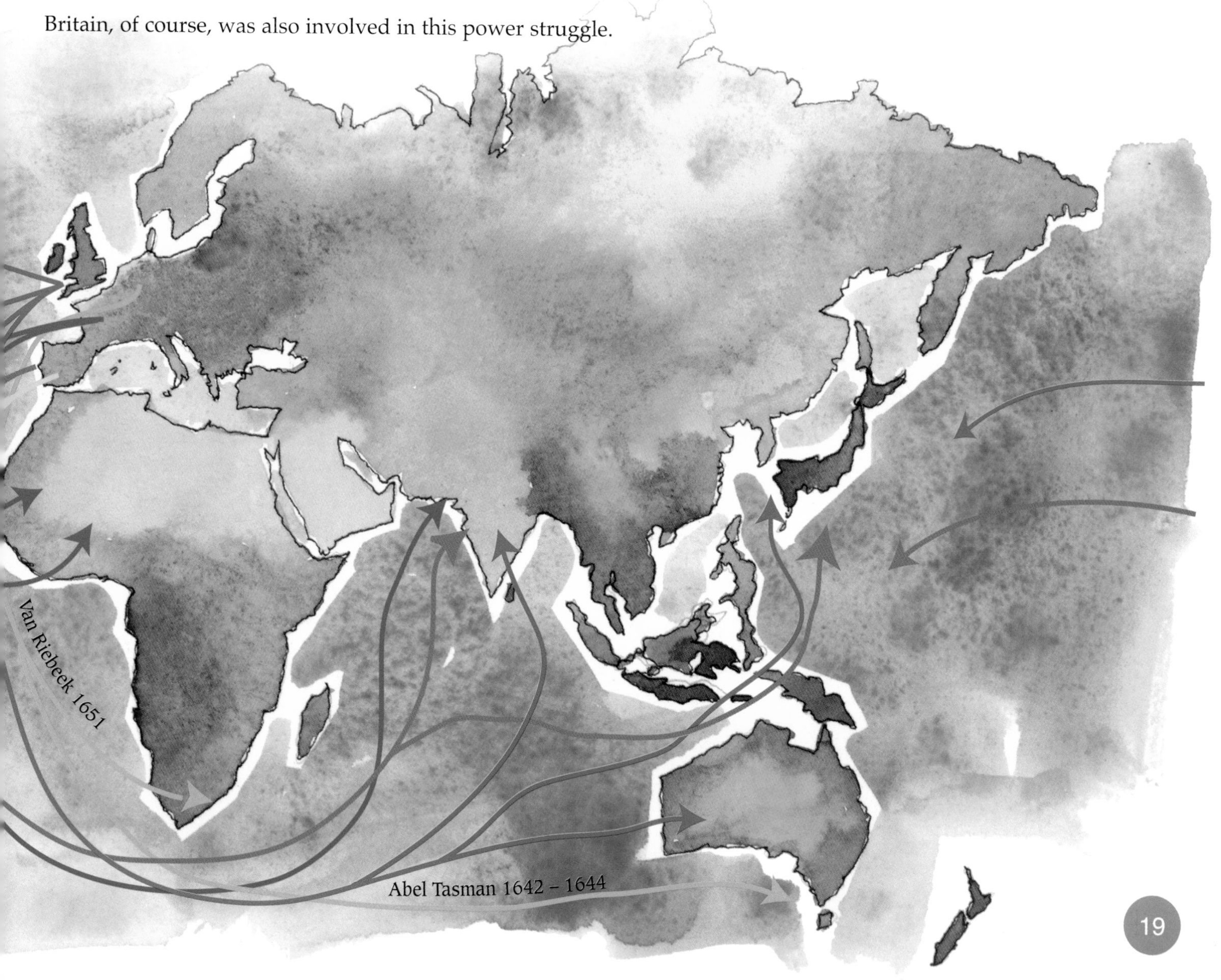

Chapter 2
An overview of the Empire

2.1 Showcasing the Empire

The British Empire was so large that people at home in Britain could not easily imagine how big it was. What do you know about:

- how people came to appreciate the size of the Empire through displays of its goods, produce and treasures?
- the Great Exhibition?

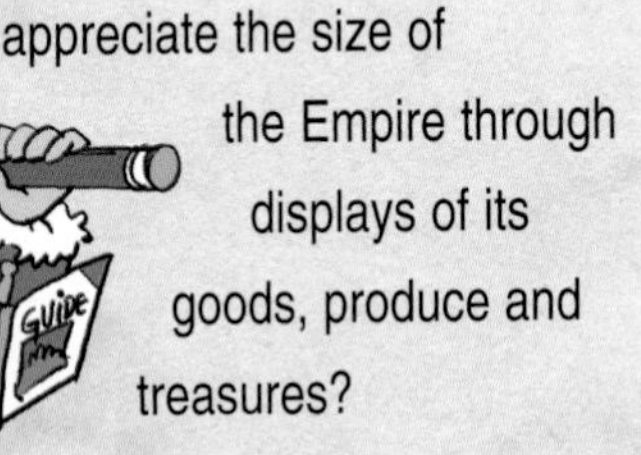

The Great Exhibition

The Great Exhibition was a display of everything there was to celebrate about the British Empire. It was opened by Queen Victoria on May 1st 1851. The exhibition near London was housed in a fantastic glass building, called The Crystal Palace, that had been built especially for the occasion. The building itself was huge, covering an impressive 19 acres and containing a massive 294,000 glass panes. Over half a million people saw the Queen open the exhibition and during the six months it was open, approximately six million people visited it. Queen Victoria herself visited many times, coming through the doors every two days on average. At the centre of the exhibition was the fabulous 'Koh-i-noor' diamond.

Source A

From www.historic-uk.com

The History and Heritage Accommodation Guide

"The exhibits included almost every marvel of the Victorian age, including pottery, porcelain, ironwork, furniture, perfumes, pianos, firearms, fabrics, steam hammers, hydraulic presses and even the odd house or two.

Although the original aim of the world fair had been as a celebration of art in industry for the benefit of All Nations, in practice it appears to have been turned into more of a showcase for British manufacturing: more than half the 100,000 exhibits on display were from Britain or the British Empire."

Source B From the National Archives website

www.nationalarchives.gov.uk

"The idea of a Great Exhibition in London was promoted by Prince Albert, Queen Victoria's husband. The main aim was to showcase British goods and skills. Albert was also keen to have contributions from around the world. He got his wish. When the Exhibition opened on 1 May 1851, over 100,000 items were on display. There were tapestries from Persia, furniture from Belgium, machinery from America, cloth from Russia and glassware from Germany, plus British industrial goods and works of art."

NB

The Elgin Marbles
Also known as the Parthenon Marbles, these are a group of famous Greek marble sculptures, controversially removed from Athens between 1801 and 1812 and brought to Britain.

The very fact that the Great Exhibition could display so many exhibits was itself an indication of the success of the British Empire. Without such control over so many far-flung places, the Great Exhibition would have had far less to call on for its displays.

The British Museum

One of Britain's national treasures, the British Museum, is full of artefacts and historical pieces from both Britain and around the world. Many of these came through the British Empire's desire for expansion. Even the Crown Jewels that are safely housed in the Tower of London contain rare, valuable reminders of the economic and monetary value of the Empire, such as the Koh-i-Noor diamond that originally came from India.

The main entrance to the British Museum.

One of the most generous donators of artefacts such as these was Sir Hans Sloane, who donated many items from classical civilisations. Famous – and sometimes controversial – objects like the Rosetta Stone, the Elgin marbles and Egyptian and African artefacts have also been added to the museum's collection.

But neither the Great Exhibition nor the British Museum managed to capture the essence of the countries themselves. To find out what the nations that were part of the British Empire were really like, people had to travel to visit them. Visits were either 'forced' through transportation or voluntary, and many people never came back to tell those at home the delights, or horrors, these places overseas actually held in store.

Discussion POINT

Do you think that the treasures in the British Museum should be returned to the countries they came from originally? What do you think, and why?

2.2 The extent of the Empire

So how did the Great Exhibition and the British Museum come to contain so many fantastic things? As mentioned before it was because of the sheer extent and size of the British Empire.

Here, you'll find out:

- How big was the British Empire at its greatest extent?
- How did the British Empire rule over the nations under its control?

The Empire at its greatest extent

The British Empire was truly magnificent in many ways. At its peak the Empire covered 12.7 million square miles of land, ruled over 430 million people and covered approximately 25% of the world's surface. Maps of the Empire showed the territory in red, which due to printing methods and the type of ink used often showed up as pink. The pinker the world got, the larger the influence of the Empire! It wasn't just the **acquisition** of land that drove the growth of the Empire. Trade played a massive part as well. Take a look at one of these maps to appreciate the size and location of the British Empire. It really did have territory in all four corners of the globe.

A wealthy nation

The Empire also made Britain wealthy, opening up many new areas of trade that could be exploited.

Source A

The industrialisation of Britain 1780-1914

Phil Chapple

"The growth of overseas trade reached unparalleled levels between 1850 and 1870. During this period the value of imports rose from £103 million to £303 million. At the same time total world trade had grown from an estimated £600 million to £2,700 million. Britain was by far the world's most important trading nation."

The Empire had an impact both at home and abroad. Britain saw goods and items that people could only previously dream of, along with new races of people who **enhanced** culture and society. The British Empire also gave a great deal to its overseas colonies, although this is often lost in tales of what the Empire took away. As the Empire grew it acquired a number of nations, categorised in a number of ways.

A selection of British stamps showing some of the many countries around the world in which British stamps were used as part of the Empire's administration.

Colony

A group of people in a foreign country who still come under British rule – in essence, a piece of Britain that had been **transposed** onto foreign soil.

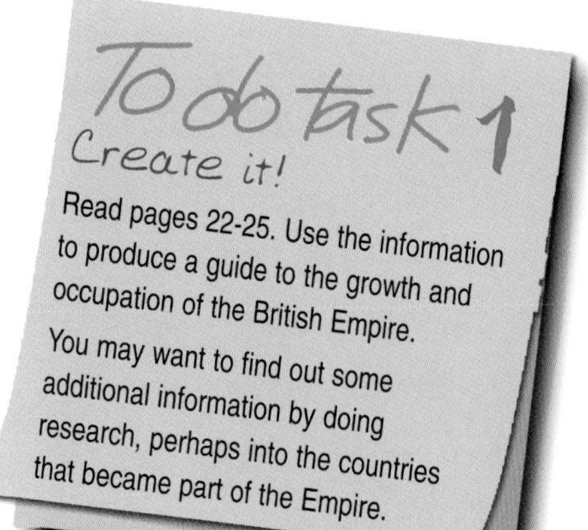

Protectorates

Areas which are governed, in part, by Britain, but still have some control over their own affairs. They are essentially "semi-independent".

Dominions

These countries are run independently from Britain, but recognise the British monarch as their own. They have their own Parliament and ruling body.

Mandates

Where a country has been placed under the authority / rule of Britain, usually after a war.

This map of the world dates from 1901, and shows the extent of the British Empire marked in red.

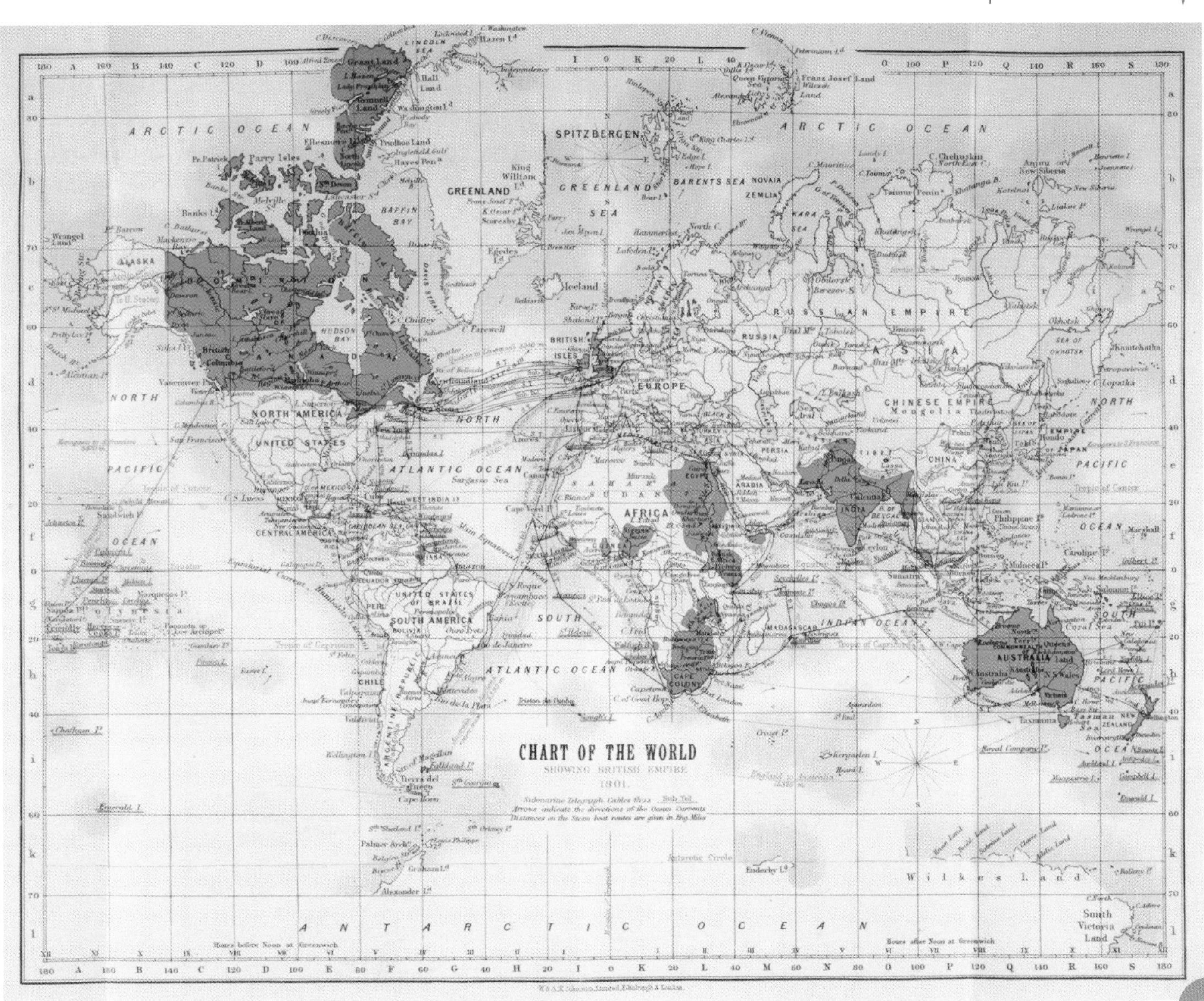

The rise and fall of the British Empire

So how did the British Empire reach such a size, and how long did it take?

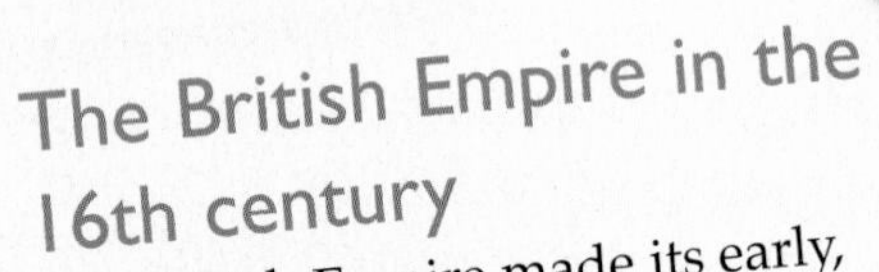

The British Empire in the 16th century

The British Empire made its early, stumbling steps in the 16th century, with the voyages of John Cabot at the end of the 15th century and the attempted settlement of Roanaoke at the end of the 16th century. From such humble beginnings came such a large Empire.

The British Empire in the 17th century

The 17th century saw the start of the real push for the colonisation of America and the West Indies, and the beginning of an interest in India and Canada.

The British Empire in the 18th century

With interest in India and America top the list of priorities, the British Empire took an interest in South Africa and the Cape of Good Hope at the very end of t 18th century, and then moved onwards t Australia. The loss of the American colonies in this century was a blow to the prestige and standing of the British Empire.

BUZZ WORDZZ

aquisition
enhanced
transposed

The British Empire in the 20th century

The British Empire began its decline fully in the 20th century, when it became a shadow of its former self, most particularly after the loss of India.

The British Empire in the 19th century

The focus for the Empire was now firmly on India, with other interests lying in Canada, the Caribbean and Australia. A new interest in Africa developed after the abolition of the slave trade.

The British Empire spread across the globe. Consider:

- Why did the British Empire expand outside Europe?

- How did private companies drive the growth of the Empire?

Where did it come from?

The British were relatively late in beginning their drive for an empire, and many people question whether the British Empire was intentionally acquired, or simply gathered along the way as a product of trade. British manufacturing and industry definitely benefited from the growth of new markets throughout the colonies. Without the ability to trade far and wide across the globe, Britain would surely not have been able to build any real amount of economic **prosperity**.

These Victorian bricks are part of a monument in Cardiff, and show the prices for shipping various goods around the empire from Cardiff port.

Source A

An Utterly Impartial History of Britain

John O'Farrell

"With British manufacturing output expanding so rapidly, new markets were continually sought and new sources of raw materials always needed. The British Empire was conquered more by market forces than armed forces. Some possessions such as Gibraltar or Cyprus were seized by the navy or acquired at the post-war conference table for their strategic military value, but on the whole the pink bits on the globe were wherever British companies happened to have landed and managed to outdo other competitors."

The Imperial Century: 1815-1914

One particular policy that enabled Britain's commercial output to grow, along with their Empire, was 'Mercantilism'. This policy allowed Britain to safeguard its own manufacturing industry by protecting it from overseas competition. It also allowed the build-up of a large and vital merchant navy and a vibrant British economy. Any goods that were imported into Britain would have to be brought in on British vessels, which made Britain a 'closed shop' for European imports and those from other rival empires.
This outlawing of foreign trade within the waters and colonies of the British Empire was largely controlled by a series of laws known as the 'Navigation Acts'.

Part of the Mercantilist policy was also to grant permission to private companies to exploit certain areas. They were, in essence, buying the right to that land and the commercial potential of it from the Crown. They would pay money to the Monarch in exchange for this right.

The gathering of colonies as part of the British Empire would certainly increase the ability of Britain to be self-sufficient and to build up vital stocks of money.

Navigation Act

Examples of the rules laid down in the Acts:

- Navigation Act 1660 – $^3/_4$ of a ship's crew had to beEnglish.
- Navigation Act 1663 – All European goods going to America had to be shipped through England first, and carried only in English ships.

Source B

The British Empire *Frank McDonough*

"The European colonial Empires which rose from 1500 onwards were run according to mercantilist principles. The aim of mercantilism, as practised by most European states, was to export more goods than were imported, thereby creating a profitable 'balance of trade' and increasing the wealth of the country, as judged by the amount of gold and silver held within it.

It was believed that this process could be greatly assisted by securing supplies of highly prized commodities such as tea, sugar, coffee, spices, and other luxury goods from one's own colonies (thus avoiding the need for imports to the mother country and its territories), and by closing off the colonies to trade with other states (thereby restricting the market for their exports). Each of the five major European colonial powers used naval power to defend the trade routes between the mother country and its colonies, not only from rivals, but also from increasing numbers of pirates who roamed the high seas in search of riches."

To do task 1

Comprehension

1. What is mercantilism?
2. Name two items highly valued by trading nations.
3. Which was the most famous of the British trading compaines?

The trading companies

Sometimes Britain was economically or politically not able to conquer new lands; at that point it turned to private companies and individuals who would do the exploring for them in return for pay and rewards. The most famous example of these companies is the 'East India Company'.

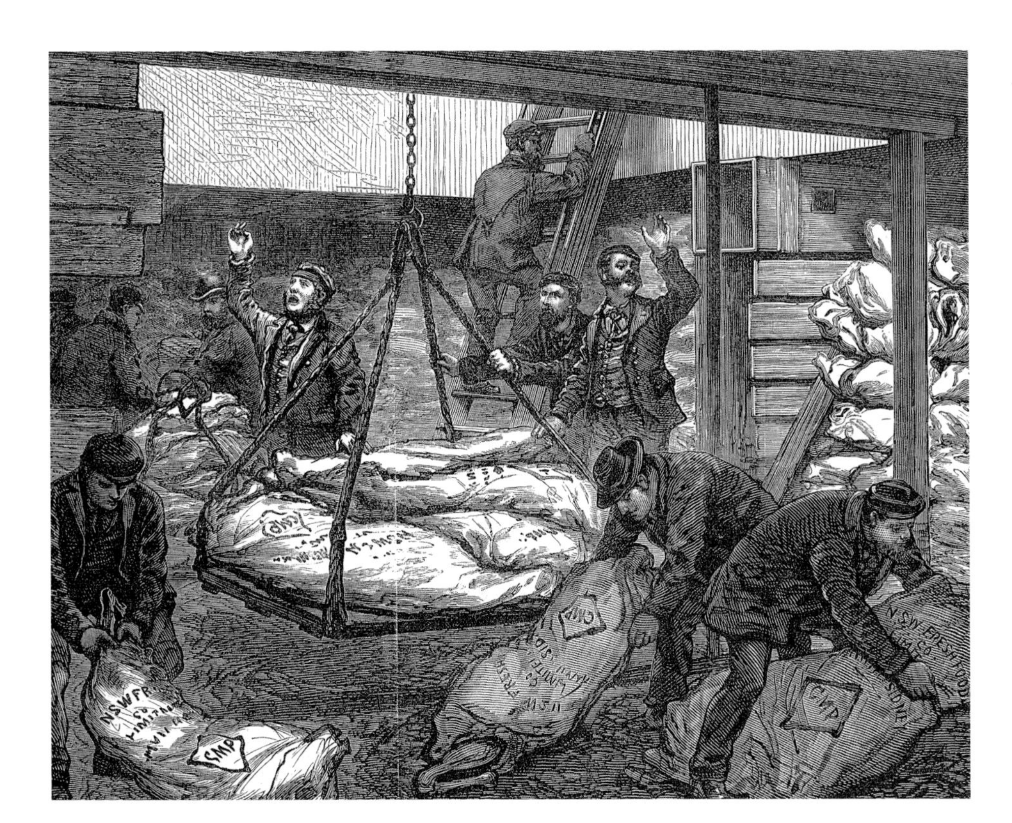

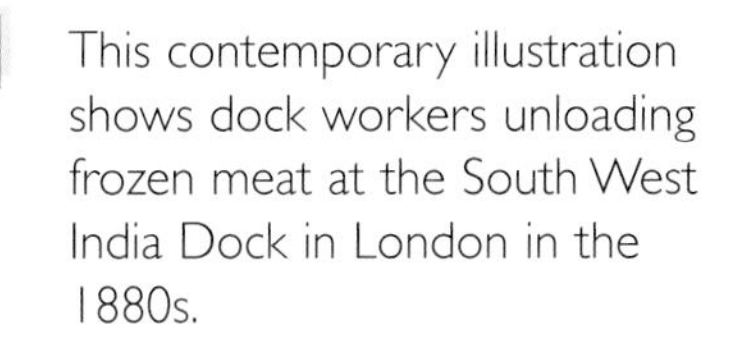

This contemporary illustration shows dock workers unloading frozen meat at the South West India Dock in London in the 1880s.

HMS Warrior – the largest, fastest and most heavily armed warship in the world when she was launched in 1860.

Britain's navy

Although the Navigation Acts did much to build up the British economy, policing these acts – ensuring that British ships were able to make the most of this British trade protection – was never going to be easy. The key to this success was the size and strength of the Royal Navy.

One piece of verse that highlights the importance of British superiority over the seas during the later part of the British Empire is 'Rule Britannia'.

"Rule Britannia,

Britannia rules the waves,

Britons never, never, never shall be slaves."

The words of 'Rule Britannia' show just how important it was for Britain to rule the waves. Without the skill, talent and hard work of famous British sailors such as Nelson and Collingwood, the ability of vital British trading vessels to navigate the seas would have been much more uncertain.

You are growing up in an age of relatively cheap air travel that allows people to go pretty much anywhere they like in the world. This might make all this emphasis on the role of the Navy hard to understand. Shipping routes and the vessels that navigated their way through them were quite simply the **lifeblood** of the nation. The only way to get goods in or out of the British Isles was by sea. Without safe trading routes Britain would essentially be isolated.

The term 'Pax Britannica' is associated with Britain holding unchallenged domination of the seas. This phrase was only used after the defeat of Napoleon in 1815, which brought in a period where Britain was unchallenged by other European and world powers. This unrivalled domination of the seas meant that Britain's Empire was also truly unchallenged.

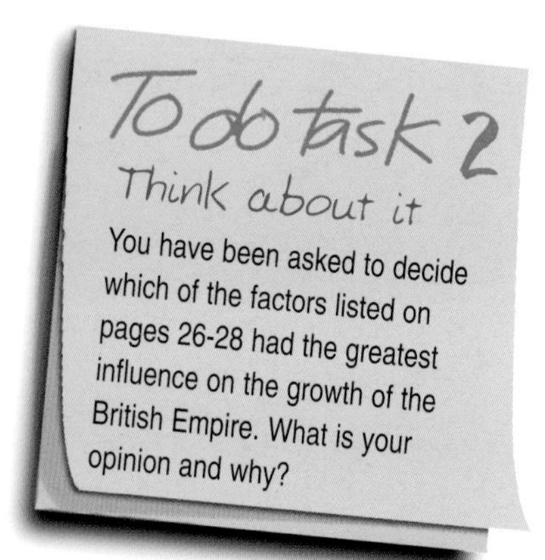

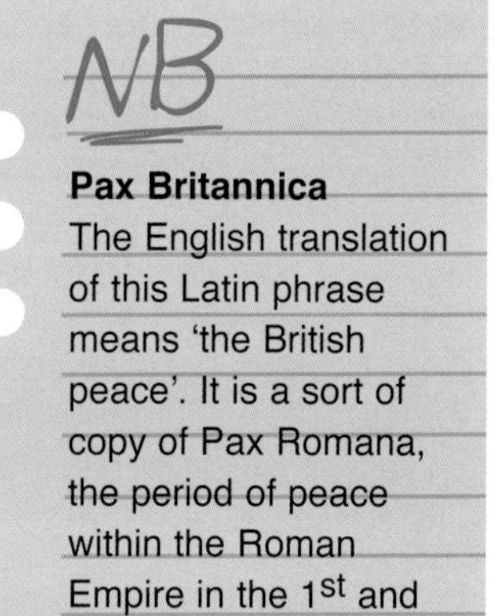

Britain's army

Although Britain's army was nowhere near as powerful, or feared, as its navy, it too was a necessary product of the Empire. Without it the British would undoubtedly have struggled to hold on to certain essential territories. Often the only way that they could stake their claim upon certain areas was through the use of force. Few nations happily give up and accept that their homes, territory or commerce will be overtaken by an overseas power. Britain's army, therefore, was vital in asserting their place in the world. Even when territory had been claimed, keeping hold of it was often not easy.

Co-operation with the indigenous inhabitants

Colonising and making the most of newly-acquired lands requires a certain amount of co-operation between the new owners and the native local people. Many of the lands that became a part of the British Empire had conditions and climates that were unusual for the people who were starting their new lives or new businesses there. Without the help of the **indigenous** people – the people who had lived there all their lives and for generations before – British ability to make a success of these new areas would be **compromised**.

Financial gain

The Empire brought increased financial revenue to Britain both through the opening up of new markets in the colonies and through taxation of the people who settled there. Both were valuable sources of income. This was important as maintaining the strength of the army and the navy, and searching for new areas to colonise, was an expensive business. Britain would not have been able to finance such expansion without taking a tremendous amount from the areas that it already held.

The Seven Years' War and the defeat of Napoleon

One war in particular allowed the British Empire to grow considerably in a short period of time. This was the Seven Years' War in the mid 18th century.

Source C

Growing the Empire

"In 1756–63 the Seven Years' War against France – which included the capture of Québec (1759) by James Wolfe, the incident of the Black Hole of Calcutta (1756), and Robert Clive's victory at the Battle of Plassey (1757), India – resulted in Britain acquiring lands in Canada and India, more islands in the West Indies, and Gibraltar. Although the 13 colonies on the North Atlantic seaboard won independence as the United States of America in the American Revolution (1776–83), Britain acquired the Bahamas in 1783, and the defeat of France in the Napoleonic Wars – including the victory at the Battle of Trafalgar (1805) by Admiral Horatio Nelson – enabled Britain to add Malta, St Lucia, Grenada, Dominica, St Vincent, Trinidad, Tobago, part of Guiana (now Guyana), Ceylon (now Sri Lanka), the Seychelles, and Cape Colony (now part of South Africa) to its empire."

2.4 What has the Empire ever done for us?

The expanding Empire resulted in many new products being available at home.

- Which desirable products were grown in parts of the Empire?

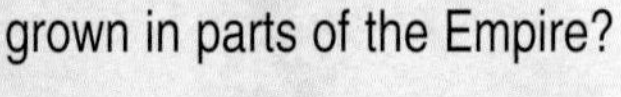

- What were some of the positive aspects of the Empire for the people in Britain?

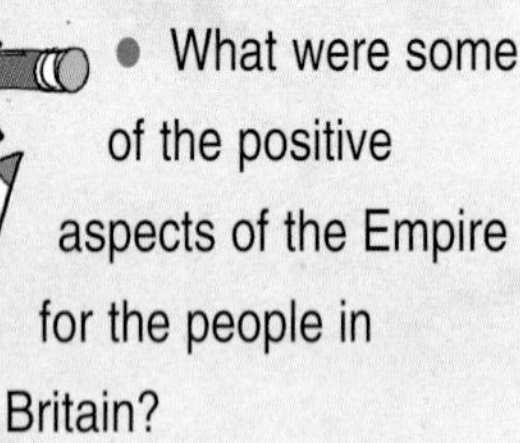

We want chocolate and we want it now!

Some historians believe that a major factor behind the rapid expansion of the British Empire was the huge demand for sugar, caffeine and nicotine. Because of its geography and climate, Britain is not well-suited to the growth of sugar, tea or coffee. The only access to these is through imports from other nations or from colonies acquired through expansion. Chocolate too, is an example of a high-demand product impossible to produce in Britain, so some historians consider that the British desire for chocolate may have been a factor in the continuing growth of the Empire.

Tobacco

The British desire for tobacco, long before its risks to health had been identified, meant that enormous amounts had to be imported – possibly as much as 17 million kilos by the end of the 17th century. The importation of tobacco in Britain and Europe ever since has provided necessary revenue for British traders and taxation for the British government.

Chocolate

First brought to Europe by the Spanish, the British were relatively slow to catch on to this now favourite food. In Britain it was first enjoyed as a drink and it was only converted into a 'bar' during the reign of Queen Victoria.

Coffee

Drinking coffee is very popular across Europe and has been for a long time. However, it was not until the 17th century that coffee made its way into the British way of life when it became a social and business tool during meetings in 'coffee houses'. As it is not a crop grown in Europe, coffee had to be imported and in the time of the empire it came from the Middle East, via other European nations. The Muslim world had been drinking coffee for hundreds of years.

The sheer popularity of the drink, especially amongst men, meant that very large quantities had to be imported. The British government took advantage of the demand by imposing high import duties on the drink.

Tea

Whilst coffee was very much a male drink, tea was seen as a more feminine drink. It was very popular across the whole of Europe, although it is now seen as the typical British drink, despite its origins. Tea is produced from tea leaves that are mostly grown in the Far East in places such as China and India. Initially it was the Dutch who made tea a popular drink, pioneering trading in India and the surrounding areas before the British arrived.

Tea is one of the main reasons why smuggling became a major problem in Britain, as the import duties on it were so high. Only when these import duties were dropped did the problem of smuggling decrease.

Silk, spices and textiles, tropical fruits, new vegetables and...turkeys!

Forays into the East, specifically India, brought high-quality textiles onto the British market, along with valuable spices. They also brought tropical fruits such as bananas, pineapples and melons. You might also be surprised to know that the potato originally came from America, as did the turkey.

Sugar

For many people sugar is an essential partner to drinks such as tea, coffee and cocoa. The British public in general has a pretty sweet tooth and this meant that as early as 1760, 5,000,000 lbs of sugar had been imported to Britain. It became a staple crop grown in many Caribbean colonies.

Cricket

As just one of a number of team sports that were established in the colonies, cricket is a symbol of British imperialism. Many of the countries that have a history connected to the British Empire play cricket, often better than the nation that introduced it to them! You only have to look at the matches against the West Indies, Australia, New Zealand, India and Pakistan to realise that.

But it would be wrong to say that people could not have enjoyed these things if the British Empire had not existed. The other nations who provided them before the British took charge would surely have made them available even without British interference. The British Empire simply allowed the British to have a regular and often cheap supply of the goods they liked.

An end to water-borne disease

A by-product of the rise in tea and coffee drinking was a reduction in deaths caused by dirty water. For many centuries people had suffered from the effects of water-borne diseases and the influx of new drinks that required hot water meant that many of these diseases had their impact reduced. The germs and bacteria were killed when the water was boiled.

Money and employment

Naturally, the increased business and trade that the Empire generated meant that people found it easier to get a job, and British wealth increased. Many jobs were created in ports, due to the slave trade and the transportation and processing of goods such as tobacco and sugar.

Introduction

Britain's Empire

Lord Thomas Fitzgerald renounces his allegiance to Henry VIII in Ireland.

The first country to become part of the British Empire was found quite close to home. Since the Middle Ages, British monarchs had looked across the Irish Sea and tried – and mostly failed – to secure a solid foothold in Ireland. Under the reign of the Tudors (1485–1603), however, real progress was made; in particular, Henry VIII was determined that Ireland be controlled properly and he introduced a number of reforms to allow this.

Poyning's Law 1494

The first moves towards maintaining control had come during the reign of Henry VII. Poyning's Law was an attempt to bring Ireland under the control and rule of the English Monarch. Not surprisingly, the Irish saw it as a huge imposition upon them. Prior to this, Henry VII had initially attempted to maintain good relationships with Ireland, asking many of the Irish Lords to guarantee their allegiance to him by signing peace treaties. But Poyning's Law broke down this trust between the English and the Irish.

The King of Ireland – 1541

Relations became more strained when Henry VIII broke away from the Roman Catholic church in 1534, making himself Head of the Church of England. It was then a small step for him to become Head of the Church of Ireland, which he did in 1541. As Ireland was a mainly Catholic country, with relatively few Protestant settlers, this was bound to be an unpopular move with most of the Irish population. In fact, a large proportion of the Irish did not accept this at all and were still loyal to the Pope.

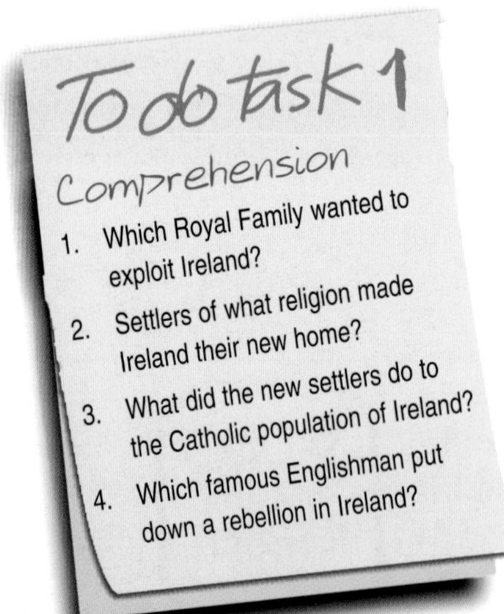

The imposition of English law

From 1541 English law was imposed upon the Irish. After all, Henry VIII was their King, and head of their church, so it was a logical step.

Persecution of the Catholics

A particularly difficult change for the Irish was a new religious focus. The English Catholic population was **persecuted** – particularly during the reign of Elizabeth I – and so too were the Irish Catholics. Their land was confiscated and handed over to the Protestant settlers, and those who did not conform to the new religious ideas of Protestantism were burnt at the stake – although Elizabeth was not the most ardent 'anti-Catholic' monarch, preferring instead to fine them.

Protestant Plantations

The real imposition upon Ireland, however, was the settlement of Protestants there. They came from England and Scotland, having been given land on which to settle. Land was allocated through a group of men known as the 'Undertakers', who were given land in Ireland which they subsequently sublet to the settlers or even to the Irish. Unfortunately the incoming English often outcompeted the Irish at their main trade of agriculture and dissatisfaction gradually overtook the Irish with this increased, enforced competition. The main area that suffered this settlement was Ulster in the north of Ireland.

To do task 2

Source work

Read Source A. Why was Londonderry given this name? What does Source A suggest about the city of Londonderry, and how do you know this? Do you think that this is a reliable source of information for a historian to use?

Source A

From the website www.londonderrychamber.co.uk

"The 'Plantations in Ulster' required the colonising of the area by loyal English and Scottish migrants who were to be predominantly Protestant in religion, unlike the Catholic Irish. One part of this colonisation was to be organized by the ancient and wealthy trades' guilds of London. The new county granted to the Londoners and its fortified city, built on the site of the recently destroyed settlement, were renamed Londonderry in honour of this association. The city of Londonderry was the jewel in the crown of the Ulster plantations. It was laid out according to the best contemporary principles of town planning, imported from the continent (the original street lay-out has survived to the present almost intact). More importantly, the city was enclosed by massive stone and earthen fortifications."

The settlement of the Ulster plantations led eventually to a Catholic uprising against the Protestant settlers and the English monarchy, ultimately resulting in the arrival of Oliver Cromwell in Ireland in 1649, who crushed this Irish rebellion.

Although this is only a snapshot of the history of the strained relationship between England and Ireland, it shows the lengths to which Britain would go to secure new land. The experience in Ireland demonstrated that colonisation would not be easy. It prepared would-be colonisers further afield for what was to come. It also established the means by which the British would go about their colonisation in future – using force, religion and law as their main tools.

3.1 Early exploration and colonisation of America

Britain and America have close ties. Across the Atlantic Ocean is the most powerful nation on the planet. This is all about how the first British settlers came to America:

- Which part of America was colonised first?
- What did it take to make the break from Britain?

What do you know about American colonies?

Have you ever been to America? Even if you haven't, you are probably aware of the impact of this great nation. Given that the power of America today is so huge, it may surprise you to realise that it was once part of Britain's Empire.

13 American colonies

The American flag is instantly recognisable, but did you know that the 13 stripes on it represent the original 13 **colonies** of the eastern seaboard of America? These were:

Georgia, South Carolina, North Carolina, Virginia, Maryland, Delaware, New Jersey, Connecticut, Rhode Island, Massachusetts, New Hampshire, New York and Pennsylvania.

The British were mostly responsible for the formation of these colonies, and the American flag is a reminder that American history is very much intertwined with British history. The expansion of British interest over the Atlantic to America was in many ways the next logical step after events in Ireland. The British experience in Ireland had taught them a great deal about conquest and colonisation, and they anticipated similar problems and issues in America. In a way, Ireland had been the ideal 'test' before the colonisation of America, and the area on the eastern seaboard that would become known as 'Virginia'.

To do task 1

Comprehension

1) How many states are there on the Eastern seaboard of America?
2) The colonisation of which nation had helped the British learn valuable lessons before they reached America?
3) Which European nation had already made inroads into America?

Early exploitation of the Americas

Early domination of the Americas went to the Spanish and Portuguese Empires, with the British close behind. The north-east coast of America, being the closest part to Britain and Europe, was the first to get attention from the Europeans. The Southern colonies of the eastern seaboard were settled first, with the Middle and Northern colonies settled slightly later.

The Spanish had already visited America but had really only concentrated on South and Central America, particularly Florida. The French had also taken Canada, around the St Lawrence River, as part of its own Empire. These European nations were more interested in the natural resources and valuable commodities found in America than they were in colonising it. It was the British who had interest in both trade and colonisation.

Initially, Britain lacked both funds and sufficient ships to be able to fully **exploit** the potential for colonisation in the Americas. Recognising this problem and not happy to just leave America to the other European nations, monarchs such as Queen Elizabeth I sought a solution. Licences or grants were issued to private companies and individuals that would give them the right to explore areas and to set up settlements on behalf of the crown. In return they could reap any profits gained. This meant that the British

Empire was already beginning to expand without any real effort on behalf of the nation itself. The brave, intrepid men who were mentioned earlier in this book were the ones who were the real **pioneers**.

The granting of a licence by a monarch to an explorer was not only done by English kings: this picture shows Louis XIV of France granting a licence.

The main map shows the Eastern seaboard of the United States; the insert shows the original 13 colonies

Source A

The conquest of America

From the website www.worldalmanacforkids.com

"St. Augustine, Florida, the first town established by Europeans in the United States, is founded by the Spanish. Later burned by the English in 1586."

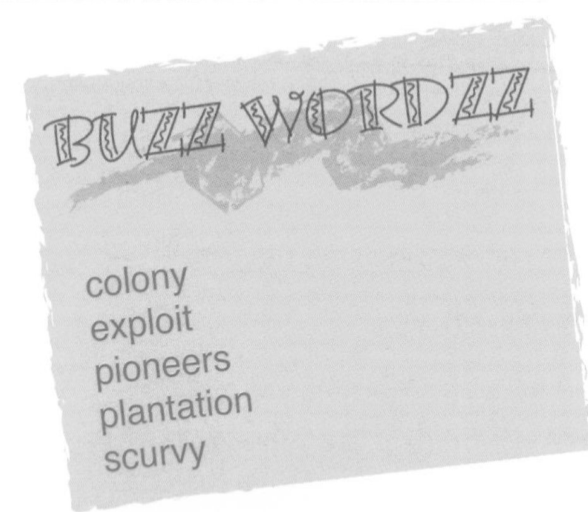

The journey to America

The journey to America was not to be taken lightly. If you have ever been on a long haul flight to America, you may have found it to incredibly long. Imagine how difficult it would be to have to make this journey by boat, which was the only option at this time. An average crossing could take anywhere between eight and twelve weeks depending on the conditions. The Atlantic Ocean has always been dangerous; it is a huge expanse of water, with great variations in weather and heights of waves. Sailing conditions were made even worse by the way that the passengers were squashed aboard the small boats. Many people suffered from terrible seasickness and some suffered from **scurvy**. Scurvy is an illness that is caused by not having enough Vitamin C in the diet.

Source A From the NHS Website www.nhs.uk

"Symptoms of scurvy will appear one to three months after vitamin C intake stops. The exact period depends on how much vitamin C the body has stored.

Symptoms include:

- *a feeling of discomfort,*
- *tiredness,*
- *nausea,*
- *muscle and joint pain,*
- *easy bruising,*
- *swollen and bleeding gums,*
- *loosening of teeth,*
- *wounds healing slowly and poorly,*
- *dry skin and hair, and*
- *bleeding into muscles and joints, causing pain."*

Scurvy was common because passengers had to endure rations like those consumed by Royal Navy sailors, fish and meat preserved in salt being the main diet. Water quickly went stale. Those that survived this ordeal could have been helped by thinking about the new life full of opportunities that would hopefully begin when they arrived in America, praying that the provisions they had on board would last, and just holding on for dear life!

To do task 2

Descriptive writing

Imagine that you have set out on the journey as one of the early settlers in America. Why are you going? What are you hoping for? What emotions have you gone through on your journey? Write a letter home to your loved-ones that describes what you have been through and felt.

Plantations

The aim of those travelling to America at this point was not to take on a different way of life, adapting to the customs or circumstances of another nation. It was to transfer a little part of Britain and a large part of the British way of life to America. This tendency led to an interesting name that was used to describe the colonies. They were given the name **plantations**. The term plantation makes reference to how English tendencies, laws and governance, and the English people, had been 'transplanted' or moved to another continent. Like some British people abroad today, they made little or no attempt to adopt the culture and ways of the country that they were colonising. Instead they tried to manufacture a 'little Britain' abroad. (The name Plantation has also been used in describing the settlement of Ireland.)

If the colonists believed that they would be able to establish themselves quickly in America, they were mistaken. Establishing a new colony is never easy, especially without the modern technology that we use today to set up water supplies, irrigation, sewage facilities, comfortable buildings and homes, etc. The early settlements in America were little more than makeshift camps until more permanent foundations for a society could be laid.

The many problems involved in establishing a permanent settlement are highlighted well in the story of the settlement at Roanoke later in this chapter.

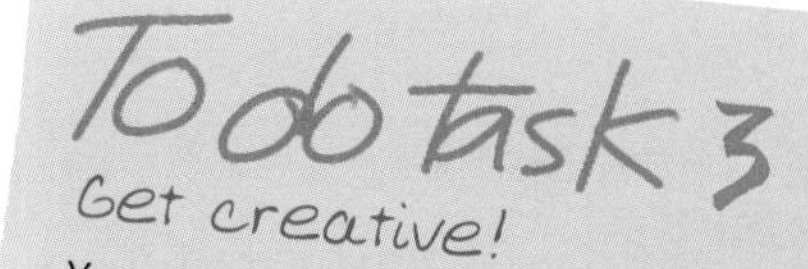

You are acting on behalf of a company who wants to make a fortune from the new venture that is America. You must design a poster that will advertise what can be gained through a journey to America. How will you persuade people that they really can find a new life in America?

Financing colonisation

The voyages to America were not generally undertaken at a person's individual expense. Instead, they were usually financed by entrepreneurial companies or rich merchants. They wanted to bring goods back home from America on the same ships that took colonists out, and sell them at a profit in the English and European markets. This meant that while the trading companies had an interest in the colonies that would mature nicely over the coming years, they would be able to make a profit while they waited for their longer-term investments to come good. These profits would enable them to finance even more voyages transporting even more colonists to America, and so on.

3.2 Why America?

Once the initial decision had been taken to make the journey to America, a suitable area had to be found to settle in:

- What was on offer in America and who was in direct competition to the British?
- Who travelled to America?
- Why were some of the first settlers criminals?

Source A

Empire Niall Ferguson

"What began as a hunt for gold and silver quickly acquired an agricultural dimension. Crops from the New World could be exported, including maize, potatoes, sweet potatoes, tomatoes, pineapples, cocoa and tobacco; while crops from elsewhere – wheat, rice, sugar cane, bananas and coffee – could be transferred to the Americas. Even more importantly, the introduction then of hitherto unknown domesticated animals (cattle, pigs, chicken, sheep, goats and horses) greatly enhanced agricultural productivity."

To do task 1

Comprehension

1. What did the East coast of America offer the people who were willing to make the journey?
2. Where is 'Cathay'?
3. What types of people travelled to America?

Competition with Spain

As the British began to consider colonisation of America, the Spanish had already claimed Florida as their own. The Americas became of special interest to the British because they knew that the Spanish were plundering the area and that gold was to be found there. In fact they stole a huge amount of it off Spanish treasure ships via privateers like Sir Francis Drake and pirates like Sir John Hawkins.

What was on offer in America?

Most seamen and explorers saw the colonisation of America as a profit-making venture, handily placed close to the Spanish Empire thereby allowing it to be used as a base for attacking Spanish trading routes. But there was much more to it than that. The east coast offered a large variety of products that settlers could make use of. Exploitation of America and the Caribbean was absolutely vital to the further growth and success of the British Empire.

America really was a land of opportunity. Nearly everyone who went to America was free to make their living in whatever way they wanted, despite the considerable risks in even getting there! And once in America, settlers faced hard work, disease and unexpected problems with the Native Americans.

Why move at all?

When people travel abroad to begin a new life today, often they do so to take advantage of an up-turn in circumstances. People knew that there was a huge amount of land available in America and traders knew that America would provide a vital stopping point on a valuable route to 'Cathay' – China. Speculators were convinced that they would be able to grow Mediterranean-style goods in America, which would provide valuable trade with Europe. (See Source A.)

Those involved in promoting colonies on the eastern coast of America knew that to get people to travel they had to make it attractive enough to be worth such an upheaval. The problems around land availability and ownership in Ireland made some people cautious about potential issues that they might encounter in America. To help the transition, most settlers in Virginia were guaranteed 50 acres of land for each person in their party. This was not just given away, though. In return, the settler had to pay rent for this land to the company that had financed their voyage.

This is a realistic modern-day reconstruction of the sort of homes the first colonists made for themselves.

Source B

Britannia's Empire

Bill Nasson

"Promotion of the eastern seaboard of North America did not skimp on promises. Through improvement and diversification, potential settlers and investors were assured of coming fortunes in tobacco, silk, hemp and fruit."

Who travelled to America?

The majority of those who emigrated were young – under 25. With their youthful exuberance and relatively 'happy go lucky' attitudes, they felt they had nothing to lose. And they came from all over Europe. They may be loosely described as 'pioneering folk', people with the 'get up and go' to take a risk and put their past lives behind them.

Source D

The rise and fall of the British Empire

Lawrence James

"Hard times in Britain encouraged movement to America and between 1760 and 1775, 30,000 English, 55,000 Irish and 40,000 Scots crossed the Atlantic."

Then, after 1680, England ceased to be the chief source of immigration, as large numbers of pioneers came from Germany, Ireland, Scotland, Switzerland and France. Thousands fled Germany to escape war; the Irish, Scots and Swiss were escaping from poverty. By 1690 the American population had risen to a quarter of a million. After that, it doubled every 25 years until, in 1775, it numbered more than 2.5 million.

Most non-English colonists adopted the English language, English law and many English customs, but these had already been modified by conditions in America. The result was a unique mixture of British and European ideas conditioned by the environment of the New World.

America as a prison colony

What cannot be forgotten, and will be mentioned later in this chapter, is that Britain used America as a prison colony – a dumping ground for the most undesirable people from the overcrowded British prisons. So some people travelling to America did not do so of their own free-will. This was known as transportation.

Source C

Modern history

J.M. Roberts

"The English colonies were very diverse. Strung out as they were over almost the whole Atlantic seaboard, they contained a great variety of climate, economy and terrain. Their origins reflected a wide range of motives and methods of foundation. They soon became somewhat ethnically mixed, for after 1688 Scottish, Irish, German, Huguenot and Swiss emigrants had begun to arrive in appreciable numbers."

To do task 2

Reasoned argument

You have been asked to rate the effectiveness of the punishment of transportation. Draw a table with two columns, the left one headed 'Positives' and the right one headed 'Negatives'. In each column, write down all aspects of this punishment. Do the positives outweigh the negatives, or is it the other way round? Why do you think this?

3.3 Roanoke: 'The lost colony'

The first settlement established in America was at Roanoke, a venture surrounded by mystery and intrigue.

- Where is Roanoke?
- Why did the settlement fail?

Sir Ralph Lane had relinquished a promising career in the army in order to travel to America.

The first settlement in America

The first steps towards a permanent colony in America were made under the guidance and inspiration of Sir Walter Raleigh, at Roanoke Island in 1584. Hopes were high for the success of the colony.

On arrival in **Virginia**, patriotically the British called the area after their glorious monarch Queen Elizabeth I – The Virgin Queen. The first 100 or so colonists, organised by Raleigh, were all men who were sent purely to establish the colony. The man who was charged with governing and running the new colony was Ralph Lane.

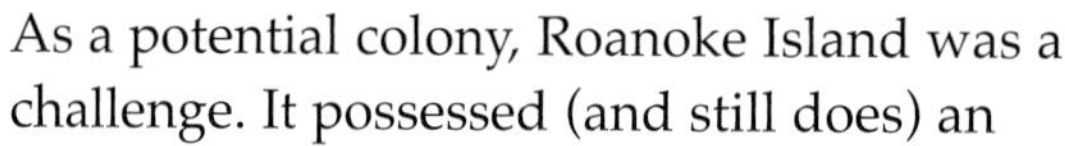

As a potential colony, Roanoke Island was a challenge. It possessed (and still does) an interesting but dangerous coastline, with numerous sandbanks making landing there tricky. Without knowledge of how to navigate these dangers many ships were lost approaching Roanoke, and so experienced sailors and crews were required. Any failure to establish the colony properly would mean that the settlers would be terribly **isolated**. This isolation soon became a distinct disadvantage as it was not at all easy to get supplies to the settlers.

Tough times at Roanoke

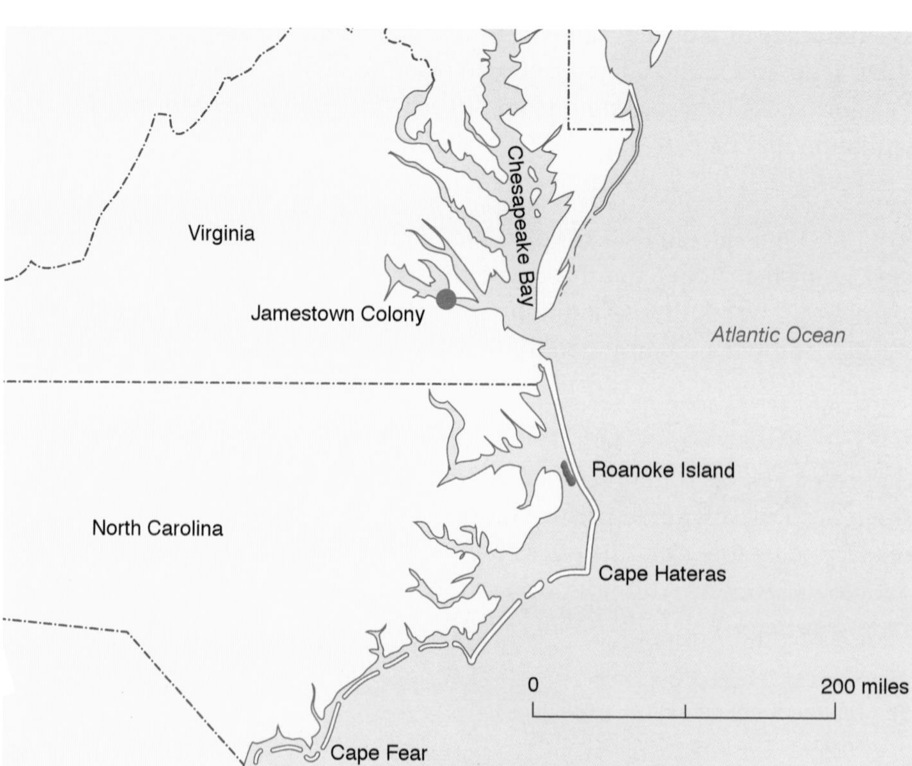

To do task 1

Comprehension

1. Why was 'Virginia' given such an unusual name?
2. Where was the first attempt made at a permanent settlement?
3. Which Native American tribe inhabited the area?

Roanoke Island also turned out to be poorly suited to agriculture, with relatively infertile soils that had few nutrients. With very few supplies available from Britain to help them out when times became hard, the only people that the new settlers could turn to were the indigenous inhabitants of the island – the Native Americans.

The colonists believed they could gain food supplies from the **Algonquian** tribe. Initial co-operation was good, but the colonist's leader Ralph Lane ruined this by killing the Algonquian Chief, Wingina, after their food stocks ran low. As a result the Algonquians felt that they were unable to help the colonists any further without risking their own chances of survival. The English had no choice but to abandon the colony and were removed from the island by boat in 1586, by Sir Francis Drake.

The venture had been a massive failure, and failure to learn from the mistakes made meant that they would be repeated in later ventures as well.

The area around Roanoke today – quite different from when the first colonists landed!

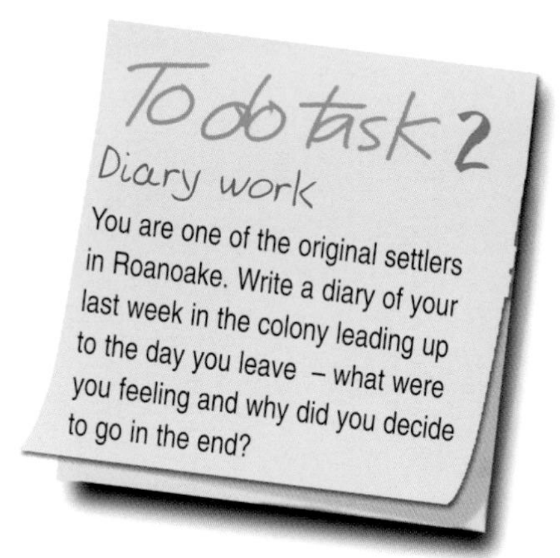

The Cape Hatteras Lighthouse, built in 1870, is still the tallest lighthouse in the USA. It replaced the first unsatisfactory lighthouse that was built in 1803, and was designed to warn ships of the dangerous currents and sandbars that extend many miles offshore. Little wonder the first colonists suffered many shipwrecks as they approached Roanoke!

Despite this poor start, the English were determined to see a successful settlement in America, and they continued with their attempts to establish a colony. Their next attempt in 1587 was once again led by Raleigh, but this time he placed the expedition in the hands of an artist called John White. He also included men, women and children in the party, aiming it to become a **self-sustaining** colony. The new settlement was to be called the 'Cittie of Raleigh' after Raleigh himself.

These mounds and ditches are the remains of the Chesapeake colony, now a national park.

Difficulties again...

A contemporary map showing the coastline and approaches to Chesapeake Bay.

The location of this second colony did not entirely go to plan. A decision had been made before the ships left Britain that the colony would be at Chesapeake Bay, the largest estuary in the USA. It would have provided a fantastic location for a settlement, with plenty of food resources and opportunities for shelter and agriculture. This would prevent a repeat of the supply problems that had hit Roanoke, with the colonists becoming self-sustaining rather than having to rely on British imports.

Unfortunately, due to an ill-fated choice of crew for the ship taking the settlers to America, the men, women and children were not deposited in Chesapeake Bay. In fact they were dropped off at Roanoke Island once again. The crew was more interested in **plundering** Spanish treasure ships in the Caribbean and were impatient to get to work, feeling that they couldn't spare the time to get to the Chesapeake area.

And so once again the settlement faced a challenge. White knew that the problems that had caused the collapse of the original colony would face him. He subsequently made the decision to return to England for supplies and help. Having returned to England, however, his departure back to America was delayed by England's war with Spain. The battle in 1588 with the Spanish Armada had hit naval resources and shipping hard, and this prevented White from finding a ship that would take him back to Roanoke.

Disaster!

While he was away, starvation hit the colony but this time there was nobody to come to the rescue. When White finally managed to return to Roanoke in August 1590 he could find no sign of his relatives or the original settlers. The only indication as to what had happened was a carving of a single word on the trunk of a tree: CROATOAN. This was a reference to Croatoan Island, today called Hatteras Island, which White believed to be a message about where the settlers had fled to. Before White had left for England he had agreed with the settlers that if they encountered difficulties and had to leave, they would carve into a tree the name of their destination so that White could locate them.

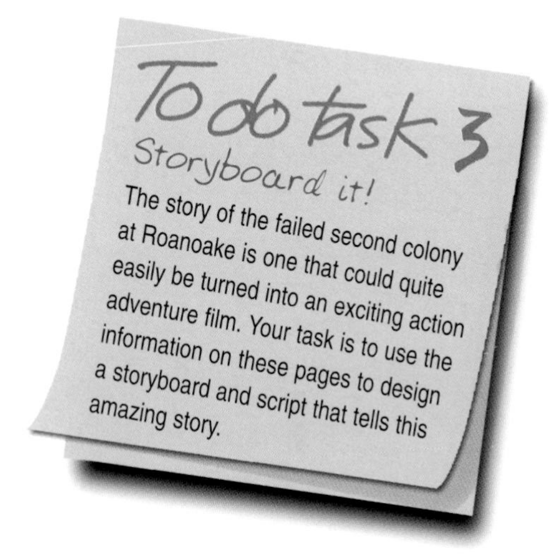

White, however, was once again delayed in his attempts to get to the settlers when bad weather hit the coastline, damaging the ship he was travelling on. In fact he never managed to reach Croatoan Island and the fate of the settlers has never been discovered. Some people believe that the settlers may have made their way to Chesapeake Bay and asked the local tribes for help, where during a period of unrest they were murdered by a local chief named 'Powhatan'. Archaeologists and historians are still unsure of the fate of the colonists, so any idea about what happened to them is still speculation.

After the successful conclusion of the war with Spain, the English no longer had to rely on private individuals to colonise America and they could take a little more interest in it as a nation. Well-financed companies, established or sponsored by the Crown and led by rich merchants from London, now took an active role in colonisation. Subsequently the Virginia area became the main colony, with large numbers of British people arriving there. Despite problems along the way, the colonisation of Virginia would become a British success story.

3.4 The Southern Colonies

The first attempt to establish a major, permanent settlement was in the southern colonies, centred around Virginia.

- Why was a settlement established at Jamestown?
- What problems did they face in Jamestown?
- What other colonies were established in the south?

The Virginia Company

One company that tried to establish a permanent colony was the Virginia Company, originally known as the London Company. Despite the failures at Roanoke, James I granted a charter in 1606, with instructions for the company to set up a permanent settlement in Virginia. The main impetus behind all of this was profit. To be successful the company had to have a good supply of quality citizens and labour filtering through to the colonies. The Virginia Company was not a Government-run company. It was in essence privately run acting on behalf of England and was financed by a group of **shareholders**. It was therefore in the best interests of their shareholders that the company made sure the colonies prospered.

Source A

The Rise and Fall of the British Empire

Lawrence James

"The companies which financed the first colonising projects wanted profits from rents and the sale of land, and therefore a greater part of their initial outlay was spent on shipping and equipping a substantial labour force whose efforts were expected to repay their investment."

To do task 1

Comprehension

1. What was unusual about the Virginia Company?
2. Where was the James River colony established?
3. What dangerous conditions met the settlers when they arrived there?

Jamestown

The permanent settlement was established on the James River in 1607 at Chesapeake Bay – the intended site for the earlier colony. The James, York, Rappahannock and Potomac rivers all converge in the Bay, making it a very fertile area of flood plains and alluvial soil. So it was expected that people would be able to farm crops and herd livestock quite successfully in this area. Hunting and fishing would also be easy and plentiful. Despite these advantages, however, the area also had the potential for disaster.

The Chesapeake Bay area today.

A commemorative coin minted to celebrate the founding of Jamestown.

The settlement was hit hard by disease early on, because the site for the settlement – essentially an island – was surrounded by marshy, swampy ground. Most of the settlers died within the first year, mostly from malaria. This killer disease was rife in the swampy lands, carried by mosquitoes that bred quickly. The colonists also struggled to find sufficient drinking water. What little they found was often contaminated by salt, as the area was largely **brackish**. It was simply beyond the understanding of the colonists to keep the water clean, and salt poisoning therefore saw off a large number of the colonists as well.

Because of the fears of attack by local Native Americans, Jamestown at first resembled a fort with high fences all around. The settlers were well armed with a range of weapons, including some cannons, to defend themselves from attack.

NB

Brackish is a term that describes water that is neither fresh, nor salty, in fact a mixture of the two.

Hard times

Despite these precautions the settlement would still face hard times. This was in part because the initial settlers did not have the right attitude towards work. Many of them were not working class, being rather relatively well-off gentlemen, so they weren't particularly keen on hard physical work. They were more interested in entertaining themselves and hunting for gold and treasure. A lack of basic farming and **agricultural** knowledge also hampered them. In the first season they simply did not plant enough crops to get them through the year.

You may think that this first attempt at a colony was considered to be unsuccessful with so many people dying. However, it did not put off the Virginia Company and more settlers would arrive in 1609 to boost the **floundering** settlement. Without such 'topping up' the settlement would have been doomed, as the inhabitants were slowly dying from starvation. In fact they were so hungry that stories of cannibalism blight the history of the settlement, with one settler being executed for this crime. Famine was definitely not what people had come to America for!

The new 'Americans' were in need of help and they turned to the Native Americans, despite their fears. They needed help with their farming and more often than not they actually required the Native Americans to give them food in order that they could survive. What the English failed to understand was that the Native Americans did not have enough food to feed themselves, let alone the English as well. This often led to attacks by the Native Americans to defend their rights and food.

Success in the James River colony was never going to be easy. As many as 10,000 people made the journey in total over the years, but only 2000 survived to make a go of it.

The salvation for Jamestown was tobacco, which had been grown with success in another area of British colonisation, the **Caribbean**. The American climate was well-suited to this crop which had a very high profit margin of up to 500%. Plantations and farms had a huge impact on the lifestyles of the Native Americans: the search for new land on which to grow tobacco meant that many Native Americans were forced off their land or saw it destroyed by pigs and cattle which ate their crops.

Tobacco, however, was not going to solve the issue of providing enough food. This would take hard work and dedication.

An antique map showing the areas of Virginia and Maryland.

Maryland

Building on the growth of Jamestown, there was interest in setting up a Catholic settlement in the Chesapeake Bay area. In 1642, two ships – the 'Ark' and the 'Dove' – made the long journey across the Atlantic to look for a suitable site for the colony. Twelve million acres of land were eventually acquired, purchased from the Yaocamicoe Indians. George Calvert was put in charge of the settlement which was named Maryland after Henrietta Maria, the Catholic wife of King Charles I. To entice people into making the journey there was a generous allowance of 100 acres of land per settler, more than had been granted in Jamestown. This land grant is probably the reason why many of the settlers were not actually Catholics. Experience had shown that a good settlement needed a wide variety of people and skills. Many people made the journey from other parts of Virginia, and made the most of what they had learned from the problems faced in Jamestown. They also cultivated the same profitable crop – tobacco. In 1649 a Toleration Act 1649 was passed to ensure the close association between the people of different religions – in this case Catholic and Protestant.

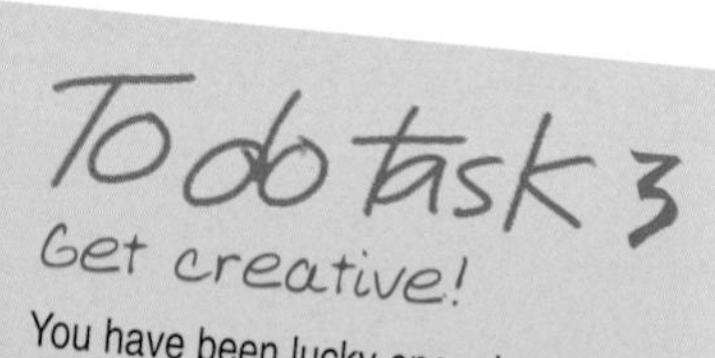

You have been lucky enough to have been granted a large amount of land in the Carolinas – 400 acres. What will you do with it? What crops will you put on it? What livestock will you put on it? Draw a sketch or plan of your new property.

North Carolina and South Carolina

The Carolinas, named after King Charles II of England, looked to be very good areas for profitable colonisation: the large, open land was flat and suitable for farming. The wide, muddy rivers in the area meant that large flood plains provided fertile alluvial soils. Very large plantations were established, averaging over 400 acres each in size.

A reconstruction of a colonist's hut similar to those built in the Carolinas colony.

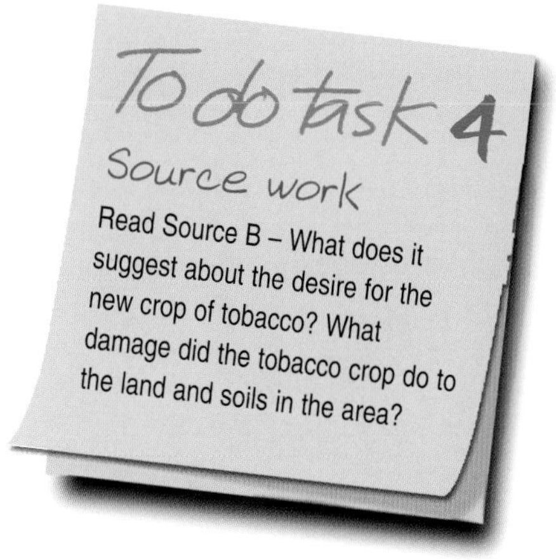

Land was given out to new settlers by wealthy noblemen from England – a group of eight men known as the Lord Proprietors. The settlers were also promised religious toleration if they settled in the Carolinas, and many came from the Jamestown colony, just as had happened when Maryland was established. The problems faced by the colonists were familiar, including swampy land infested by mosquitoes. The air was humid and tropical, and disease spread quickly. The colonists had to call on large amounts of slave and indentured labour to establish the area properly.

Georgia

Georgia, like many American colonies, was named after a monarch – George II. Set up by the Georgia Trustees, the colony offered the opportunity for very large plantations. Again, these would require the use of slave and indentured labour. However, the initial idea was to shun the slave trade and to rely on small estates using families as labour. These very rarely measured more than 50 acres, but over time the size of estates grew and soon came to rely on slave labour. The geography and the climate of the Carolinas and Georgia made it very much like the Caribbean in terms of life on the plantations, with lots of hard work and semi-tropical conditions.

The eventual success of the colonies in the south of the eastern seaboard meant that the Virginia Company's monopoly was ended in 1624 when it was taken over by the Crown. Virginia was now seen as such a valuable commodity that it could not be left in the hands of private individuals.

Tobacco, the saviour of Virginia

Without the ability to cultivate tobacco, the Virginia colony would probably have failed very early on. Without its profitability, there was little reason for the people to stay in such torturous, dangerous conditions.

NB

An indentured labourer would essentially be tied into a contract, having swapped passage to the Americas for a pre-determined period of service on the land.

Source B The Penguin History of the USA

"Tobacco could be sold at a profit, though the profit might be uncertain, irregular and low. Anyone could grow it. To the unskilled Virginians these two arguments were irresistible. They took the plunge, and soon the first great boom in American history was under way. At one stage even the streets of Jamestown were sown with tobacco; and the zeal to plant more and more greatly encouraged the spread of population up the James River…up and down the coast, on every inlet between the river Potomac and the Dismal swamp. This movement was in part caused by the fact that tobacco exhausted the soil in seven years, so that tobacco planters were constantly in search of new lands. This explains also the steady move westward of the Virginians in the seventeenth and eighteenth centuries…"

3.5 The Middle Colonies

The relative success of the southern colonies prompted many new ventures in other areas of the Eastern seaboard, most notably in New York.

- What colonies were established in the middle of the Eastern Seaboard?
- Who did the British face competition from?
- What made these areas suitable for colonisation?

A Quaker is a member of a religious group known as the 'Society of Friends' set up by George Fox in the 17th century. They were often persecuted.

Delaware and Pennsylvania

The histories of the colonies of Delaware and Pennsylvania are inextricably linked. Both are located on the Delaware River (pictured here), named after Lord de la Warr (Sir Thomas West) the first Governor of Virginia. The Delaware Bay area was first discovered by the explorer Henry Hudson and the first Europeans to settle the area were Dutch and Swedish. Hence previously the area was known as New Sweden.

The area only became an English colony when William Penn was granted the rights to the area by King Charles II, and it eventually became an English colony in 1664. Pennsylvania and Delaware were originally one area but were split during the Charter of Pennsylvania. signed in March 1681. Pennsylvania was primarily a Quaker settlement.

Source A

The Penguin History of the USA

"The coastal plain, gently sloping a hundred miles inland from Philadelphia to the feet of the Appalachians, watered by three great rivers – the Susquehanna, the feet of Schuylkill and the Delaware – was ideal country for European farmers, whether Palatines, English, Scottish or Irish. The temperate climate made it possible for them to grow the crops they were used to: wheat above all, but also rye, oats, barley, hemp and flax; maize was the only new grain being attempted. The immense fertility of the soil, and the large acreage to be had for the asking, ensured large harvests for everyone, although Pennsylvanian methods of agriculture were distinctly backward."

New York

New York was one of the most multi-cultural settlements, with settlers arriving from Switzerland, Scandinavia, Holland and Ireland, as well as Britain. The first European nation to colonise the area, though, was the Dutch. New York was originally called New Amsterdam because of its links with the Dutch, who had originally exchanged the area with the Native Americans for around £10 worth of goods.

But the English believed that, as they had already settled the majority of that part of the coastline, they should also be able to claim New Amsterdam as theirs. Technically it fell between their present colonies of Virginia and New England. They only managed to formally acquire the area, however, during the Second Dutch War of 1664.

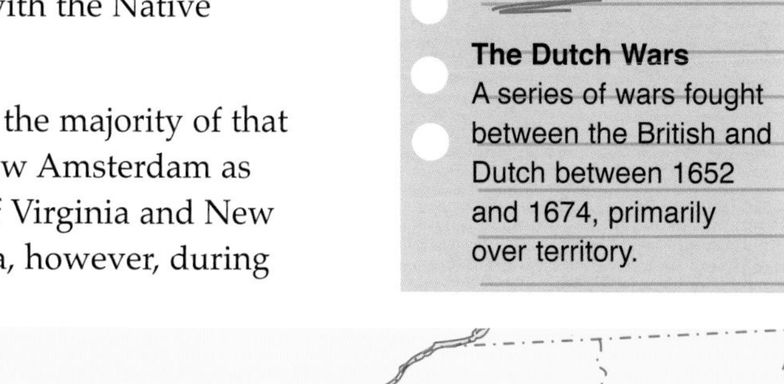

New Jersey

New Jersey, unlike many of the other American colonies, grew with an emphasis on farming and industry. The manufacture of iron, paper and textiles took root and the area was originally called New Netherlands. It was later named New Jersey because the governor of Jersey, Sir George Carteret, is credited with acquiring the area.

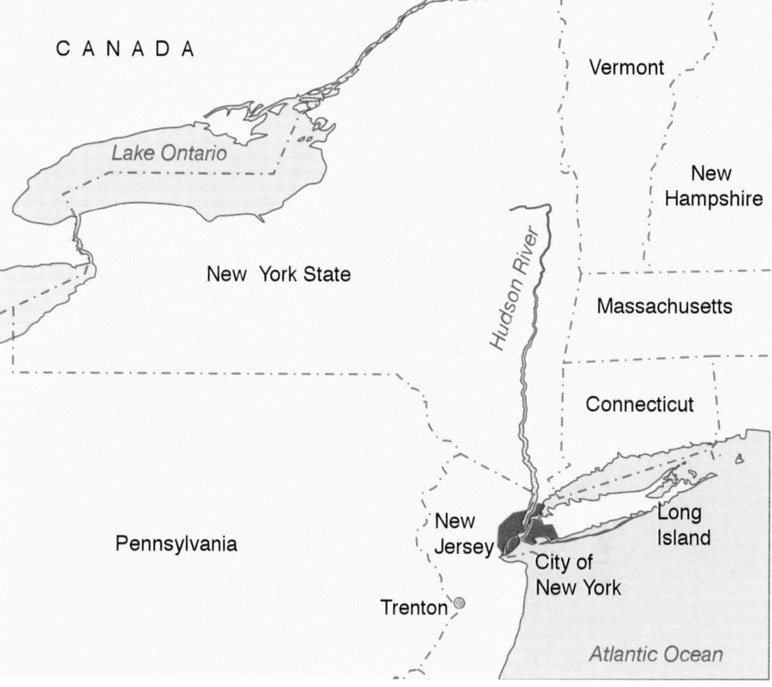

Source B From the website www.state.nj.us

"In 1664 the Dutch lost New Netherlands when the British took control of the land and added it to their colonies. They divided the land in half and gave control to two proprietors: Sir George Carteret (who was in charge of the east side) and Lord John Berkley (who was in charge of the west side). The land was officially named New Jersey after the Isle of Jersey in the English Channel. Carteret had been governor of the Isle of Jersey.

Berkeley and Carteret sold the land at low prices and allowed the settlers to have political and religious freedom. As a result, New Jersey was more ethnically diverse than many other colonies. Primarily a rural society, the colony grew to have about 100,000 people. Eventually, governing power was transferred back to England."

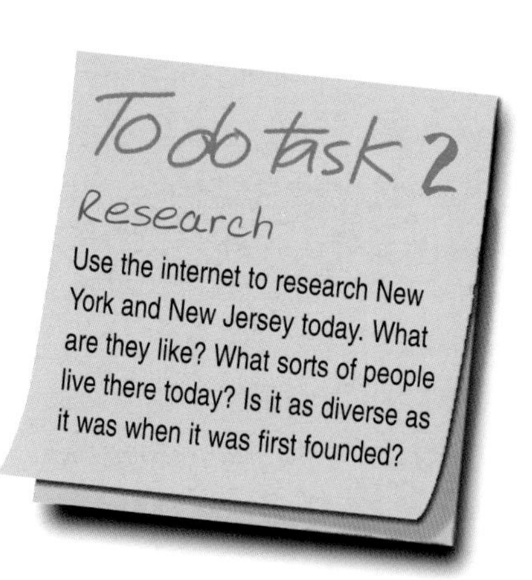

3.6 The New England Colonies

One of the most famous journeys to America was on a boat named the Mayflower. People left Britain because of a religious conviction to lead a new life.

- Why did people travel to America on the Mayflower?
- How did people make their living in New England?
- Why were people able to find toleration in this part of America whilst they couldn't in others?

New England colonies – who went there?

The New England colonies of Rhode Island, Connecticut, Massachusetts and New Hampshire took on very different characteristics to those in Virginia and the Middle colonies. Colonists in New England were on the whole wealthier and better educated, and among them were many religious radicals, including numerous Puritans.

The Plymouth Company

The Plymouth Company was another private company that had wanted to establish a colony in the Virginia area. One member of the company – Sir Edwin Sandys – had managed to get some land set aside for a group who were seeking **sanctuary** from persecution in Britain. They became known as the **Pilgrim** Fathers and they came to America on a famous ship called the Mayflower.

Source A

History – The Definitive Guide *Adam Hart Davies*

"Many English colonies on the eastern seaboard were religious in origin: Puritans settled in Massachusetts in 1630, Catholics in Maryland in 1634, religious free thinkers in Rhode Island in 1636, and Quakers in Pennsylvania in 1682. Dutch and Swedish trading companies also joined the colonials scramble. The Dutch West India Company, started in 1621, established Fort Orange (present day Albany) on the Hudson River in 1623. It then purchased Manhattan from the native Canarsees for 40 guilders in 1626. Further south, the Swedish West Indian Company set up New Sweden on the Delaware in 1638. The Dutch ended Swedish rule in 1655, but were then conquered by the British in 1664. English rule thus stretched the length of the east coast, from New England in the north to the Carolinas and, in 1724, Georgia in the south."

A modern artist's impression of the Mayflower.

The Mayflower

The Pilgrim Fathers sailed from Plymouth to America in September 1620 to escape religious persecution. Initially they had wanted to settle in Holland, but cultural and language barriers proved more difficult to overcome than expected so they decided on America. The previous use of their ship in the wine trade meant that the pleasant odour made the voyage a little more bearable!

On board the Mayflower were 103 settlers, mostly Puritans who lived their lives according to strict religious beliefs. As America seemed to allow them to worship and tolerated their beliefs, they were hopeful that their lives would be a lot more peaceful than they had been in England. The journey from their homes in Scrooby in Nottinghamshire was to be a long one. The name Pilgrim Fathers did not apply to all the people aboard the Mayflower, as not all passengers were Puritans.

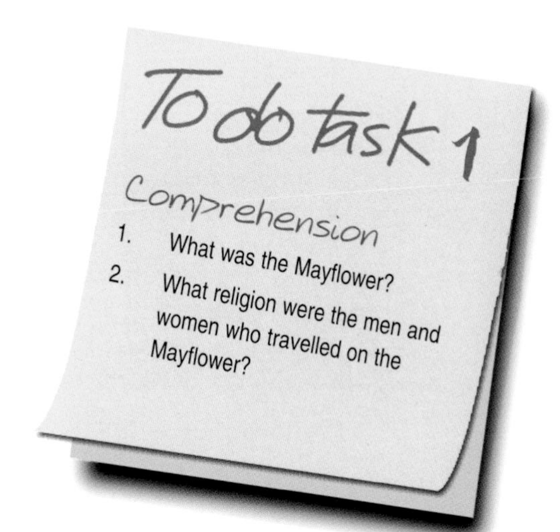

As they were sponsored by the Virginia Company of Plymouth, their intended destination was Virginia. However they landed instead in Massachussetts, and at the time nobody had staked a claim to New England. The Pilgrims were expected to work to pay for their travel that had been financed by the Virginia Company, so you wonder quite what the company thought about them landing in New England.

Difficulties for the colonists

Although the climate was better than that in Virginia, life was still hard. As temperatures in New England were generally lower than in Virginia, there was less chance of picking up diseases. However the land was also hillier and harder for farming.

Surviving in a foreign country, with little knowledge of the surroundings and the best ways to farm, fish and find fresh water, was very difficult. The first houses were little more than rough structures built on campsites, with the early days even tougher than had been experienced in Chesapeake Bay. What made the colony successful was that, unlike the Virginians, the settlers in New England were willing to work hard.

The local Native Americans had been hit hard by disease and the Pilgrims were able to take advantage of the situation by using the now vacated land. The settlers did need some help, to show them how to make the most of the **climate**, the soils and the terrain. This time the tribe that offered assistance were the Wampanoag tribe.

Source B

From the website www.timepage.org

"Finally, on December 21, they decided on a location…which they named Plymouth. Nearly half of the colonists and crew died from illnesses that first winter as they struggled to build their town. The following spring they were visited by a local Wampanoag native named Samoset who, surprisingly, spoke some broken English. Eventually he introduced the settlers to another native named Squanto whose village had occupied the area before the Pilgrims arrived. Squanto taught them many valuable skills that enabled them to survive in their new country."

While tobacco represented a 'get rich quick' plan for many in Virginia, there was no comparable crop in New England. Fishing provided a vital source of food and farming was centred around more traditional crops such as corn and wheat. As in other colonies, the settlers still relied on a huge amount of produce coming from England to keep themselves going. Due mainly to the lack of profit from tobacco, New England would never be as rich as the Virginian plantations, but there were still many positive aspects to life there.

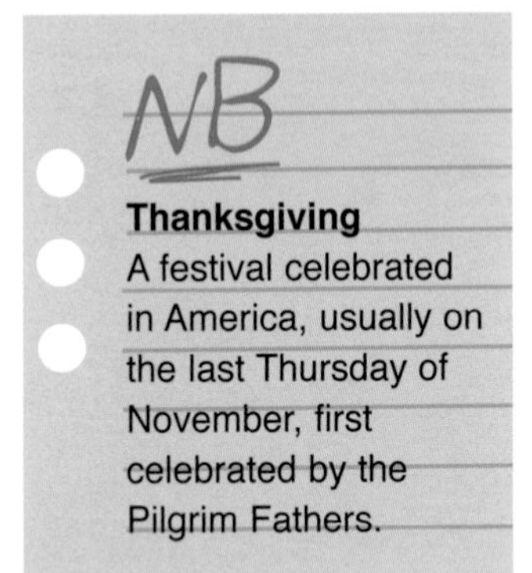

Even so, many of the original settlers did not survive their first winter. Those who did gave thanks for their survival of the first year in a new settlement. This is the origin of the modern 'thanksgiving' celebrations in America. After that first winter, the arrival of more **immigrants** soon allowed the colony to thrive.

The colony grows

Many people came from Virginia to make the most of what would be an improved lifestyle and way of life. People tended to live longer in New England, mainly because of the easy availability of fresh water from clean rivers. On average settlers lived into their 60s, whereas people in Virginia had an average age of around 45.

Those who came to New England came to work hard. They brought fewer servants with them and slavery was of little significance. Rather than buying in labour, people were more inclined to use their own large families to tend the land.

Source C

Text of the Mayflower Compact

"In ye name of God, Amen. We whose names are underwritten, the loyall subjects of our dread soveraigne Lord, King James, by the grace of God, of Great Britaine, Franc, and Ireland king, defender of the faith, etc.

Haveing undertaken, for ye glorie of God, and advancemente of ye Christian faith, and honour of our king & countrie, a voyage to plant ye first colonie in ye Northerne parts of Virginia, doe by these presents solemnly & mutualy in ye presence of God, and one of another, covenant & combine our selves togeather into a civill body politick, for our better ordering & preservation & furtherance of ye ends aforesaid; and by vertue hearof to enacte lawes, ordinances, acts constitutions, & offices, from time to time, as shall be thought most meet & convenient for ye generall good of ye Colonie, unto which we promise all due submission and obedience.

In witnes wherof we have hereunder subscribed our names at Cap-Codd ye 11th. of November, in ye year of ye raigne of our soveraigne lord, King James, of England, France, & Ireland ye eighteenth, and of Scotland, ye fiftie fourth. Ano: Dom. 1620."

The Mayflower Compact

To ensure a degree of **regulation** within the colony, a formal agreement was drawn up. The Mayflower Compact was an agreement signed by all the settlers to ensure that they were all governed by a reasonable set of guidelines and boundaries.

Great Migration

The Pilgrim Fathers were not the only religious group moving to this area. Many more arrived in Massachusetts during what was known as the 'Great Migration', when more than 20,000 settlers arrived between 1629 and 1640.

Rhode Island colony

The Rhode Island colony was founded by Roger Williams in 1636 and was located on Narrangansett Bay.

Source E

From the website www.visitrhodeisland.com

"Roger Williams founded the first permanent white settlement in Rhode Island at Providence in 1636 on land purchased from the Narragansett Indians. Forced to flee Massachusetts because of persecution, Williams established a policy of religious and political freedom in his new settlement. Other leaders advocating freedom of worship soon established similar communities on either side of Narragansett Bay. These communities united, and in 1663 King Charles II of England granted them a royal charter."

Dutch settler land on Manhattan Island.

Rhode Island was unusual in that it contained a number of very radical Puritans and others with extreme religious beliefs who had not been able to find toleration in any of the other settlements. The colony had a number of towns that housed these groups in an early 'multi-faith' society. Many Quakers found that they could seek **tolerance** in this area, but despite their religious beliefs some Rhode Island settlers had no qualms about taking an active role in the slave trade. They also made profit from fishing, agriculture and the exploitation of wood and timber.

BUZZ WORDZZ

climate
immigrants
pilgrim
regulation
sanctuary
tolerance

Source D

From the website
www.greatmigration.org

"New Englanders had a high level of literacy, perhaps nearly twice that of England as a whole. New Englanders were highly skilled; more than half of the settlers had been artisans or craftsmen. Only about seventeen percent came as servants, mostly as members of a household. In contrast, seventy-five percent of Virginia's population arrived as servants. Great Migration colonists were primarily middle class, and few were rich or poor. ...those already rich saw little opportunity to increase their wealth in a harsh region with no obvious cash crop...and the result of this exclusion was...colonists sharing similar backgrounds, outlooks, and perspectives."

3.7 An American labour force

The settlers themselves were very hard working, but at other times people were forced to work – either as prisoners, or as slaves.

- What was transportation and why did it make recruiting labourers for the American colonists easier?
- What was slave labour?
- What was indentured labour?

Let's get to work!

Would-be colonists soon realised that establishing a successful colony required planning. Working the land, planting and harvesting crops and building homes and towns was never going to be easy. The settlers needed strong, male workers that they could either rely on, or at least force to work in a generally hot, humid and exhausting climate. The British Government had the solution: they sent inmates from Britain's prisons and poor houses as forced labour. First introduced in 1717, it was called '**Transportation**' and the name tells us the basic aim – to transport people to another country.

Source A — White Cargo

Don Jordan and Michael Walsh

"To the extent that it is better to live than to die, it was an act of mercy in some degree to send convicts to the colony rather than to the scaffold. Perhaps the 'scum' would prove useful members of the colonial community and one day even earn their freedom in Virginia. But that was not the underlying intention. Four years later, in 1619, the Privy Council made the intention clear. It ordered that convicts sent to 'parts abroad' were to be 'constrained to toil in such heavy and painful works as such servitude shall be a greater terror than death itself.'

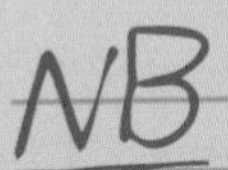

NB

The Bloody Code is the name for a system of law enforcement that relied on overly harsh punishments, usually death, for over 200 crimes, designed to scare people out of committing crimes.

British courts used transportation to America to make a break from the long -established 'Bloody Code', and British prisons at the time were horribly overcrowded. Transportation was a partial **solution** to these problems for 140 years, between 1717 and 1857.

Many people from the prisons were untrustworthy and unreliable' and included some hardened and dangerous criminals. Despite this, transportation did offer one benefit: many transportees were 30 years old or less. This gave the colony a potential **influx** of young people who would start their own families in America, producing a self-populating society.

A love token sent by a transported convict to his mother in the mid 19th century.

To do task 1

Comprehension

1. What was the British Government's solution to the lack of a labour force in America?
2. What was the name of the legal code that the British Government had used that condemned so many people to death?
3. What did the new punishment bring to America – good and bad?

The people who were transported did not have many rights until their sentences had lapsed. They were there to be exploited. Transportation was seen as a sensible way to get rid of troublesome individuals from Britain. To avoid criminals running away, colonies had to develop a system of rule that was brutal to frighten convicts into staying put.

People were usually transported for a period of seven or fourteen years and they were forced to work, in chains, without wages and in harsh conditions in which many died.

Transportation, however, did cause an upsurge in crime and disorder and the growth in the population meant that the once **idyllic** vision that was America was becoming slightly blurred and fuzzy around the edges.

Slave labour

Although not originally intended to be a part of the East Coast colonies, it was not long before the first slaves arrived in Jamestown in 1619. By 1700 they numbered 13,000, and the benefit of them was that they were relatively cheap to purchase and were also **plentiful**. There was no problem replacing them when they died or escaped.

The Virginia area was a haven for slave traders who made the long journey to the Chesapeake area, knowing that they would have little trouble selling their cargo.

Indentured labour

The Virginia Company needed willing and able men and women to farm, cultivate and colonise the land. Anybody who could get themselves to the colonies, or pay for their own travel, was given an amount of land for their own use.

These modern actors are dressed in authentic clothing of the type worn by indentured labourers in the colonies.

However **indentured** servants were still needed to work the land. These people went from England to work in the colonies and they paid back their passage through work for an agreed length of time, anywhere between four and ten years. Then they were able to begin their own lives in a new country. Indentured servants were paid a wage for their work and could save for their future lives.

For those people who had not actually chosen to go to America, but had been transported, it must have been a terrifying experience to be taken away and deposited in a strange country. The people who had volunteered to go must have felt similar emotions when they arrived. Many of those who agreed to work in exchange for the passage to America would face long years of hard labour with very little return. Often people died during this period of service, or were unable to realise their dreams when the time was over.

To do task 2

What's your opinion?

You have been asked to report on the effects of the new punishment of transportation on both Britain and America. Has this been a positive move for the colony? Write a report for the Government that evaluates its successes and failures – in your opinion.

BUZZ WORDZZ

idyllic
indentured
influx
plentiful
solution
transportation

To do task 3

You are an indentured labourer who has made the journey to America and you are writing your first letter home to your relatives. What has your life been like since you arrived? What have you got to look forward to?

3.8 The Native Americans

The British were not the first people to make America their home. The Native Americans also had a very definite claim to the continent.

- What tribes were living in America when the British settlers arrived?
  - How did the British and the Native Americans interact?
    - What impact did the settlers have on the Native Americans?

Who were they?

The Native Americans had been in America long before they were first encountered by the Europeans, although they may have been immigrants themselves. Evidence shows that they may initially have migrated from Siberia and Canada.

When the Native Americans were first encountered by Christopher Columbus, he believed that he had reached India. He mistakenly identified the Native Americans as 'Indians' because of this belief, which is actually a wholly inaccurate description of their origins. The **continent** that the Europeans initially viewed as being largely unpopulated was home to over two million people who were dispersed widely across the land.

Native Americans harvesting maize, one of their staple foods.

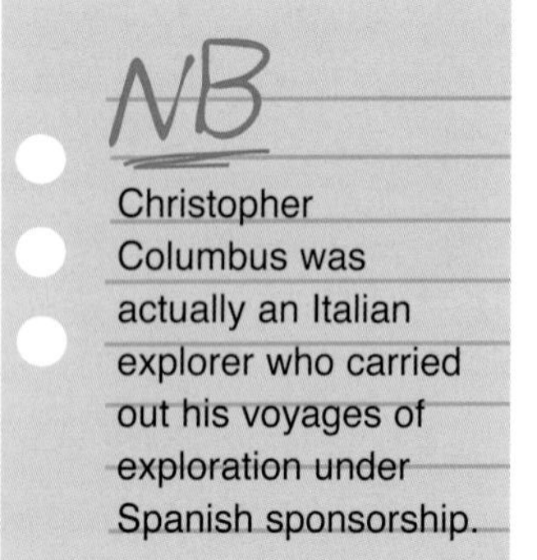

Source A

American Colonies *Alan Taylor*

"The broad coastal plain sustained about 24,000 Indians divided into thirty tribes but united by an Algonquian language and the rule of a paramount chief named Powhatan. They lived by a mix of horticulture, fishing, hunting and gathering. During the winter the natives dwelled in many villages consisting of one to two hundred inhabitants, occupying twenty to thirty houses. In the spring, they dispersed into still smaller and scattered encampments to fish and gather shellfish and aquatic tubers from the rivers, marshes, and bay. During the summer they returned to their village to cultivate fields of beans, maize and squashes. In the fall, they scattered again to hunt for waterfowl in the wetlands and for deer in the broad forest of immense deciduous trees, while the women and children gathered edible nuts, roots and berries."

Native American tribes

Native American tribes cannot be described universally. This is because the tribes were relatively isolated across the continent and had developed separately from each other, developing unique characteristics, cultures and languages. They were largely **nomadic** groups of people who did not establish permanent settlements. Instead, they preferred to wander to where the stocks of food were greatest and establish their camps there.

What we know about early encounters between the settlers of Virginia comes from detailed drawings done by John White, who we last heard of in the 'Lost Colony of Roanoke'. His descriptions, though, were only broadly indicative of the Algonquians, because of the huge variations in dress and characteristics between isolated tribes.

Listed here are just a few of the tribes that populated the continent of America:

The Cree Hunters, the Narragansetts, the Penobscot tribe, the Malecite tribe, the Iroquois League (incorporating the Mohawks, the Onondaja, the Seneca, the Oneida and the Cayuga), the Secotan, the Cherokee, the Chickasaw, the Creek, the Choctaw, the Seminole, the Sioux, Powhatan **Confederacy** and the Wampanoags.

NB

The Algonquian Indians The Algonquians were one of the most widely dispersed tribes and were frequently encountered by the settlers.

This map shows the areas within America where Native Americans tribes mainly lived.

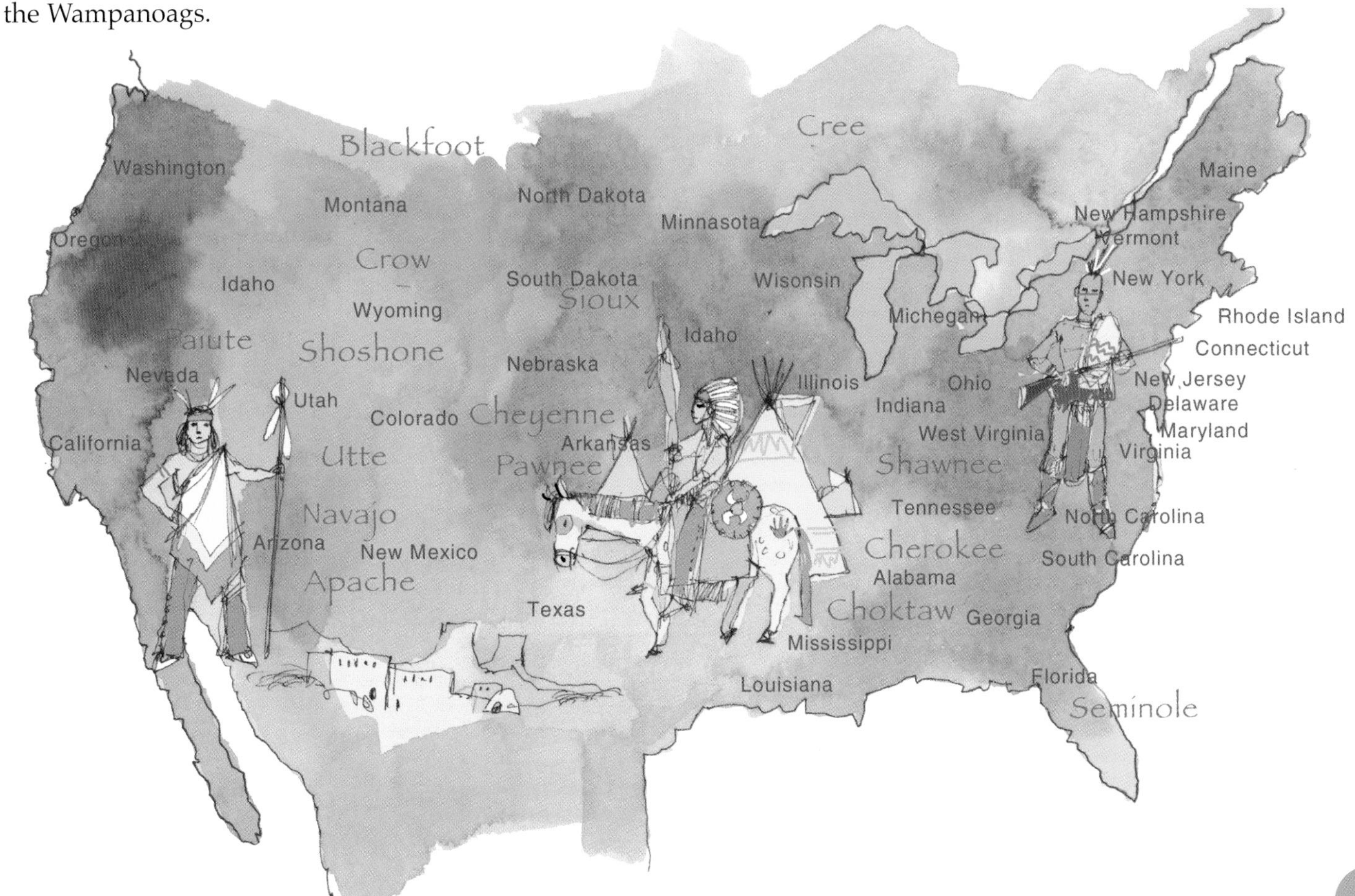

Source C

From a historical website,

www.preservationvirginia.org

Pocahontas was an Indian princess, the daughter of Powhatan, the powerful chief of the Algonquian Indians in the Tidewater region of Virginia. She was born around 1595 to one of Powhatan's many wives. They named her Matoaka, though she is better known as Pocahontas, which means 'Little Wanton', or playful, frolicsome little girl.

Relationships between the Native Americans and the settlers

Despite there being so many Native American tribes, only a small number had an impact on the English settlers. The colonists only encountered those tribes that were prevalent along the eastern seaboard. Other tribes would not be 'discovered' until after the settlers had begun to move inland to establish further colonies.

As we have seen, the early colonists needed the help of the Native Americans to successfully establish their colonies.

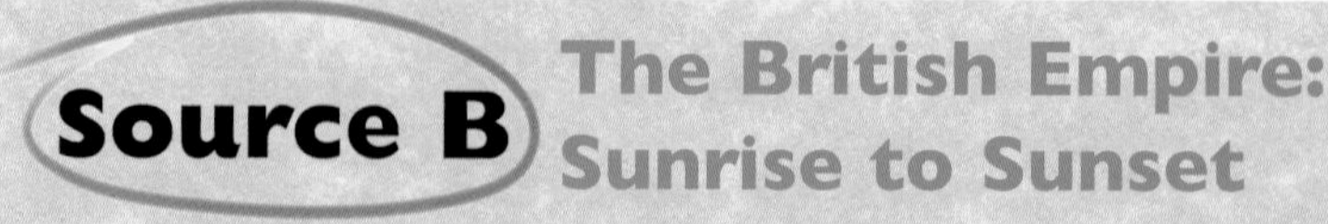

Philippa Levine

"The modern American Thanksgiving table owes much to what settlers learned from the locals: turkey, corn on the cob, maple syrup and pumpkins were all foodstuffs that settlers learned how to prepare from Native Americans."

Despite initial co-operation, the relationship between the settlers and the Native American tribes was not a happy one. In general the Europeans did not treat the Native Americans with respect. Many viewed them as little more than an inconvenience that had to be dealt with as part of the whole process of settlement. The settlers were often brutal towards the Native Americans and many were killed or even **massacred** without reason.

Relationships with the Algonquians in Virginia had been friendly at first, but then turned sour, despite a strategic marriage between John Rolfe and the Indian Princess Pocahontas in 1614.

A contemporary portrait of Pocahontas and her son.

Pocahontas was the daughter of the Algonquian chief, Powhatan. She was used by the Virginia Company as a bargaining tool in their negotiations with the Native Americans and even as a publicity tool in England. Pocahontas and her new husband made their way to England and she advertised the good relationship between the Native Americans and the settlers. She even took an English name – Rebecca. Her fame was short-lived though, as she died in 1617 at only 21 years of age, another victim of deadly European disease.

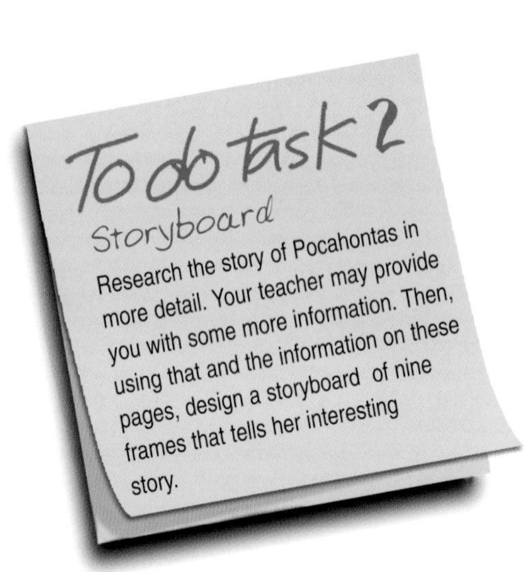

When Powhatan also died, those few relationships that had been built up between the Native Americans and the settlers took a turn for the worse with the appearance of a new leader of the Algonquians – Opechancanough (pictured below). He had very little time or respect for the settlers.

Despite the generous acts shown by the **indigenous** Americans, the settlers showed a nasty, vicious side to their character far too often. They often attacked and destroyed both crops and villages, leaving the tribes even more hungry and destitute than the new colonists themselves.

Massacres

Disagreements were largely over land: both groups had a claim to it, but you could easily argue that the claim of the Native Americans was morally stronger. Neither group was going to back down if their survival – or in the eyes of the British, their profit – was in danger.

During the American Indian uprising of 1622, the new Powhatan chief, Opechancanough, plotted to hit the settlers hard. He gave them a false sense of security by giving them land that they had not previously been entitled to. This cunning plan actually divided the settlers up and there by made them weaker in any one area. The Indians were able to attack some of the settlements that were now left relatively unprotected, and around 350 of the settlers were killed.

Hostilities between the colonists and the Algonquian Indians finally came to a head in 1644, when Opechancanough and his tribe murdered a further 500 colonists. This resulted in virtual open warfare and in 1646 Opechancanough was caught and executed.

Although violence did break out with deaths on both sides, on most occasions the Native Americans chose a more peaceful solution: they would rather leave the area and create distance between themselves and the new settlers.

Source D

From the NHS website

"Measles is caused by a very infectious virus. Nearly everyone who catches it will have a high fever, a rash and generally be unwell. Children often have to spend about five days in bed and could be off school for ten days. Adults are likely to be ill for longer. It is not possible to tell who will be seriously affected by measles. The complications of measles affect one in every 15 children. The complications include chest infections, fits, encephalitis (swelling of the brain), and brain damage. In very serious cases, measles kills."

Colonists were also victims of disease, as well as Native Americans. These graves are of three children who died during a smallpox epidemic in South Carolina.

The impact of the arrival of the Europeans

Diseases

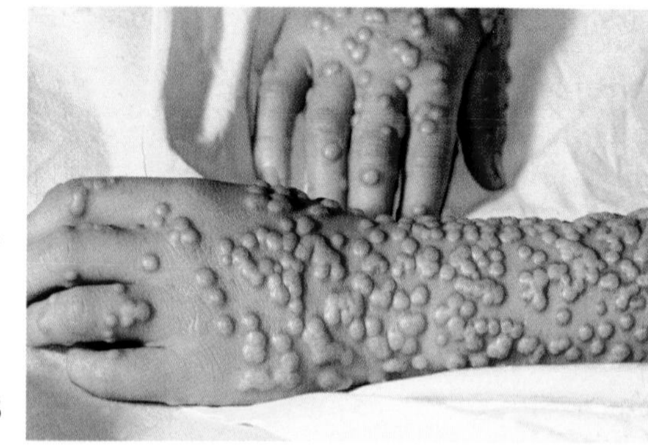

Smallpox causes severe blisters which often leave permanent scars.

The Native Americans, like many indigenous peoples who encountered the Europeans, had little immunity to disease. They were hit particularly heavily by European diseases such as smallpox, measles, influenza, TB and diptheria, along with venereal diseases.

So **devastating** was the impact of these diseases that whole societies and groups were wiped out in a very short time period. Before vaccination policies had been introduced there was simply no way that these diseases could be beaten.

Disagreement over land use

With so much land available in such a large continent, you wouldn't think it could cause so many problems! However, it was by far the main cause of conflict between the two groups. The ways in which Europeans used the land also created problems for the Native Americans,who relied on being able to move from place to place depending on the seasons. As the settlers fenced off land for their own use, or chopped down trees and planted new crops, this affected many of the wild animals that naturally inhabited the area. The introduction of new animals and livestock from Britain also had a significant impact.

Native American ways of life were often unintentionally changed; they were forced to adapt to a way of life based around trade and with the colonists at the centre of it, rather than one based around agriculture and where they moved around the area to hunt game.

Source E

The Rise and Fall of the British Empire

Lawrence James

"The Indian tribes were sadly ill-equipped to understand, let alone take action to prevent what was happening to them. They could never wholly grasp the alien, European principle of land-ownership and all the legal paraphernalia of deeds of sale and titles that went with it."

Alcohol

The Native Americans had a low tolerance to alcohol, and this was often used to force many people off their lands. They drank alcohol excessively when it was available and then regretted it for many reasons, not just the hangover the morning after! For example while drunk they were liable to make decisions about land for instance that couldn't be reversed when they sobered up.

Guns

The influence of the European settlers was felt far and wide across America. One of the unforseen consequences was the proliferation of guns that arrived in America. Firearms seriously changed the nature of the relationships between the Native American groups, as described in the source below.

"The introduction of European style firearms was also destabilizing; the power of guns made them a valuable commodity, and Native American groups competed with one another for possession of them. Such competition led to an increase in inter-tribal conflict, itself made deadlier by the growing use of guns."

The type of matchlock rifle used by the colonists and settlers, seen here handled by a modern-day actor.

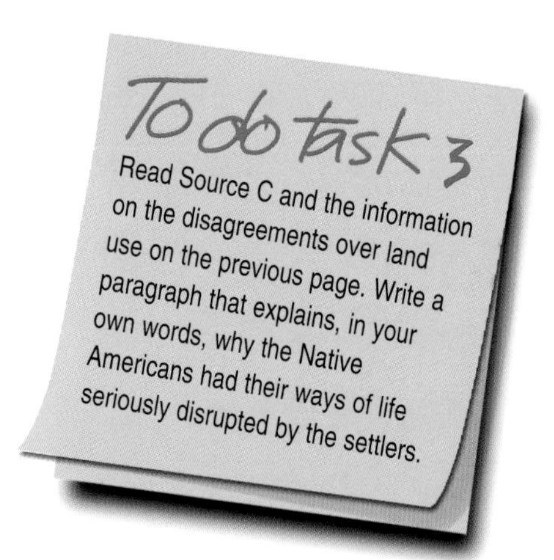

3.9 The loss of America

Independence Day in America marks the break from British rule, where the American colonies became 'independent'.

- How had the relationship between Britain and America deteriorated?
- What was the Boston Tea Party?
- When was the Declaration of Independence signed?
- Why was Canada important to the British?

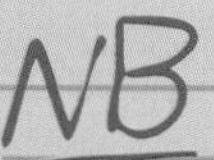

For many Americans, Mount Rushmore in South Dakota symbolises how they feel about America as a great nation, embodied in some of its greatest leaders. Carved from the mountains between 1927 and 1941, over 400 workers blasted and carved the 60-foot high busts of Presidents Washington, Jefferson, Roosevelt and Lincoln.

British control over the colonies

The British Government needed the colonies to be a vital area of trade for the British Empire; this fact alone meant the British would never willingly change their policy of direct control over the colonies. The methods used to rule each one were more or less the same: a colonial assembly was elected by the people living in the colony, presided over by a Governor. The overall process was overseen by the Government in London. Major issues such as taxation were controlled by the British. Although most colonists thought of themselves as British, some were beginning to think that independence from Britain might be desirable.

These men included such notable characters as:

Samuel Adams

Samuel Adams had been a student at Harvard University before he became heavily involved in the quest for American independence, being a participant in the Boston Tea Party. As a member of a group that campaigned for the independence of the American colonies from Britain, known as the 'Sons of Liberty', Adams was an expert speech writer and speaker, and was one of the men who signed the Declaration of Independence.

Benjamin Franklin

Benjamin Franklin's life and career could have followed many different paths, with him exhibiting considerable skills in writing, science and politics. He was also a signatory to the Declaration of Independence.

Thomas Jefferson

Thomas Jefferson came from a career background that was heavily influenced by politics. He had been a magistrate and had become involved in colonial politics. Jefferson made a real name for himself by being the main man behind the wording and formatting of the Declaration.

Reasons for the loss of America

The Navigation Acts

The desire for independence received a major blow with the introduction of the Navigation Acts, which effectively said that goods could only be imported to the Americas on British boats which had come via British ports. In reality this hugely restricted the type and amount of goods that could be brought into America, and reduced competition in the market which would have normally helped force down prices. This resulted in a huge rise in smuggling as American colonists were supplied with what they really wanted – cheap goods. In response the British mounted patrols of coastal waters and seized the smuggling vessels, and by doing so they protected British trade. Their actions affected the colonists' ability to be independent m and cost the British Government a lot in lost taxation.

Britain relied heavily on income from its colonies. As an expanding industrial nation, Britain needed money from whatever sources it could.
Its colonies were the ideal places from which to get this revenue.

The British Government tried to protect their markets even further by imposing high import duties on foreign goods such as sugar, that had been produced by other European nations. However, quite often the prices that had to be paid for the British-supplied goods pushed them out of the reach of normal Americans. American colonists were forced to pay large amounts of money for basic goods.

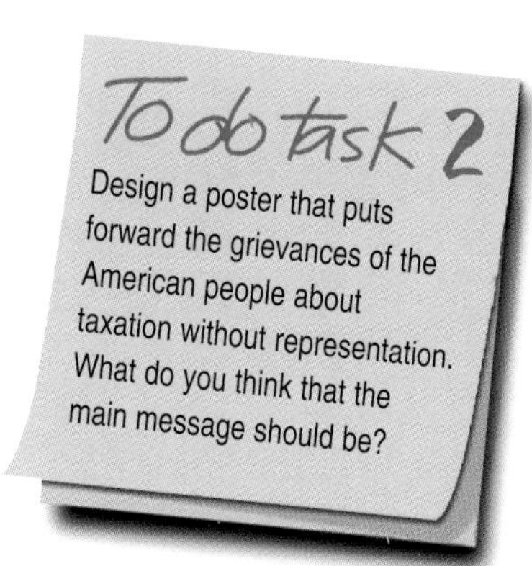

No taxation without representation

While all this was going on the colonists had another **dispute**, because they came under the financial control of the British through direct taxation. The objection to this was quite simple: if they were going to be part of Britain through being taxed by Britain, colonists felt they should be represented in the British Parliament and have a say in British affairs of state. This was just not the case, and out of this came the famous phrase that became a changing point in colonial rule: 'no taxation without **representation**'.

The Seven Years' War

The Seven Years War had been raging between Britain and France and one of the places that it was fought was in North America. Defending America cost money and an army had to be permanently stationed there, despite the cost. The only obvious way to pay for this army was through taxation, and so the American colonies were taxed to take advantage of the funding available from the 2.5 million people who now lived in America. Again, not surprisingly this proved an unpopular decision.

Stamp Act

Yet another tax was the Stamp Act of 1765 which said that a special paper, officially stamped, was the only one that could be used for any important documentation. This paper cost money – a tax.

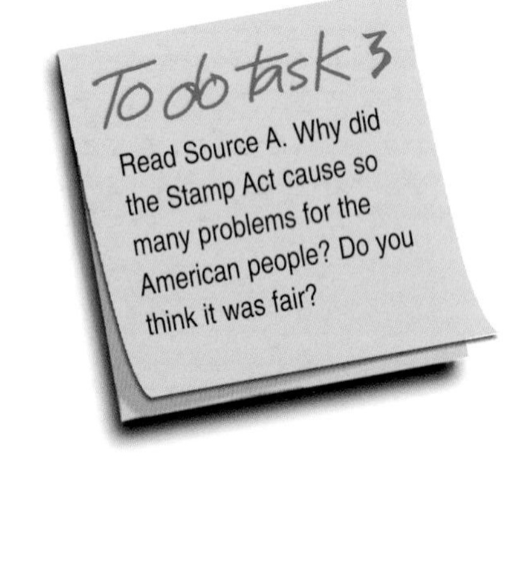

Source A

From the BBC website
www.bbc.co.uk

"Among the items covered by the tax were wills, deeds, diplomas, almanacs, advertisements, bills, bonds, newspapers, playing cards and even dice. Anyone who was involved in any legal transactions, purchased a newspaper or pamphlet or accepted a government appointment would have to pay the tax. In short, the Stamp Act would affect nearly all Americans. Grenville intended, with the full agreement of Parliament, that the Stamp Act should not only raise revenue, it should clearly demonstrate that the British government through Parliament exercised political sovereignty over the colonies."

Unrest comes to a head: The Boston Tea Party 1773

As you can see, the colonists felt they had plenty of cause for complaint and there was little chance of them discussing their problems with the British Government. Instead they chose direct action, and one of the ways that they did so was through the Boston Tea Party.

The infamous Boston Tea Party of 1773 was the result of anger over this taxation without representation. 342 chests of tea were thrown into the sea from a ship called The Dartmouth, amounting to around 5 tonnes in weight. This tea was enough to make 24 million cups of tea and was valued at approximately £10,000. Many taxes had been withdrawn by the British Government, except for the tax on tea.

Source B From a website covering the history of tea

www.tea.co.uk

"During the eighteenth century, tea drinking was as popular in Britain's American colonies as it was in Britain itself. Legally, all tea imported into America had to be shipped from Britain, and all tea imported into Britain had to be shipped in by the East India Company. But during the 1770s the East India Company ran into financial problems: illegal tea smuggling into Britain was vastly reducing the amount of tea being bought from the Company... the Company asked the British government for permission to export tea direct to America, a move that would enable it to get rid of its surplus stock of tea. Thus in 1773 the Tea Act was passed, granting the Company's wish, and allowing a duty of 3d per lb to be levied on the exports to America.

The British Government did not anticipate this being a problem – by being exported directly to America, the cost of tea there would actually become cheaper. But it had underestimated the strength of the American resistance to being taxed at all by their British colonial masters.

Ordinarily taxes do not lead to war, but in America the strength of these disagreements over taxation linked directly to questions about where America should be ruled from. This period of conflict soon escalated into a period known as the American War of **Independence**.

The Declaration of Independence

At the end of the wars the American colonies were declared independent from Britain when the **Declaration** of Independence was signed on 4th July 1776. This meant that they would now function as an independent nation, distanced from Britain by the sheer scale of the Atlantic Ocean, but still connected by the history of many of the people who had colonised the Eastern Seaboard. The way had been opened up for further expansion and the exploitation of this vast continent.

The famous signing of the Declaration of Independence. painted by John Trumbull (1756-1843).

NB

The Seven Years' War, between Britain and France amongst others, was a conflict that was unusual for that period in that it was essentially split, with fighting taking place in both Europe and America.

An engraving from the 19th century showing General Wolfe landing with his troops in Quebec in 1759.

NB

Wolfe was a young but inspirational leader of men, who was unlucky enough to meet his death just as his forces grasped victory against the French during the Battle of Quebec.

Canada

The loss of the American colonies, however, was not the end of the British in America, because they had control of Canada as well. Canada had traditionally been a French colony but this had all changed during the Seven Years' War of 1756–1763, as is explained in Source A.

Source C

Atlas of World History
Patrick K O'Brien

"During the 18th century territorial rivalry between the French and British in North America gradually increased, coming to a head in the Seven Years War of 1756–63. Although the British initially suffered defeats, by 1760 they had effectively defeated the French. France surrendered Canada to Britain in the Treaty of Paris in 1763, and Britain found itself in the unprecedented position of having a colony with a large white population of approximately 6500, who were non-English speaking and Roman Catholic. The British parliament passed the Quebec Act in 1774, which greatly enlarged the territory of Quebec, guaranteed freedom of religion to French Canadians and recognized the validity of French civil law. These measures succeeded in securing the loyalty of the Canadians at a time of increasing discontent in the British colonies elsewhere in America."

The major city of Quebec, and with it Canada, had been surrendered to the British in 1760, as the British forces led by General Wolfe had defeated the French.

Source D

From the website www.historic-uk.com
The History and Heritage Accommodation Guide

"In 1758 Wolfe was dispatched to Canada, sent by William Pitt (the Elder), the Prime Minister of England, to capture the city of Quebec.This was not going to be easy as the French, led by the Marquis de Montcalm, were strongly entrenched along the cliffs that bounded the city's river frontage. Wolfe then laid siege to the city, which dragged on through August, and by now Wolfe was extremely ill with tuberculosis and in great pain. On the night of 12th September Wolfe landed 5000 of his men across the river west of Quebec, and under the cover of darkness he and his troops scaled the steep cliffs, known as the 'Heights of Abraham'. To ensure the element of surprise, Wolfe had ordered that his men remove their shoes and boots before the climb, and they reached the cliff-top without the French defenders even being aware of their presence!"

During the battle that followed, Wolfe was wounded three times and he died at the peak of the battle. The French commander died the next day. The French fled and Quebec surrendered on 18th September 1760 to Major General Amherst, who had taken over the army after Wolfe's death. Montreal did not hold out for long, and the rest of Canada surrendered.

Canada was an area of the world that was attractive to many different nations, mainly because of the great natural resources it possessed. The most attractive of these were the many types of fur and animal products that could be harvested – including the ever-popular cod. Britain would not want to lose this part of their Empire as well, which was now even more important after their defeat in the American Wars of Independence.

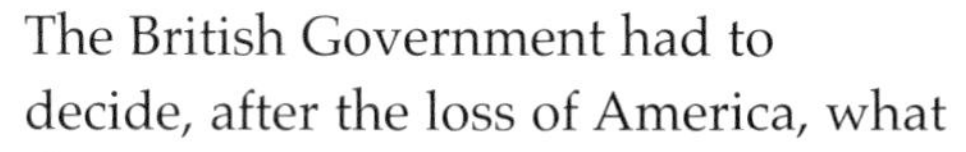

The British Government had to decide, after the loss of America, what the best way to rule Canada would be – by force and through imposing British Law, or through forming policies that benefited both parties. If they made the wrong decision it would surely mean that the British would risk losing another important colony. Eventually, after much deliberation, Canada was made a Dominion of the British Empire – essentially a self-ruling colony.

To do task 4

Draw up a table with 2 columns, one headed Rule by Force and the other headed Allow Self-Rule. Your task is to think about whether the British Government made the right choice in allowing Canada to become a dominion... What advantages and disadvantages can you think of for each type of policy the British had to chose from? Based on the factors you list in each column in your table, what decision do you come to and why?

Source E

From the Learning Curve website www.learningcurve.gov.uk

"Throughout the 1800s huge numbers of European settlers from Britain, Ireland and other parts of Europe poured into British North America (as it was officially called). They soon outnumbered the Native American peoples and turned much of Canada's open plains into fenced-off farms. By the mid 1800s British North America was a collection of separate provinces - Newfoundland, Upper Canada (modern Ontario) and Lower Canada (modern Quebec). By the 1860s the settlers who lived in British North America felt that the time was right for Canada to rule itself. Britain was anxious that Canada did not rebel against them like the USA had done in the 1770s. In 1867 Britain passed the British North America Act. The provinces of British North America became a federation called Canada."

BUZZ WORDZZ

Declaration
dispute
Independence
representation

4.1 Why India?

Did you know that India was a vital part of the British Empire? Its colonisation was as important, if not more important, than America's.

- Why was India so important?
- Who did Britain have to compete with in order to secure a hold over India?

The Jewel in the Crown

India played a huge part in the British Empire. For this reason it is often referred to as 'The Jewel in the Crown'. After losing the valuable American markets, the British searched for a new area of trade to compensate for this. India proved to be an ideal replacement.

Rivalry with the other European Empires

Initially, British traders had looked at The Spice Islands for business, but fierce competition from the Portuguese made this too difficult, so they turned instead to India.

The Portuguese had been interested in Asia for many centuries. When Vasco de Gama landed there in 1498 they had finally been able to exploit a very lucrative market for spices, silks and textiles.

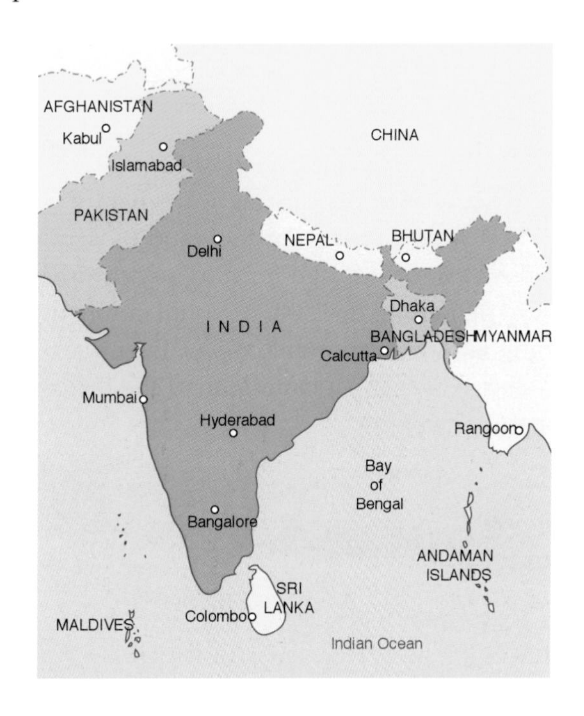

India

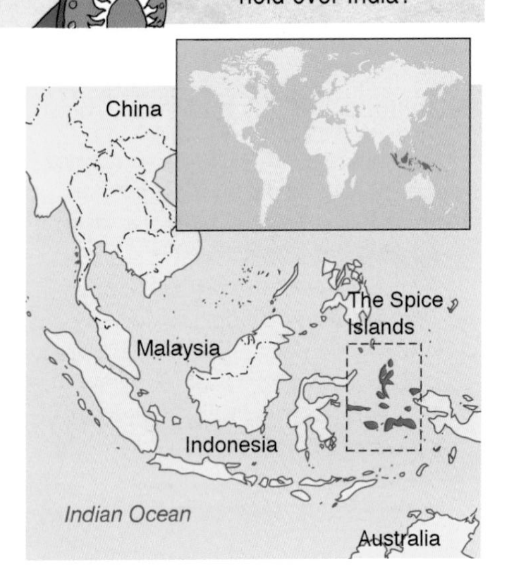

The Spice Islands

Source A

From *The Independent* newspaper website

"It is currently inadvisable to venture to the area that was first dubbed The Spice Islands by European explorers. The thousand or so islands of Indonesia's Maluku and North Maluku provinces are now very troubled."

©www.independent.co.uk/travel/asia

To do task 1

Comprehension

1. What was India also known as?
2. Why were the Spice Islands avoided by the British?
3. Why did the Europeans believe that India would be easy to exploit?

The expansion of trade routes by sea meant that commodities no longer had to be transported over land. The Portuguese built up a number of trading outposts and forts from which they could command the vital trade routes and they had become the dominant force in this area throughout the 16th century. Then the emerging British East India Company began to make their trading presence felt.

The British were not the only European nation who wanted to challenge the Portuguese. The Spanish and the Dutch also had considerable interest in the area. The Dutch East India Company, especially, was a real threat to the Portuguese. So successful were the Dutch that they were able to import lots of Asian goods into the European market. The value of this trade was not lost on the British.

The emphasis for trade

Many goods were of interest to the Europeans, most specifically silk, calico, dyes, saltpetre, cotton, pepper, cardamom, other spices and tea.

India, the Europeans believed, would be easy to exploit because it already had a developed and successful economy, based around relatively small-scale industry and their craft workers. Trade within India and with other nations was not unusual for the people there, who had been trading with other Asian nations for many years.

Trade into India

Control over the trade of goods coming out of India was not the only thing that attracted the Europeans. They also viewed India as a potentially lucrative market for their own goods, hoping to export cotton, iron and steel in particular.

However, trading with Asia was not without considerable risks – this was not an area that would be easily conquered.

Source B **The Evil Empire – 101 ways that England ruined the world** Steven A. Grasse

"Along with silk, cotton and indigo, tea was the main commodity that drove the British East India Company to make India its slave and China its captive. Tea was the reason tens of thousands of acres were razed; the backs of able bodied men were broken working them. All for tea. A drink."

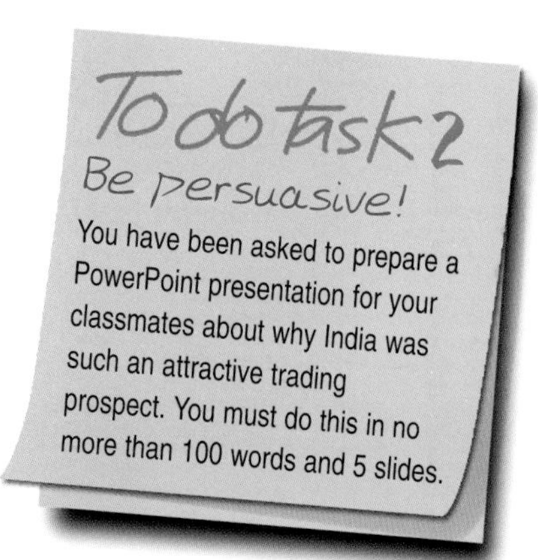

4.2 The Mughal Empire

Before the British reached India, the Indian people were ruled by a group known as the Mughals, who were very powerful and in many ways ahead of many European nations:

- Who were the Mughals?
- How did the British overcome them and take control of India?

NB

A Hindu is somebody who follows the religion of Hinduism, the majority religion in India.
Sikhs follow the religion known as Sikhism, based on the teachings of Guru Nanak.

To do task 1

Comprehension

1. What religion were the Mughal Emperors?
2. Name an example of architecture from the Mughal Empire.
3. Who was the last Mughal Emperor?

The Kings of Kings

Before the arrival of the British, India was relatively well-controlled and was united by one particular group – the **Mughals**. They were a Muslim group in a mainly Hindu country. Their dynasty had begun with the rule of Babur in 1526, and they were known to be a powerful force who had resisted aggressive attempts at expansion by the Dutch and the Portuguese Empires.

The Mughals did not rule totally over all of India. They were actually just a group of Kings who were seen as the 'Shah-an-Shah' or 'King of Kings'. This meant that they were the most important people in India, but their control over India relied on co-operation with a number of Princes who presided over the network of small kingdoms within India.

Tax collection and the administration of the country depended on a series of regional revenue collectors and administrators who made sure that the systems that had been put into place worked properly.

As the Mughal **Emperors** were Muslim, and the majority of their people were Hindu, this meant that the majority of the nation held different beliefs to their rulers. So, if the majority had decided to overthrow the minority, the Mughal position might easily have been undermined. However, groups such as the Hindus, Sikhs and the Marathas tolerated the Mughals, which was how they remained in power for so long.

Source A The decline and fall of the British Empire

Piers Brendon

"The Mughal Empire was a byword for might, majesty and magnificence. Its court was a self-proclaimed paradise of gems, silks, perfumes, odalisques, ivory and peacock feathers. The Mughals' cities were larger and more beautiful than London or Paris. Their bankers were richer than those of Hamburg and Cadiz. Their cotton producers clothed much of Africa and Asia, and their hundred million population matched that of all Europe. Their Elephant cavalry would have intimidated Hannibal and their trains of artillery would have awed Louis XIV. What is more, the 17th century was a golden age of Mughal art, poetry, painting and agriculture."

The Marathas are renowned as warriors. They originally came from an area of India known as Maharashtra. They could have made a push for power against the Mughal.

One of the finest examples of Mughal architecture is the world-famous Taj Mahal. (see below)

The Taj Mahal is one of the most famous buildings in the world and is located in an area of India known as Agra. It was built by a Mughal Emperor – Shah Jahan – for his wife, Mumtaz Mahal.

The Mughal Emperors listed here are cosidered to be the greatest in the dynasty. After the death of Aurangzeb in 1707, their power began to decline.

Babur (1526–30)

Akbar (1556–1605)

Jahangir (1605–27)

Shah Jahan (1627–58)

Aurangzeb (1658–1707)

One of the major factors in their decline was the impact of Europe.

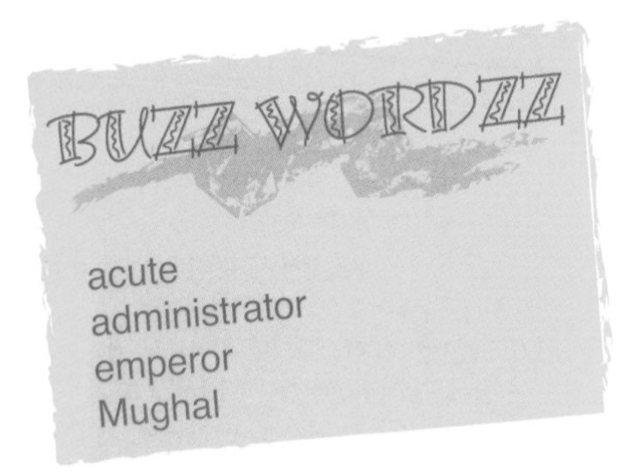

The organisation of India

The sheer size of India meant that the Mughals had to rely on a network of **administrators** and regional rulers to retain their power. A huge population spread over a large area needed close contact with a ruling body and hierarchy, and the network of administrators and regional rulers provided this.

The Mughals were at the top of this ruling hierarchy, with a group known as the Mansabdars just below them. These people were also sometimes known as Nawabs. They were essentially an administrative class, fundamentally loyal only to the Mughals. Next down were the Rajput Chieftains – who ruled over the general Hindu population in the many states – and Rajas the who ruled over the provinces. These groups were collectively known by the British as 'Princes'. Below these classes, at the bottom of the social scale, were the ordinary Indian people.

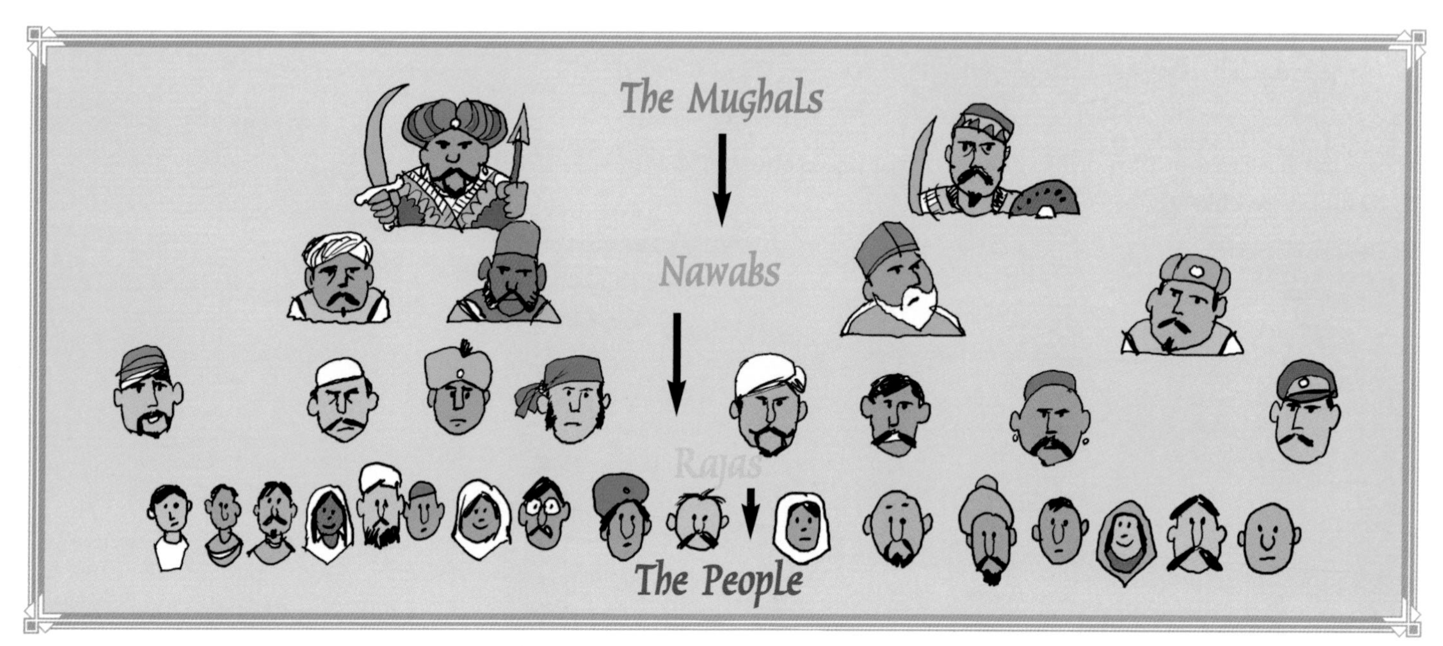

The nature of this ruling alliance through the 'Princes' meant that the way India was ruled varied considerably from place to place. Although the 'Princes' were loyal to the Mughals in essence, they also liked to think that they could rule their own areas independently. They were by no means without authority of their own. There was a large variety of languages spoken across India and each area had marked differences which were most obvious in religion and culture, as well as different methods of administration and rule. India at the time can be thought of as a collection of lots of small, independent states.

Any nation that wanted to rule over India would therefore have to tackle these internal issues as well. Winning over one area would not necessarily mean that the whole of India had been won over.

The decline of the Mughal Empire

From 1707, the Mughal Empire fell into decline as other groups who had previously worked with them battled hard to take over their own areas. The resulting conflict spread across India. The power of the Mughal Emperors was reduced and they finally disappeared in 1858 when the last Mughal Emperor, Bahadur Shah, was exiled to Rangoon, in Burma.

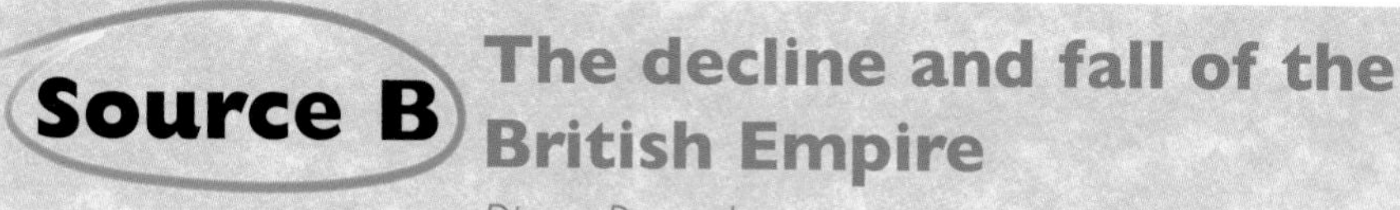

Source B The decline and fall of the British Empire

Piers Brendon

"They sauntered away life in secluded palaces, chewing bang (cannabis), fondling concubines and listening to buffoons."

Making the most of the situation

The British and French managed to exploit the internal problems that had weakened the Mughal Empire. The groups that were fighting each other for supremacy often needed money or supplies so that they could continue these battles, and the British and French were able to supply both. Guns in particular were highly sought after.

To do task 2

How did the British Empire exploit the situation in India? What problems within India allowed this to happen? Draw a spider diagram to show your explanation.

Source C

From the BBC website

www.bbc.co.uk/history/british/empire_seapower

"The Mughal empire had disintegrated and was being replaced by a variety of regional states. This did not produce a situation of anarchy and chaos, as used once to be assumed. Some of the regional states maintained stable rule and there was no marked overall economic decline throughout India."

There were, however, conflicts within some of the states. Contestants for power in certain coastal states were willing to seek European support for their ambitions and Europeans were only too willing to give it. By the 1740s, rivalry between the British and the French, who were latecomers to Indian trade, was becoming **acute**. Private ambitions were also involved. Great personal rewards were promised to the European commanders who succeeded in placing their Indian clients on the thrones for which they were contending.

A British company was perfectly placed to take advantage of this turmoil, and the way was clear for a new power to take control of India. Usually, in such circumstances, a group that was born and bred in a country would take control of the country. However, in this instance, a business company assumed the position and ran India as a business interest. That company was known as the East India Company.

An artist's impression from the mid 19th century showing the capture of Bahadur Shah.

4.3 The East India Company

The East India Company successfully ruled India for many years. Does it surprise you that a company took charge of a whole country?

- How did the East India Company come to hold this position?
  - Who was Robert Clive?
  - How did the East India Company overcome their enemies in India?

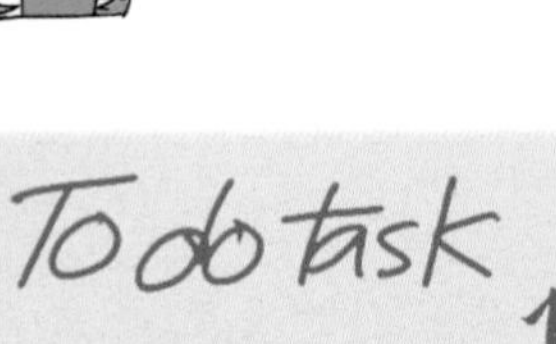

Comprehension

1. When did the East India Company arrive in India?
2. Which two other nations were also interested in India?
3. What was the Black Hole of Calcutta?

The history of the East India Company

The East India Company's initial ventures into India took place in 1608. Their main objective was to break into the lucrative spice and textile trades, which they did successfully, making most of their money from trading in textiles.

India's **geographical** position meant that it would be a vital link between Britain, Europe and Asia. As the East India Company grew, it found ways in which trade with nearby China could be cultivated. It was here that great fortunes could be made through the lucrative opium trade. The British needed India as a close base from which to trade with China effectively.

A contemporary print showing the building in which the East India Company was formed: Founders Hall in London.

East India Company monopoly

Although the company had been given a **monopoly** over British trade in India, this ended in 1694 when the Indian markets were opened up to allow **Free Trade**. However the East India Company proved to be so strong that they continued to be the major force in trade in India until 1773. Then the British Government stepped in and limited their power through the Regulating Act of 1773. But how had a business company become so strong, and why did the Government have to take such an extraordinary step?

Rivalry with the Dutch and French

From the establishment of their first trading post in Surat in 1613, it was vital for the British that they alone controlled trade in India, rather than just being one of a number of nations involved in it. Their main rival was the Dutch East India Company. The Dutch, although they had been trading fairly successfully with the Mughal Empire, did not have a trade monopoly, and the British knew that it would be profitable for them if they could force the Dutch out.

This objective was soon achieved. They overcame most attempts from other European powers, and gained a monopoly over trade and commerce in India. The profits of the East India Company therefore increased immensely.

Acting as 'Kingmakers'

The East India Company was eventually able to improve its position even more. This happened not just because of increasing trade, but also through influencing the internal affairs of India. This was achieved mainly because they were used by the warring factions in India as a way of securing their own positions. The Company's gradual advancement across India was as much down to this 'helping out', as it was down to aggressive **expansionism**.

When the British offered assistance to the Indian princes, they protected their investment by signing an agreement with them. If any of these agreements were not maintained, the East India Company was able to use its large army to seize territory from these 'defaulters'. The army was also a significant defence against any smaller states who resented the British control and proved to be overly aggressive towards the Company.

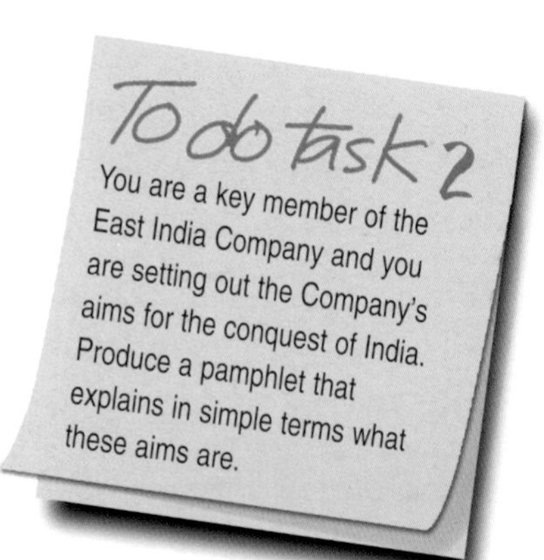

What was the aim of the company?

The British viewed India as a base for trade rather than a permanent colony like America. Conquering and monopolising its trading potential was sufficient to satisfy them. They set up trading outposts that were called 'factories'. These would provide a relatively safe and stable base from which to launch their trade.

An artist's impression from the late 19th century of the sort of forces the East India Company had to fight against. These are small cannon mounted on a portable wooden platform moved by oxen.

The Presidencies

The East India Company maintained its hold over India through three Presidencies that were based in Bombay, Madras and Calcutta. The first to be acquired was Madras in 1634, Bombay followed in1674 and Calcutta in 1690. Each **Presidency** was able to defend its position by using its own personal army.

A military presence

As we have already seen, the British were more than willing to use aggression to guarantee their foothold in such a valuable economic market, even if it meant war. By using their military strength they could hopefully push out competitors and defend themselves against Indian groups who were unhappy about the presence of the British in their country. The British built up a large contingent of forces within India, and Indian soldiers who served the East India Company were called 'Sepoys'.

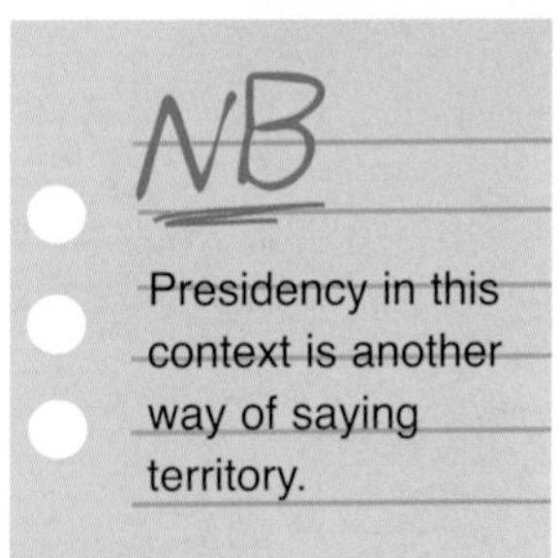

Gradual advancement

British expansion across India was gradual and often slow at times, which is a product of the fact that this was a trading venture rather than a colonisation venture. This gradual advancement, however, was accelerated by the Company's military strength and in particular by a man named Robert Clive.

Who was Robert Clive?

Robert Clive (pictured alongside) made the giant leap from the role of simple office clerk to the commander of the East India Company's armies in a relatively short period of time. Born in 1725 into a relatively wealthy English family, he had lived in India since 1744 when he moved to forge a successful and respectable career for himself.

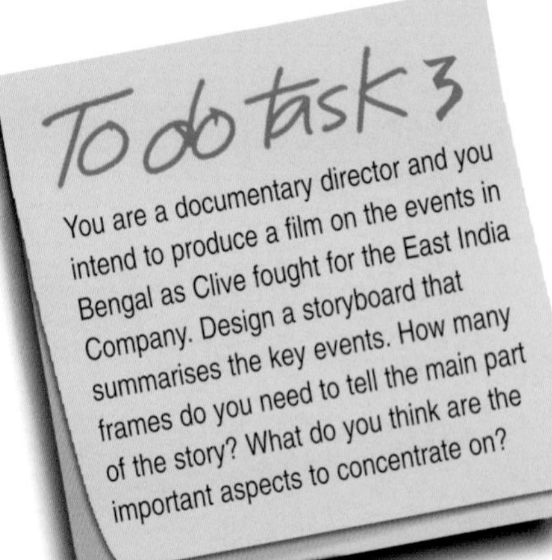

Bengal

British arrogance and desire to dominate trade was sure to lead to conflict. One of the areas that the East India Company was particularly interested in, and where conflict became inevitable, was Bengal, where they had initially been granted trading rights by the Mughals. Following the decline of the Mughal Empire, however, the local Prince had decided that the British presence was unacceptable as it was depriving him of vital trade for himself. The local Prince was named Siraj ud Daula, (his official title was the **Nawab** of Bengal) and he made a move to force the English out of Bengal.

An artist's impression of conditions inside the 'Black Hole of Calcutta.

The Black Hole of Calcutta

The British had expected to defeat the Nawab quickly but this proved not to be the case. Calcutta fell to him rather quickly, largely thanks to the cowardice of Roger Drake, the Governor of Calcutta. Instead of staying to face his enemy, the Governor fled Calcutta by boat leaving his troops alone and without a leader. They were quickly captured by Siraj's invading forces, who imprisoned a number of these British soldiers in what became known as the Black Hole of Calcutta. This infamous event occurred between the 20th and 21st July 1756.

The Black Hole was in fact a small, dark, sweaty room (of around 4m by 5m in size) into which between 100 and 200 men were squeezed. The men suffered terribly in the confined space and many died. The British saw this as an atrocity and sent their best man, Robert Clive, to rectify the situation and restore Calcutta to British rule. Clive seized control of Calcutta by force, thereby placing the area back in British hands – but the East India Company intended to push Siraj and his troops out of the area forever.

The resulting Battle of Plassey took place on 23rd June 1757. The rather one-sided conflict saw the Bengalis badly beaten. Having effectively removed the threat from the Nawab of Bengal's forces, the way was relatively clear for the East India Company to progress further across India.

Clive of India (on the left) meets Nabob Mir Jafar of Bengal at the Battle of Plassey.

Source A

The British Empire *Frank McDonough*

"The real drive to extend the British interests in India began with the annexation of Bengal – the largest Indian province – following the Battle of Plassey in 1757. This occurred shortly after the East Indian Company had appointed Robert Clive, who became known later as "Clive of India", to extend the territory under its control. He brought Calcutta and Bengal under the control of the company, negotiated important trade agreements with the numerous independent regional princes, pushed the French out of India, and persuaded the Mughal Emperor to grant monopoly trading rights to the East India Company. By the late eighteenth century the East India Company... had also emerged as a major political power in India with responsibilities for law, order, administration, trade, defence and diplomacy. By this time the Company – run by London merchants – resembled a state more than a private company."

By 1764, thanks largely to Robert Clive, the whole of Bengal was under the control of the East India Company.

Tipu Sultan – the Tiger of Mysore

However, this was by no means the end of the East India Company's problems, and one of the most interesting opponents they faced was Tipu Sultan, also known as The Tiger of Mysore. Tipu's forces were only finally defeated by the East India Company in 1799. Sources B and C tell a little more about him.

Source B

From the website www.storyofpakistan.com

"Tipu Sultan was born on December 10, 1750 at Devanhalli. Right from his early years he was trained in the art of warfare and at the age of 15 he used to accompany his father Haider Ali, the ruler of Mysore, to different military campaigns. In addition, he also learnt different languages, mathematics and science. His personal library consisted of more than 2,000 books in different languages. He took over the kingdom of Mysore after the death of his father in 1782, who died of a carbuncle in the midst of a campaign against the British. He continued fighting the British and defeated them in 1783. As long as the British fought alone, Tipu always defeated them."

A painting showing the defeat of Tipu Sultan at the Battle of Seringapatnam in 1799.

Source C From *The Independent* newspaper website

"Tipu Sultan ruled the southern Indian state of Mysore for the last 20 years of the 18th century. With his stubborn defiance of Britain's East India Company and his insistence on governing his ancestral land his own way, he proved to be Britain's toughest Indian foe. It took four wars before they broke him.

So passionately did he hate the English that he had a French instrument maker construct him a large model of a tiger crouched on top of a Redcoat, eating him. When the mechanism is operated the tiger utters terrible roars while the soldier moans and feebly waves his arms. On Tipu's death, his mechanical tiger was looted from his palace at Seringapatnam, and has long been a popular exhibit (still in working order) in the Victoria & Albert museum in London.

Despite this evidence of bloodthirstiness, Tipu was by the standards of the time a model ruler, progressive, cultured, "a sophisticated man", according to one Indian scholar, "who understood what Europe's entry into India signified". His fault for the British, in the first flush of empire building, was simply that he refused to bend the knee."

Peter Popham, 23 May 1999 ©www.independent.co.uk

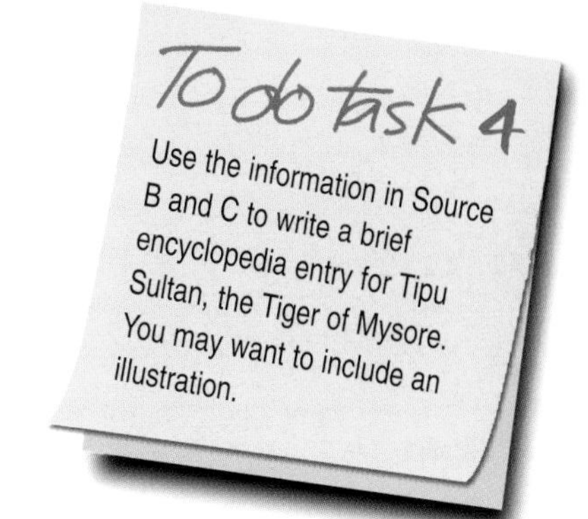

The Maratha Confederacy

Another group that the East India Company had to fight was the Maratha **Confederacy**.

Source D

From the website www.muscatmarathimandal.com

"The 17th century heralded the sudden rise in power of the Marathas – the Marathi speaking warriors of the region. The Marathas emerged as a strong power under Shivaji, who ruled from 1646 to 1680. The Peshwas who succeeded Shivaji built up a Maratha empire which extended from Delhi in the north to Tanjore in the south until the 18th century after which the British exercised their influence in this region."

Despite these issues with the regional forces, who were keen to assert their own dominance, the East India Company became stronger. And as we have seen before, one of the principal reasons for their success was their large, permanent army. It was expensive to run and administer but vital for securing their trading interests. The Company therefore needed a well-trained, well-educated administration service to make sure that it all ran smoothly. To foot the bill for the army and the administration system, the East India Company had to make the most of every opportunity to trade and make a profit. They did this extremely successfully.

4.4 Commerce, trade and administration

India is a country that is full of natural resources, many of which were exploited by the British. One particular commodity, however, has become infamous – opium.

- What is opium?
- Why was opium so important to the British?

Opium

Initially Indian trade had been focused on textiles and spices. But experience soon showed these to be less profitable than expected. Instead the British focused their attention on a product that was notably more controversial than any other so far.

Source A **Atlas of World History**
Patrick K O'Brien

"From the second quarter of the 18th century trade relations between England, France and India began to change. Many European states put up tariff barriers against Indian textile imports in order to protect their own domestic industries. This increased the importance to the English of trade with China, and, in turn, placed greater emphasis on their ability to gain access to Indian silver and Opium."

Selling to China

In order to break into the lucrative Chinese market, the British needed something that the Chinese would actually buy. China was more than capable of competing with British manufacturing, therefore having no real need to buy anything from the British. They were in fact very keen to export their own goods into areas where the British were trading themselves. Opium seemed to fill this gap and was to become an excellent source of income for British traders.

It was the Governor General of India, Warren Hastings, who, in 1780, first had the idea to import opium into China. Chinese interest in it was not initially very significant, but grew quite quickly towards the turn of the century.

What is opium?

Opium is made from opium poppies and is a highly addictive drug. The British were quite willing to exploit Chinese addiction to it. Bengal, in particular, invested considerable time and effort in cultivating its opium fields. The sale of opium was particularly profitable because it brought large amounts of silver into both Britain and India.

The Opium Wars

Over time the Chinese authorities became unhappy that the British should be profiteering from the exploitation of an addiction, and they made every attempt to make sure that these British imports were outlawed. This meant that they tried to forcibly turn away British exports of opium and punish the British merchants who had brought it from India. The sanction for any British merchant found to be importing opium was imprisonment.

This conflict between the Chinese authorities who were trying to prevent or limit the importing of the drug, and the British who were seeking to make even more profit from its trade, became known as the Opium Wars. They took place over two distinct periods:

First Opium War – 1839–42

Second Opium War – 1856–60

Source B

Britannia's Empire

Bill Nasson

"Always confident that it could more than hold its own at sea, Britain was glad of a pretext upon which it could bombard and subdue Chinese coastal opposition to its encroachments. The Opium Wars ended in treaties which diluted China's sovereignty by obliging it to grant increased access for Western trade. The gains of these conflicts were followed by the later seizure of Hong Kong and Kowloon, along with the securing of other outer headlands from which to aim European market capitalism at the Chinese economy."

In 1839, the Chinese authorities seized a shipment of East India Company opium in the port of Canton. In reponse British warships attacked and blockaded Chinese ports. The Chinese eventually signed the Treaty of Nanking (1842), which opened Chinese ports to British trade.

It is clear that the British relationship with China was a strained one, with Britain fully exploiting a rival nation for its own gain. This trade in a lucrative, but deadly, commodity like opium is a part of British and Indian history that many today see as both dubious and immoral. What it served to do, though, was provide vital revenue for a company that was finding the rule of India increasingly expensive.

The geography of China, with major cities and rivers marked.

4.5 The Indian Mutiny

Nations asserting their authority and power upon other nations will always lead to resentment. You can see this, in India, with the Indian Mutiny.

- What was the Indian Mutiny?
- Why did it show that the British did not fully understand the nation that they controlled?

In the army now

The nature of the East India Company's control of India meant that a large army was needed, and a significant proportion of these troops were Indian. This Indian army could also be used in other parts of the Empire if it was needed. The Indian soldiers, or 'Sepoys', were vital to the British control of India.

British attitudes to Indian culture

The Indian people were doubtful that the British had their best interests at heart, as the British had attempted to westernise India in many ways. For instance, they tried to outlaw some Indian customs that they saw as less than civilised. One such example was that of the Suttee (pictured left). This was where a recently-widowed Hindu woman committed suicide by burning herself to death on the funeral pyre used to cremate her husband's body. Was it really the role of the British to ban such a custom? Nevertheless, they had done so in 1829 and behaved similarly with their harsh treatment of the group of people known as the Thugees.

A contemporary illustration showing Thugees.

Source A

Thug: the true story of India's murderous cult

Mike Dash

"Thug is an Anglo-Indian word referring to a cult of wandering highwaymen, adept in the art of strangulation by a piece of material no more than 1m in length. This organised, ruthless, swift and elusive fraternity was active in India for nearly two centuries until Major William Henry Sleeman, a British officer, led the successful campaign to eradicate the practice. Between 1830 and 1840, Sleeman pursued, meticulously documented and eventually captured more than 3,000 Thugs. Some were hanged, the rest transported. He rightfully became a hero of the Raj."

As you may understand, many Indian communities were not pleased about the way that the British were imposing themselves on their nation. They felt that the British too often worked from a position of little cultural or overall understanding. After all, they were not ruling Britain but were presiding over the affairs of another country: India. As such they should have been more respectful of traditions that they did not necessarily understand. What other parts of their culture, religion and ways of life would be at stake if the British rule continued?

The Enfield rifle and its bullets

Although it may seem odd at first, one of the main sources of friction for the Indians and the Sepoys was a ruling over the type of rifle ammunition that they used. This led to the Sepoys taking a stand over what they saw as a lack of cultural understanding on the part of the British. This became known as the Indian Mutiny, and it raged between 1857 and 1859. A new rifle called the Enfield had been issued to the troops and the bullets that the gun used were greased to enable smooth loading. However, possibly due to their ignorance, or an inability on the behalf of the British to respect the traditions of the Indian soldiers, the grease was made from animal fat. The animal fat came from pigs and cows, which caused religious offence to both Hindu and Muslim soldiers.

This is because cows are special to the Hindu religion and are not eaten by Hindus. Muslims view the pig as being an 'unclean' animal that may not be eaten. So the new bullets managed to offend both groups!

The main focus of the rebellion was the 19th Bengal Infantry who had refused point-blank to use the new greased cartridges. Those who had refused to use them faced prison, but this was seen as a risk worth taking for a conflict that essentially pitted religion against military authority.

Loading a rifle at the time meant soldiers had to bite open the cartridge which was in a small packet, pour the gunpowder down the barrel, then ram the cartridge (including the bullet) down the barrel. It was also recommended that if the grease around the bullet had melted then the bullet should be put in the soldier's mouth and the saliva would serve the same purpose as grease.

Source B — A History of India

John Keay

"Known to the British as 'the Sepoy', 'Bengal' or 'Indian Mutiny', to Indians as 'the National Uprising' or the 'First War of Independence', and to the less partisan of both nations simply as the 'Great Rebellion', what happened in 1857 defies simplistic analysis.

A new rifle was being issued for which the cartridges, which had to be rammed down the barrel, were being greased with a tallow probably containing both pigs' fat and cows' fat. Moreover the cartridge had first to be bitten open with the teeth. To cow-reverencing Hindus as to pig-paranoid Muslims the new ammunition could not have been more disgusting had it been smeared with excrement; nor had it been dipped in hemlock, could it have been more deadly to their religious prospects."

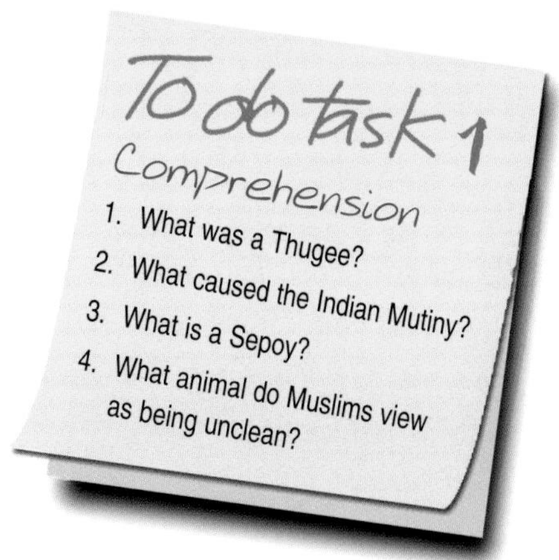

Source C From The National Army Museum website

www.national-army-museum.ac.uk

"The rising was not confined to sepoys, so it was not just a 'sepoy mutiny', thousands of ordinary civilians took part.

They were united in wanting to rid India of the British, but they were not looking to unite India. The rising was geographically limited, and when British rule in northern India temporarily collapsed, there was no unified nationalist revolt, but rather a struggle for succession by different local rulers. Other Indian soldiers were crucial in putting down the uprising, so the Indian people cannot be seen as united."

Source D

From the BBC website

"British public opinion was profoundly shocked by the scale of the uprising and by the loss of life on both sides – involving the massacre by the rebels of captured Europeans, including women and children.

When the sepoys refused to acknowledge British authority, the way was left open for disaffected princes and aristocrats, and for village and town people with grievances, to revolt alongside the soldiers.

After the rebellion had been put down, the new royal government of India that replaced that of the East India Company promised that it had no intention of imposing 'our convictions on any of our subjects'. It distanced itself further from the Christian missionaries."

The results of the Mutiny

The Indian Mutiny had a number of repercussions, but one of the most important was that the British decided that it would be in their best interests to keep a permanent army present in India, numbering around 60,000 men. Also, an effectively-controlled Indian army could now be utilised by the British and the Indian troops could be sent across the world to defend British interests in time of need. This is indeed what happened, with around 150,000 troops available for British use at its peak.

4.6 The Golden Age of the Raj

In this section you will learn about the Raj and the changes the British made during its Golden Age.

- Why did the raj have a Golden Age?
- What happened during that Golden Age?

Discussion POINT

You have been asked to decide whether the British were truly in the wrong regarding the Indian Mutiny. What do you think and why?

NB

A Durbar is a commemorative celebration.

Delhi Durbar

The Delhi Durbar (a huge procession through Delhi) of 1903 celebrated the coronation of Edward VII, and showed off the magnificence of British India. These celebrations marked not just the coronation of a King, but the ascendance of a new Emperor of India. Huge crowds gathered to see the elephants and the Maharajas ride past, and the colourful performers and artists lining the streets. This celebration capped a remarkable period in the British rule of India – known as the 'Raj', which is the Hindi word for 'rule'.

A parade of decorated elephants at the Dehli Durbar of 1903.

Source A

From The British Library website

"On New year's day 1903, Edward the VII was declared Emperor of India. The occasion was marked by a grand ceremony held at the Delhi Durbar - a spectacular and elaborate festival organised by the British government. The Durbar was intended to highlight the supposed glory of the monarchy and its Empire. The festivities involved an enormous procession which included a line of Indian princes riding on jewelled elephants."

To do task 1

Comprehension

1. What was the Delhi Durbar?
2. Who was the Empress of India?
3. What were the seven large provinces that the British maintained control over?

Although, in general, the British tried to make India a home from home, they did try to work with the Indians wherever possible. For many, though, the feeling remained that they were superior to the Indians. Because of the importance of India to the British Empire, Britain was unsure about the best way to rule the nation.

They could either rule India strictly, treating the Indian people as inferior citizens, or they could be more lenient and treat the Indian people as equals. Whatever method they tried it was important that they looked after India, as it was vital to the Empire.

Source B **Empire** *Niall Ferguson*

"The British were able to use India to control an entire hemisphere, stretching from Malta all the way to Hong Kong. It was the foundation on which the entire mid-Victorian Empire stood. Yet behind the marble facade, the Raj was the conundrum at the heart of the British Empire. How on earth did 900 British civil servants and 70,000 British soldiers manage to govern upwards of 250 million Indians?"

The Empress of India

The Empress of India was Queen Victoria. Although a very capable Queen, it was not possible for her to rule over such a large country without efficient administrators. The complex nature of the Indian states meant that ruling over them would be a difficult matter. Yet the British managed to rule India using a combination of a relatively small number of administrators and a relatively large army. To do this there had to be a good deal of co-operation between the British and the 601 states. The British maintained control over seven large provinces: Bombay, Bengal, Madras, the Punjab, the Central Provinces, the North-Western Provinces, and the North-West frontier. The states were run by the 'Princes', who were often known by the British as 'Maharajas'. These Princes co-operated with the British, but were gradually stripped of their power by the Raj.

Queen's Victoria's head on the reverse of an old British coin.

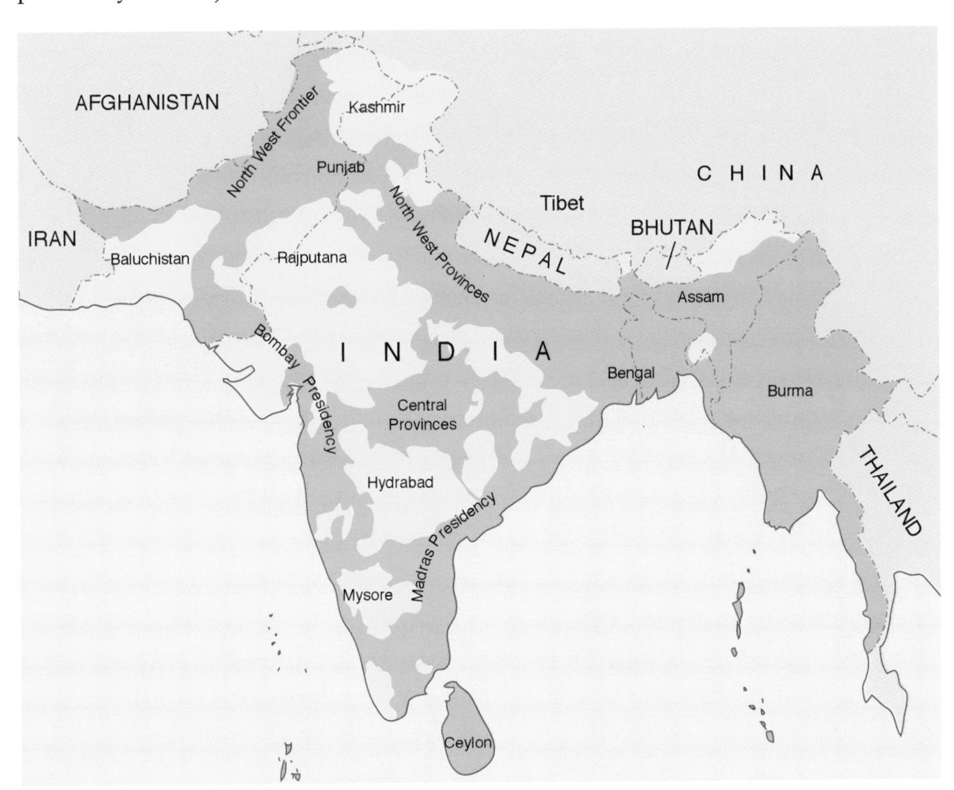

India and it's provinces.

At the peak of British expansion the British Empire presided over two thirds of India and, clearly, India became a very expensive country to run.

Nabobs

As the years passed, it became clear that British rule in India was in need of an overhaul. They had spent so long presiding over Indian trade and commerce that they had developed bad habits. The most exceptional example of this complacency was a group of individuals known as the Nabobs. These provincial governors had made a lot of money from trade in India.

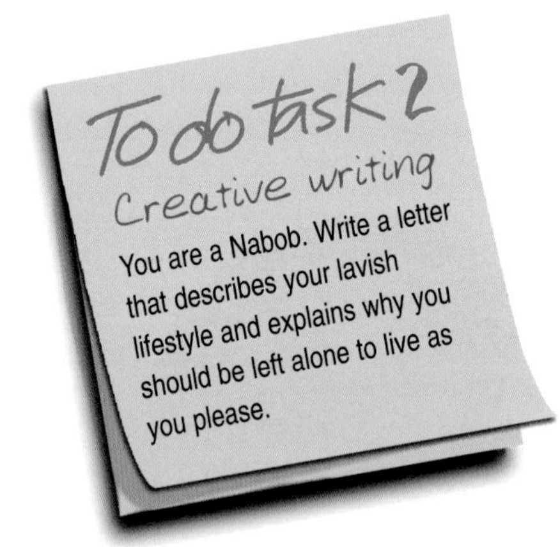

They were controversial figures who lived a life of luxury in huge mansions surrounded by acres of land. They were viewed with suspicion by many who were unsure how they had come by their wealth. Many people believed that these men had made their money through extortion, excessive taxation and by accepting bribes from Indians who wanted to climb quickly up the ladder of power. Others were concerned that Nabobs increasingly chose to leave India, taking their huge fortunes with them, and setting up again in England.

At a time when the East India Company was struggling financially, the actions of the Nabobs were making matters worse. They were essentially living their lives at the expense of the East India Company and India, and were one of the many reasons why the East India Company eventually had to ask for help from the British Government.

The Nabobs had no desire to enter into the spirit of life in India, instead choosing to shut themselves away from the outside world in their splendid mansions. Therefore they had relatively little impact on Indian ways of life, and had actually absorbed few if any of the Indian traditions and cultures to which they had been exposed.

Their way of life contrasted greatly with other British settlers, some of whom had made real attempts to fit in with the Indians. They had become 'Anglo-Indians', marrying Indian women and learning the language. This in turn helped them to expand their trading influences. The Nabobs, however, exemplified all the bad points of the East India Company.

Government of India Act

As the East India Company appealed for British Government help, it did so at a time when it was clear that the control of India was too important to the British Empire to leave in the hands of one private business. And so the Government took specific steps to protect the place of India in the Empire.

Source C

White Cargo Don Jordan and Michael Walsh

"The British Government responded by taking several measures between 1773 and 1833 which served to place the East India Company in a ***subservient*** *role. The 'India Act' of 1774 gave the British Government 'the power of guiding the politics of India with as little means of corrupt influence as possible'. The Company retained ownership rights over its captured territory, a trade monopoly and existing responsibilities over civil administration and defence. A British Governor General was given overall political, legal and diplomatic control over British territory in India. In 1813 the British Government ended the Company's monopoly over Indian trade – except the trade in tea with China."*

Source D

Britannia's Empire Bill Nasson

"East India Company servants were banned from wearing anything other than European dress, company army officers and tax collectors who had fallen into Indianised ways were barred from participating in Hindu festivals, and anyone with an Indian parent was denied employment in the company's civil, marine or military branches. Curry was now frowned off the table at English parties in Calcutta. Replaced by hostess rituals of imported salmon and cheese, and pyjamas became a garment solely for sleeping in."

Warren Hastings, the first Governor General of India.

In November 1858 the 'Act for the better government of India' saw the East India Company finally dissolved and the country placed under the direct control of the British Government. Rule would now come directly from the India Office in London, with the Governor General – or Viceroy – in charge. This was an extension of the position adopted by the East India Company, whose first Governor General of India had been Warren Hastings (1773-1784).

The Indian civil servants

The Governer General could not rule alone, however. He had to rely on a network of Indian civil servants to administrate effectively. At its peak the British in India numbered less than 50,000 and the Indian population was as large as 150,000,000. In ordinary circumstances this would have been impossible. But, somehow, miracles were worked.

Containing around 3000 people, this system of bureaucracy and administration nevertheless managed to keep British control over India running smoothly. Many civil servants were well educated, with degrees from Oxford or Cambridge universities. They needed this high level of knowledge and education as running a country as large as India was an extremely complex task. The people of India often referred to these civil servants as the 'Bengali **Babus**'.

The Maharajas

The last bit of Indian independence and power lay with the **Maharajas**. These Indian Princes were meant to be loyal to the British. but had the responsibility for their states taken away from them as they had been placed under British administration. They were now symbolic figure-heads of a way of life that had disappeared.

It ain't half hot!

One of the major problems that the British encountered, other than the cultural, language and geographical problems, was the heat. To people used to the mild climate of Britain, many often found it intolerable, declaring that it was just too hot for them. This meant that many of the British were forced to leave the low-lying coastal areas and cities and travel to cooler places in the mountain ranges.

One of the most popular mountain 'retreats' was in Shimla. It was so popular and so much more comfortable than the hot, sticky cities that many British took the opportunity to spend extended periods of time in the mountains.

A preserved example of one of the lavish mountain retreats to which the British went during the hot Indian seasons.

Source E

From *The Daily Telegraph* website www.telegraph.co.uk

"Exactly 100 years ago, Wildflower Hall, my sumptuous hotel, was the mountain eyrie of Lord Kitchener when he was commander of the British Army in India. It is just a few miles from Shimla, the remote hill station 8,200 feet above sea level, which, in the 19th century, became the official summer capital of the Raj.

When Delhi became too hot for comfort, the whole colonial shooting-match, from the viceroy down, upped sticks and migrated to the foothills of the Himalayas, where they stayed until the weather cooled. While the cities of the plain baked, the business of empire carried on amid the pine forests and the mountain streams.

Never in the field of human bureaucracy were so many filing-cabinets carted such long distances for such a short period."

To do task 6

What does the tendency for the British to move away from the industrial cities to the coast suggest about their willingness to adapt to life in India? What do you think they should have done?

It is clear that aspects of British life in India were not always comfortable. Behind the beauty of places like Shimla, and covered by the dust and heat of the cities, lay a discomfort and an inability or unwillingness to fit in. Little attempt was made to fit in with the 'ordinary' way of life in India. Instead the British just attempted to make India more hospitable and suitable to the British way of life.

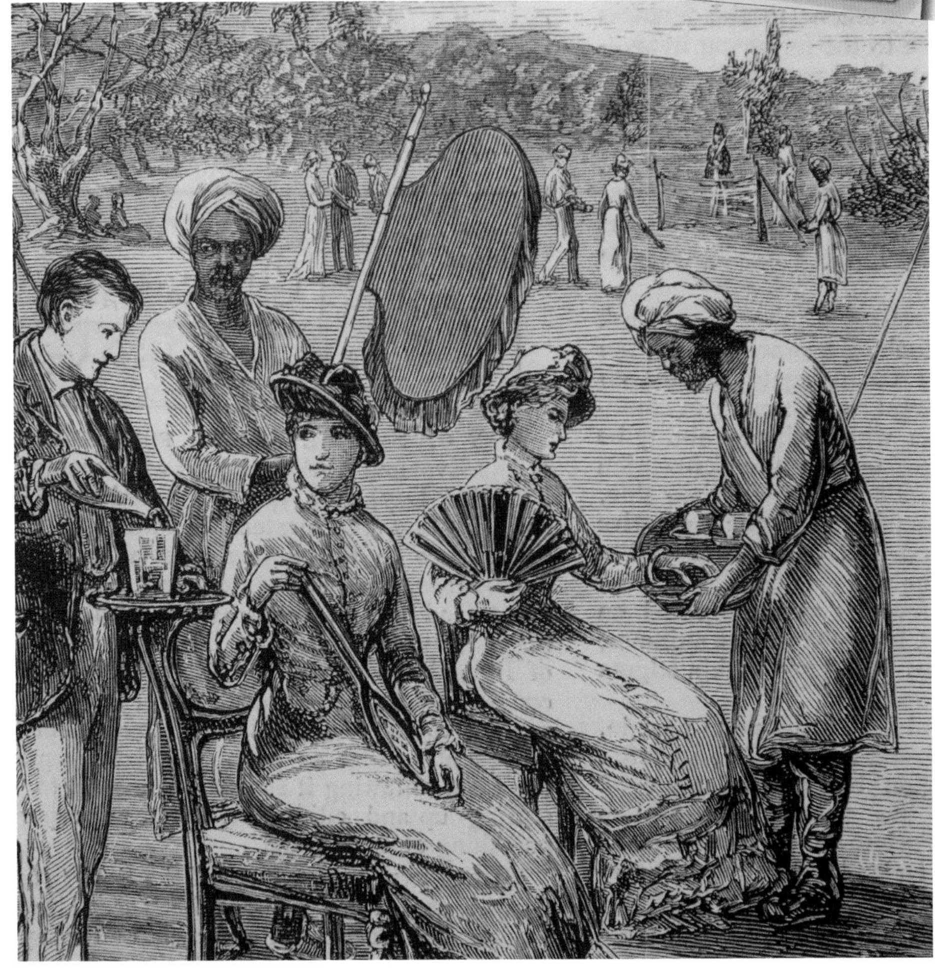

An illustration from the late 19th century showing English ladies taking afternoon tea, served by their Indian servants.

4.7 The British impact on India

Many people think that the British must have had a harmful impact upon the Indian nation. This is not necessarily the case:

- What impact did the British have on India?
- Did it add or detract from Indian life?

For better or worse?

The British had a massive impact on India, not least in their attempts to introduce Christianity to the country. This was seen as a more suitable religion for India than the majority religion of Hinduism.

Much debate has centred around whether the British Empire had a good or bad overall impact on India. Some people say that any outside interference in the development of a country is bad, while others believe that any rule that brings improvements can only be a good thing.

Whether the British impact was good or bad is really down to personal opinion. It is difficult to measure it exactly when we are looking from our view today that is so distant from the nation, the people and the period. It must be said that the British at that time – the ruling Raj – believed that they *were* 'improving' India. But do you think forcing a different way of life and culture on a nation is really an improvement?

Anglicising India

The British would never be able to Anglicise the whole of the Indian subcontinent. It was simply too big. What they could do, however, was change the nature of the areas that they had control over, even if they could not change the people. The British were guilty of exploiting the Indian resources and economy for their own gain, and their major crime in this respect was not re-investing more of the money that they had made from India back into the country. Instead, a lot of the profit simply went into the pockets of merchants, traders and investors.

A British textiles factory in India with a mostly Indian workforce on view.

However that is not to say that there was no British investment in India. There was a large amount of investment, specific in certain areas, with total British **expenditure** in India amounting to more than £400 million by 1914. And yet poverty was widespread in India despite British influence.

Historians have pointed to investment in the railways, canals, mining and agriculture as being positive, while famine, poverty, taxes, the decline in traditional industries and a lack of any real investment back into India have been highlighted as negative factors.

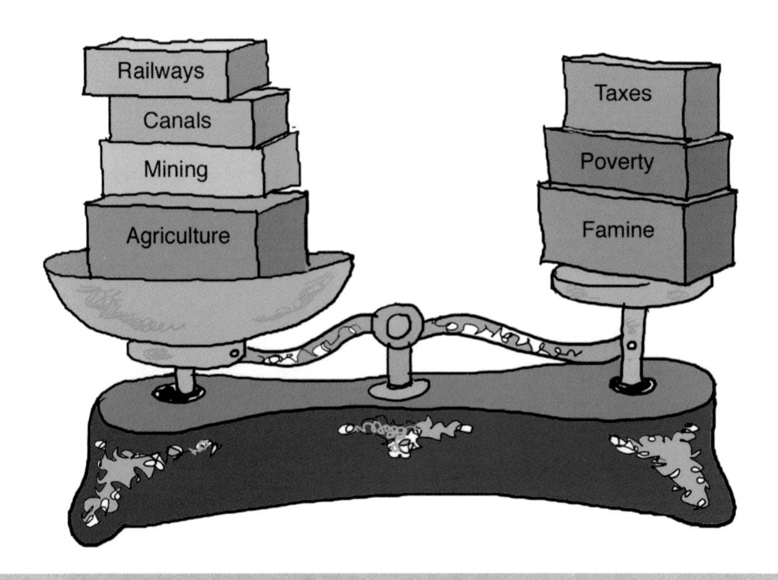

Source A

Britannia's Empire *Bill Nasson*

"Railways, roads, telegraphic and postal services, ***sanitation****, irrigation and associated public works exemplified the Victorians' notion of improvement."*

Industrialisation

Many areas were industrialised in the model of British towns and cities, becoming filled with the symbol of **industrialisation** – the factory. These manufactured similar goods and commodities to those that were located in Britain, with a booming textile trade at the centre. One place in particular that blossomed during the Indian industrial revolution was Cawnpore (now known as Kanpur) that had a number of factories producing cotton and wool cloth, and mills that produced flour.

To do task 2

Read Source B. How useful is it to a Historian studying Kanpur (Cawnpore) during the British occupation of India?

Source B

From a travel website www.indianholiday.com

"Kanpur soon became a prime military base of the British. Since then, the importance of Kanpur has been on the rise. Today, Kanpur is an important Travel Destination in India. The city offers various places of interest that ranges from Religious Places like Temples, Mosques, and Churches to ace educational institutions like the Indian Institute of Technology (IIT). Kanpur is also considered to be an effective shopping destination. There are numerous other forms of tourist attractions in Kanpur. Tours to Kanpur is also a one to look forward to, since it is easy to access. Kanpur is located beside the Grand Trunk Road, between New Delhi and Kolkata. The railway station of Kanpur connects the city with all other major cities of the country."

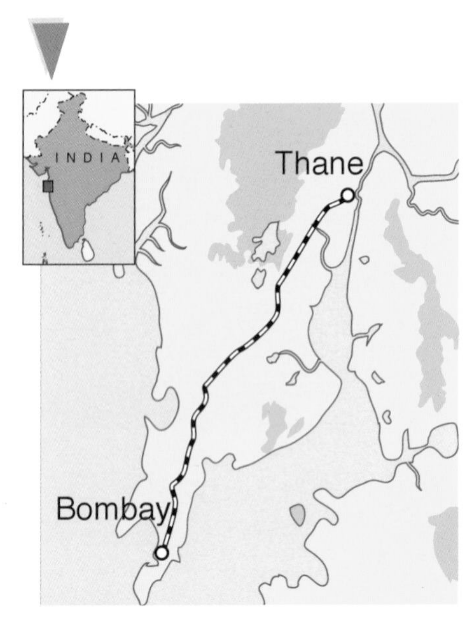

The railways

Much of the British investment in India went into building a useful railway network, which was of major importance to both British control and the expansion of India. It was also important in the development of the country itself.

This investment was often financed by individual British investors who naturally wanted to make a profit. The success of the railways was actually so great that the British investors were able to take huge profits back to Britain – not reinvesting back into India. Construction of the infrastructure, locomotives and rolling stock for the railways also usually took place in Britain, so the key manufacturing actually took many jobs away from the India.

British industrial power: heavy machinery being used to build a railway bridge in India.

The success of the railways was obvious and immediate and many people took advantage of them. Virtually everybody used them at some time or other. The railways certainly brought the distant parts of India closer together. The first stretch of railway was opened between Bombay and Thane in 1853 and by the start of the 20th century 24,000 miles of track had been laid. But conditions on the trains were far from ideal...

The Law

Another way in which the British changed India was through the anglicisation of Indian law. They did this through introducing two separate Acts in 1861 – the Code of Criminal Procedure and the Indian High Courts Act that established High Courts in Madras, Calcutta and Bombay. The law was based primarily on standard British law, both common and customary, with parts of Indian law being built into and alongside the British legal system. Both Hindu and Muslim judges helped the British make sure that they did not forget about the traditional Indian ways in every respect.

Source C

Plain tales from the British Empire

Charles Allen

"Indian trains were not free from dirt or disease. Seasoned travellers brought their own bedding and ensured that the floors of the carriages were swabbed down with disinfectant. Some even went as far as to take a bottle of Evian water to clean their teeth, because the water on the trains was considered too impure."

Improved public health

The British had a major impact on health levels in India as well. They provided a ready supply of vaccinations to the people, with quinine being especially important for fighting off the threat of malaria. However, many Indians did not like the vaccinations, mainly because they were **administered** by the British. The major illness fought through the use of a vaccination was smallpox. A disease that you may be very surprised to hear struck India, was Bubonic Plague, with the main attack occurring in 1896.

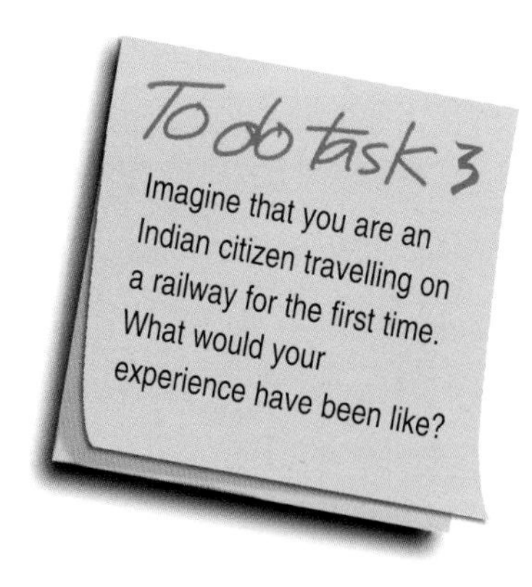

The amazingly grand building for the High Court in Calcutta.

Source D

From the Medical History of India website, with permission from the Board of Trustees of the National Library of Scotland

"The years 1898–1899 marked a turning point in the government's strategies of plague control due to an increasing realisation that the use of force in enforcing plague regulations was proving counter-productive and that it would be administratively impossible to enforce them in the large area affected by the epidemic, especially since plague was no longer confined to cities but had spread into the countryside. A further change in policy included the incorporation of practitioners of indigenous systems of medicine in plague prevention. This marked a turnaround, as Indian systems of medicine were considered unscientific and disparaged by the state. Inoculation using Haffkine's plague vaccine was also pressed, although the government made strenuous efforts to stress that inoculation was not compulsory."

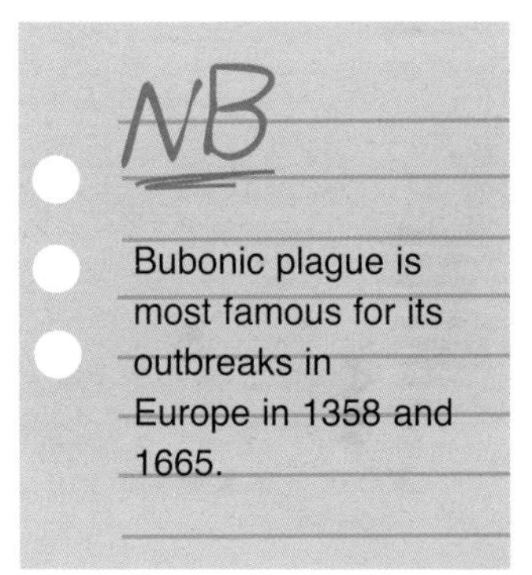

All these changes and innovations can still be seen in India, either directly or indirectly in current legislation and practices. It is hard to see whether these innovations and technological advances had a real impact on India and the Indian people. What cannot be denied is that the British invested a lot of money in India, and made a lot of money from India. It is impossible to say now what route Indian history would have taken without British involvement.

4.8 Indian self-rule

Not everybody liked British rule in India and many people fought to re-gain India's independence.

- Why did they want independence for India?
- How did they intend to get it?
- Who were the main people involved in this campaign?

The struggle for independence

The rule of the East India Company and the British Government was, as we have already seen in the case of the Indian Mutiny, not always popular.

Source A

An utterly impartial history of Britain

John O'Farrell

"It is no wonder that resentment built up, particularly from the higher castes of Indian society, as they witnessed the enormous wealth of their country being shipped back to England. The greatest diamond in history remains in the British Crown Jewels in the Tower of London. Mention the Koh-i-Noor to an Indian or Pakistani politician and they will tell you it is a symbol of centuries of imperial plunder. Mention the Koh-i-Noor to an Englishman and he will tell you it's a curry house just off the high street."

Many groups in India were beginning to campaign for an independent state. This was partly due to better standards of education, as well as a growing knowledge of world affairs which made some believe, justifiably, that they could govern themselves. Some British people living in India were also beginning to think that this was something to consider seriously.

Time to withdraw

It would take a long time before Britain finally gave up control of the nation that had brought them so much over such a long time. Despite its riches, India had become a financial burden to Britain as it was increasingly expensive to control such a large nation. Many in the British Government thought that it was **economically** wise to let India go, despite its potential. The Indian people were also beginning to seek their own independence and Indian **nationalism** was an emerging political force. The dislike for British rule resulted in the formation of a pro-Indian rule group called the Indian National **Congress**, which was established in 1885. From the formation of this group, to eventual independence in 1947, their emphasis was on breaking the ties with Britain.

Raj: The making of British India

Lawrence James

"The result was the formation of the Indian National Congress, which held its first annual meeting in Calcutta in December 1885. In essence it represented a fusing of many smaller societies from all parts of India. Its overall objective was to hold Britain to its word, which was that the Raj existed for the benefit of Indians who, under its guidance, would advance to a state in which they could manage their own affairs. No one at the time had the slightest idea of how long this process would take."

BUZZ WORDZZ

congress
economically
nationalism

Indian National Congress

The main group that campaigned for Indian independence was the Indian National Congress. This party, however, showed its own signs of turmoil with political in-fighting a common feature. They were not always united on what the best tactics were. The debate rested on whether they should be violent or peaceful. A number of key figures attracted attention during the quest for Indian independence.

Mahatma Gandhi [1869–1948]

One of the leading figures was Mohandas Gandhi, more commonly known as 'Mahatma' Gandhi, which means 'Great soul'. Gandhi was a pacifist by nature and a very well-educated man. After studying law in England, Gandhi had been involved in pro-Indian activities in South Africa, where he had been imprisoned, but released after a short period. Gandhi would also face imprisonment on numerous occasions in India, when he refused to obey British rule and legislation.

Gandhi as depicted on the Indian banknote.

Gandhi was a key member of the Indian National Congress until his resignation in 1934. Despite his resignation he was still a fierce supporter of Indian nationalism and was greatly opposed to the idea that the British might 'partition' India.

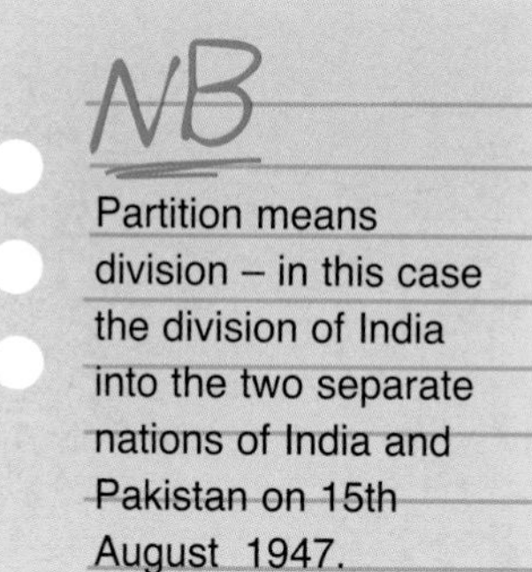

Source C

From the website The History Channel

www.thehistorychannel.co.uk

"On 11 March 1930 Gandhi and his followers set out to walk 241 mi/150 km to Dandi, to campaign against the salt tax imposed by the British government, which maintained its monopoly by making it illegal for Indians to make their own salt. After arriving at Dandi on 6 April, Gandhi and his followers defied the British government by making their own salt. On 4 May Gandhi announced that the government-owned Dharasana saltworks were to be taken over on behalf of the Indian people. Gandhi was arrested but his followers advanced on the saltworks as planned. As the marchers moved forward in columns they were beaten to the ground, offering no resistance."

Jawaharlal Nehru [1889–1964]

Jawaharlal Nehru was another key member of the Indian National Congress, although he did not become a member until 1919. Like his colleague, Gandhi, Nehru stood up for Indian nationalism and was imprisoned for his stance in the 1920s and again in the 1930s. He was a key figure in the final decision to 'partition' India, which he was forced to accept despite his personal reservations about it. He subsequently became India's first Prime Minister.

Mohammed Jinnah [1876–1948]

Mohammed Jinnah was also a member of the Indian National Congress but he later left the organisation and became a leading figure in the 'Muslim League'. He was one of the leading figures in the campaign for a partition of Muslim and Hindu India.

With the help of these key figures a number of government acts were passed that helped to reform India and to make it easier for the British to hand back the rule of India to the Indians.

NB

Muslim League
A political party that campaigned for the formation of Pakistan as a separate nation from India.

The Morley-Minto reforms

Source D From The History Channel website www.thehistorychannel.co.uk

"Announced in 1909 to increase the participation of Indians in their country's government. Introduced by John Morley (1838–1923), secretary of state for India, and Lord Minto (1845–1914), viceroy of India, they did not affect the responsibility of government, which remained in British hands, but did give Indians wider opportunities to be heard."

Source E

From the website www.britishempire.co.uk

"What emerged was 1919's Government of India Act which was a move towards double government or 'diarchy'. The Act created 11 self-governing provinces of British India and Indian ministers were given 'safe' portfolios including control over public health, education and agriculture. Power was still firmly where it had always been: British ministers controlled justice, foreign policy and the economy; moreover, the Viceroy could veto legislation, suspend provincial councils and if necessary rule as an autocrat."

Government of India Act

A number of discussions about the future of India also occurred in England, known as the 'Round Table Conferences'. These took place in 1930 and 1931 and Gandhi was one of the Indian representatives. These conferences were where the concept of a separate nation of 'Pakistan' first emerged, and they led to the 1935 Government of India Act. This Act gave even more power back to India.

However, this Act did not entirely hand over the running of India. This took many more years to come about. The process was very gradual. It was not until the end of the Second World War that India became independent from Britain.

Source F

www.channel4learning.com

"The Second World War guaranteed Indian independence. Indian troops were heavily involved in the defeat of the Japanese in Burma. The new Labour government elected in 1945 was committed to Indian independence. Sadly, the prospect of Indian independence generated horrific violence between Muslims and Hindus. The British determined that there would be a new state of Pakistan, and duly withdrew from the Indian subcontinent in 1947. India had independence and so did Pakistan, but a terrible legacy was left behind."

© Channel 4 Learning

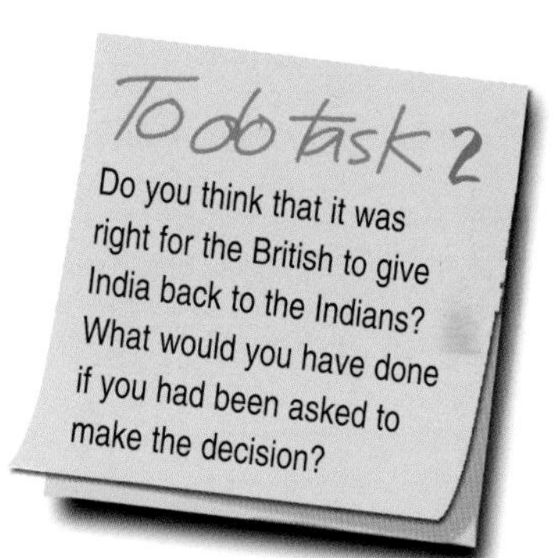

Lord Mountbatten

The man who was to oversee the handover of India back to the Indians was the Viceroy of India, Lord Mountbatten. The Mountbatten plan of 1947 saw the division of India into two separate nations – India and Pakistan.

August 1947 – Indian Independence Act

India was finally granted independence through the Indian Independence Act of 1947 and the party that was placed in charge of India was the Indian National Congress. Pakistan became a separate nation. Pakistan was a mainly Muslim nation and India mainly Hindu.

This 'independence' had been a long time in coming. Some people say, justfiably, that India should never have had to seek independence from another nation anyway. The British had no right to take their independence from them in the first place. The partition of India, like the rule of the East India Company and Britain, would also have far-reaching implications for India and the new country of Pakistan – primarily war. So how much do you think Britain is responsible for the problems that have characterised India and Pakistan since 1947?

Chapter 5
Africa, the Caribbean and the slave trade

What does it mean to be a slave?

What are the origins of slavery?

Rule Britannia was adapted from a poem written in the 18th century. It contains the famous line 'Britons never, never, never shall be slaves'.

Source A

Rule, Britannia! Britannia, rule the waves!
Britons never, never, never shall be slaves.
When Britain first, at heaven's command,
Arose from out the azure main,
This was the charter of the land,
And Guardian Angels sang this strain:

(Chorus)

The nations not so blest as thee
Must, in their turn, to tyrants fall,
While thou shalt flourish great and free:
The dread and envy of them all.

(Chorus)

Still more majestic shalt thou rise,
More dreadful from each foreign stroke,
As the loud blast that tears the skies
Serves but to root thy native oak.

(Chorus)

Thee haughty tyrants ne'er shall tame;
All their attempts to bend thee down
Will but arouse thy generous flame,
But work their woe and thy renown.

(Chorus)

To thee belongs the rural reign;
Thy cities shall with commerce shine
All thine shall be the subject main,
And every shore it circles, thine.

(Chorus)

The Muses, still with freedom found,
Shall to thy happy coasts repair.
Blest isle! with matchless beauty crowned,
And manly hearts to guard the fair.

(Chorus)
Rule, Britannia! Britannia, rule the wa
Britons never, never, never shall be slaves.

To do task 1

Comprehension

1. State one thing that people take for granted in their lives.
2. When did the British first become involved in slave trading?
3. Why was the trans-Atlantic slave trade an unusual form of slavey?

So what does it mean to be a slave? Why is it so important to the British that they do not become slaves? Well one good way to answer that is to think of the sorts of things many people take for granted.

The right to choose a job

The right to decide what route their lives take

The right to own a house

The right to live where they want

The right to make their own decisions

rights of access to clean water.

right to be free

right to a free trial

rreedom to worship

right to marry

right to vote

These are just a few of the rights that people could expect to enjoy in most modern societies. How many more can you think of? Slavery often means people have few if any of these rights, because they have been forcibly taken away from them. Their standard of living may be considerably below what we would all accept as being normal. So why is slavery such a massive part of the history of the British Empire?

Slavery throughout history

The trans-Atlantic slave trade that became a hugely profitable but highly controversial part of the British Empire's history, was really just an extension of a practice that had been going on for many years. Although the British only really became involved from the 17th century onwards, slave trading can be traced back as far as the Egyptian and Roman Empires.

In Africa as well, the Europeans were not the first people to trade in slaves: a trans-Saharan slave trade was well established by the 11th century. The only thing that was actually unusual about the European slave trade was that it had a racial aspect to it. It was a 'White' versus 'Black' situation, which was the first example of this kind of slavery.

NB

Slavery in the Roman Empire

Slaves were valued possessions in the Roman Empire and allowed the Romans who owned them to lead relaxed, glamorous lifestyles. They were often captured in battle and brought back to Italy to be sold.

Source B

A History
Adam Hart Davies

"Slavery was already part of Africa's tribal economy and society – more so than land ownership – before the arrival of the European traders. For example, women and children whose menfolk had been killed in battle were usually enslaved, becoming part of tribal ruler's extended family. The East Africa slave trade was also well established, with captured slaves transported across the Saharan desert and east into Arabia, the Middle East, and India by Arab and Ottoman slave traders."

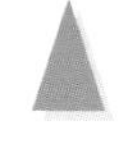

A merchant selling various goods – including a female slave – to a Roman in his villa.

Source C

The British Empire: Sunrise to Sunset
Philippa Levine

"The imperial slave trade that supplied the Caribbean and North America was distinctive in a number of ways, however. This was a trade vast in scale, and it transported slaves much further away from their homelands than was routine in other forms of slavery. Atlantic slavery was unusual in being so racially specific; freed slaves in many societies would not have been that different from those around them. For the slaves caught up in the Atlantic trade, their skin colour made them stand out, marking them as slaves."

To do task 2

Empathy activity

It is very difficult to imagine what it means to be a slave. Look at the list of things people take for granted. Draw a table with what we take for granted on the left. On the right try and summarise what it would mean to do without those things.

5.1 Africa before the Slave Trade

The people of Africa had their own way of life before the slave trade. Here you can learn:

- What was Africa like before the Slave Trade?
- What did it have by way of its own culture and history?
  - How powerful might Africa have been if it had not been interrupted by the slave trade?

West Africa

Although there was little known about Africa before the Europeans first ventured to the West Coast, this does not mean that the continent did not have a history of its own. The Europeans simply interrupted the normal shape and passage of African life. The time between the first European transportation of slaves and the end of the slave trade was substantial. During this 'lost time' what possible course could African history have taken? What would have happened to Africa and its ability to trade, if the Europeans had not intervened in the whole process?

Many Europeans at the time of the slave trade and since have been very scornful of Africa's history, viewing it as largely irrelevant. However, Africa was not 'made' by the slave trade; rather it was 'damaged', perhaps beyond repair.

One point of view is that Africa would most likely have developed at a speedy rate if it had been left alone by the Europeans, because it had so many sophisticated civilisations with the potential to become truly great. There is no doubt in the minds of many historians that the slave trade fundamentally altered African development irretrievably. Left to follow its natural course, Africa may have been one of the great regions of the world today. Among the slaves seized and forcibly removed were doubtless some of the strongest and most skilled people of the African nation, meaning that the skills and knowledge of these people were lost forever.

Africa was the victim of the slave trade largely because it was close to Europe, not because the people were the easiest to subdue, or because they were best suited to the conditions which the Europeans were taking them to. They became the victims simply because of their **proximity** to the nations who had a commercial drive to trade in slaves.

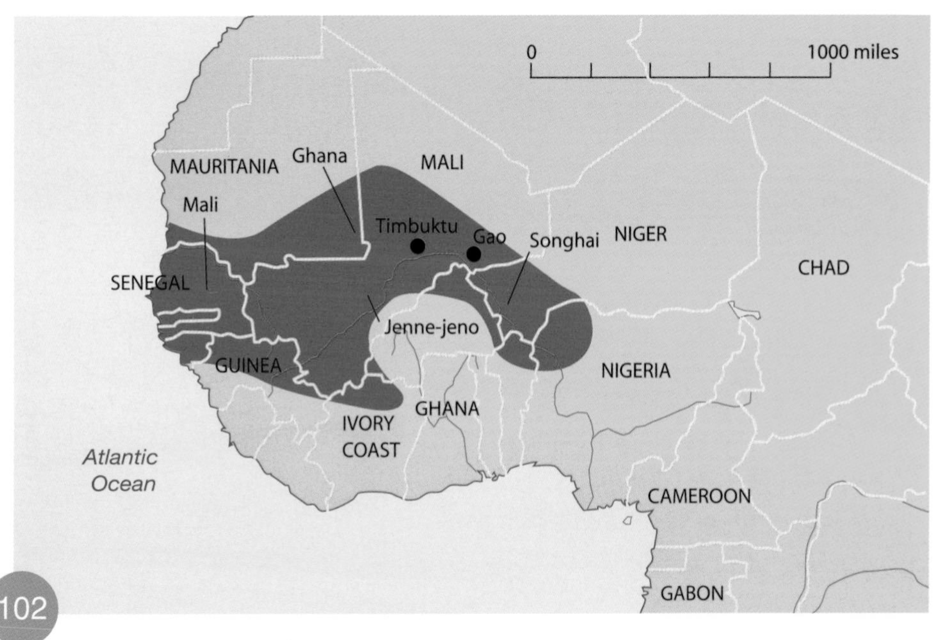

Ghana

At the heart of Africa was a series of powerful, well-developed empires such as Ghana and Mali.

Ghana covered a huge land area, was technologically developed, and had access to large gold fields.

Source A

From the website www.Ghanaweb.com

"The Republic of Ghana is named after the medieval Ghana Empire of West Africa. The actual name of the Empire was Wagadugu. Ghana was the title of the kings who ruled the kingdom. Geographically, the old Ghana is 500 miles north of the present Ghana, and occupied the area between Rivers Senegal and Niger."

Mali

Another powerful empire was Mali, based around the major city of Timbuktu, which still holds major attraction for tourists today. Rich in natural minerals including precious gold and salt, the Empire of Mali is just as famous for its quality universities which saw many scholars pass through its doors.

Source B

From the website www.Mali.pwnet.org

"Unlike the people of the older kingdom of Ghana, who had only camels, horses, and donkeys for transport, the people of Mali also used the river Niger. By river, they could transport bulk goods and larger loads much more easily than by land. Food crops were grown on the level areas by the river, not only for local people but for those living in cities farther north on the Niger River and in oasis towns along the trade routes across the desert. Thus the Niger River enabled the kingdom of Mali to develop a far more stable economy than Ghana had enjoyed and contributed to the rise of the Mali Empire."

Benin

The kingdom of Benin was very powerful and important, ruled by the Oba. Benin was renowned for its skill in metal-working.

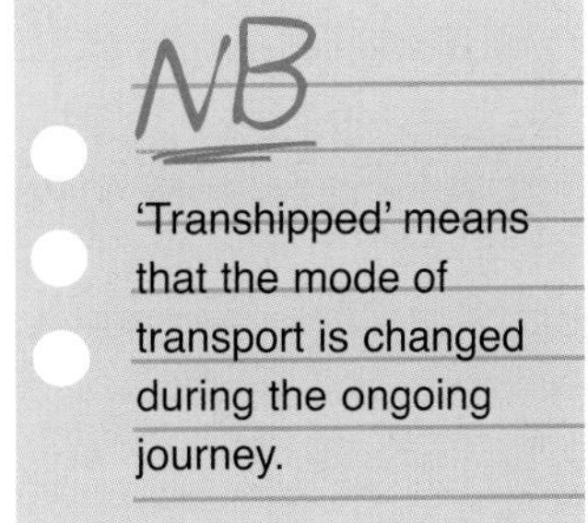

Source C

Africa: A biography of a continent

John Reader

"Timbuktu was already a trading centre of notable size in the 8th century A.D. Its origins probably lay in a cluster of farming, herding, and fishing communities, but its subsequent growth and status is almost entirely attributable to the salt that the Tuareg camel caravans brought to its markets. From the backs of camels the salt was transhipped to canoes for distribution through the hundreds of kilometres of navigable waters on the Niger River system."

Source D

From the British Museum website www.britishmuseum.org

"West Africa from the 15th century onwards, Benin came to control the trade between the inland peoples and the Europeans on the coast. When the British tried to expand their own trade in the 19th century, the Benin people killed their envoys. So in 1897 the British sent an armed expedition which captured the king of Benin, destroyed his palace and took away large quantities of sculpture and regalia, including works in wood, ivory and especially brass."

Songhai Empire

The Songhai Empire was very much the successor to the Empire of Mali, encompassing the cities of Gao and Timbuktu. Timbuktu was particularly famous for the large amount of spectacular Mosques that were situated within it.

Source E

From the website www.nationmaster.com

"From the early 15th to the late 16th century, the Songhai Empire was one of the largest African empires in history. This empire was centered around the city of Gao, and its base of power was on the bend of the Niger river in present-day Niger and Burkina Faso. Outside of this, the Songhai lands reached far down the Niger river into modern day Nigeria itself, all the way to the Northeast of modern day Mali, and even to a small part of the Atlantic coast in the West. Prior to the Songhai, the region was dominated by the Mali Empire, centered around Timbuktu. Mali grew famous due to their immense riches obtained through trade with the Arabic world, and the legendary pilgrimage of Mansa Musa to Mecca. However by the early 15th century, the Mali Empire was in decline. Disputes over succession weakened the crown and many subject peoples broke away. The Songhai were one of them, and made the prominent city of Gao their new capital."

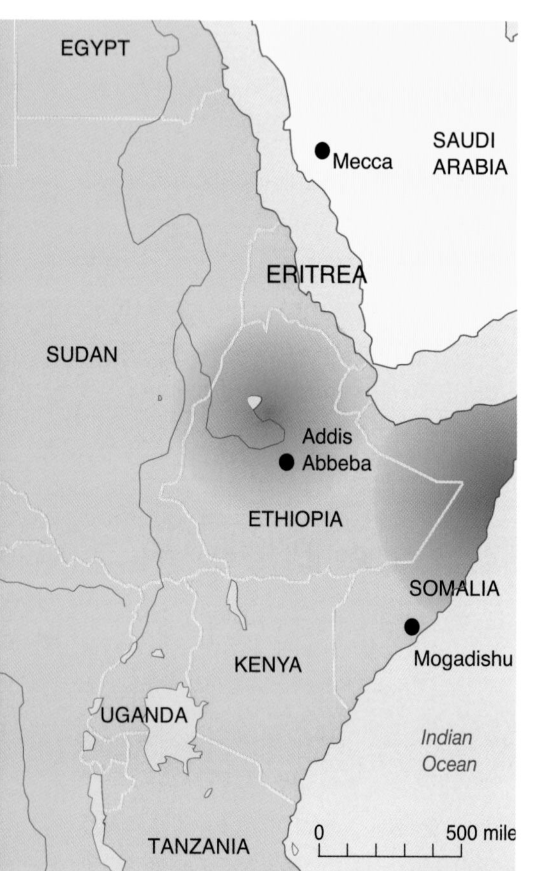

East Africa

While West Africa was highly developed, so too was East Africa. Two of the main areas were Ethiopia, a Christian nation, and Somalia, an Islamic nation. Somalia took advantage of its position near the **profitable** trade routes that entered the East Coast.

Ethiopia

The country of Ethiopia holds an important place in African history, being a Christian nation for many centuries, before it became a Muslim nation as well. Its history is long and varied, going back over a thousand years before the birth of Jesus. Its main exports and valuable **commodities** were and still are, ivory and gold.

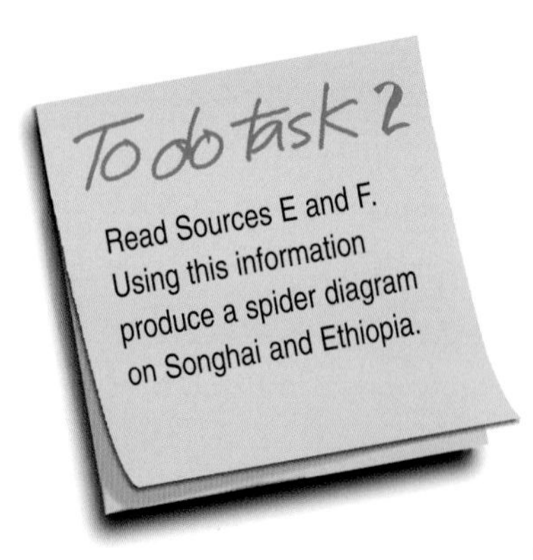

Source F

From the www.nationalgeographic.com website

"Ethiopia is a landlocked country in the northeast African region known as the Horn of Africa. The country has a high central plateau, with some mountains reaching more than 4,000 meters (13,000 feet). The Great Rift Valley splits the plateau diagonally. The western highlands get summer rainfall; the lowlands and eastern highlands are hot and dry. Most people reside in the western highlands as does the capital, Addis Ababa — the highest capital city in Africa at 2,400 meters (8,000 feet). The population is almost evenly split between Christians, living in the highlands, and Muslims inhabiting the lowlands. The Oromo, Amhara, and Tigreans are the largest ethnic groups."

Somalia

Perhaps better known recently as the base area for wide-ranging pirate attacks on merchant shipping, Somalia has a long and rich history in Africa. (See Source G).

Zimbabwe

Another powerful area was Great Zimbabwe.

Source G

From the website www.historyworld.net

"Situated on the so-called Horn of Africa, jutting out into the India Ocean, Somalia's harbours are natural ports of call for traders sailing to and from India. So the coastline of the region is much visited by foreigners, in particular Arabs and Persians. But in the interior the Somali are left to their own devices."

Source H

From the www.bbs.co.uk website www,bbc.co.uk

"Almost every local tribal group claims to be the original builders of Great Zimbabwe, but the Lemba probably have the best claim. Artefacts found at the site are very similar to those used by modern Lemba (part of the Shona group of peoples), and this is backed up both by similarities in burial customs and by folklore. Between 1100 and 1450 Zimbabwe is believed to have controlled a huge empire between the Zambezi and Limpopo Rivers, covering much of modern Zimbabwe and some of Mozambique. It is clear from artefacts discovered in the ruins that this was a great trading empire and items from as far away as China having been found. The reasons for the collapse of the empire are not clear, but the usual suspects are drought, warfare, or over-use of the local resources."

To do task 3

The trade in ivory has long been a major part of the African economy. Recently the trade has declined, for the protection of the animals involved. Research the ivory trade in more detail. What is being done to stop ivory trading today?

The goods that made the East Coast trade profitable were mainly gold, iron, copper and tin, mangroves, elephants and the fishing **industry**. Most if not all of these commodities were successfully exported across the Indian Ocean.

African trade

The majority of the trade that took place in Africa was between itself and other Muslim communities, with little venturing beyond the boundaries of the Muslim world. The Saharan trade routes were very important, with the goods transported by 'camel caravans'. Most of this trade was with Arab nations, although there was some local trade. One of the main commodities that was traded was ivory.

The salt trade was also very important to the African economy, with the salt being transported across the continent by camel caravan. Another important commodity was gold, which was very important to the development of the early African economies and their ability to trade with other nations. Africa actually supplied a lot of gold to the European economies for use in their own coins.

A typical camel caravan, still used today as a way of crossing the Sahara.

5.2 The beginnings of the Atlantic slave trade

Several European countries were involved in taking slaves from Africa and transporting them across the Atlantic. Now you will think about:

- How did the Atlantic slave trade come about?
- Which countries played a major role in it?

Major players in the slave trade

The European invasion of the West Coast of Africa was not an unusual event. Europeans were often staking claim to places that they did not have any right to. In the case of Africa, however, the Europeans did not progress very far into the continent itself, instead staying close to the coastline.

In recent years, the contribution of the slave trade to the British economy has been reviewed and much criticised. However, the British did not start the process of trading in African slaves, and 'trading' is the most accurate description of the whole process – for it was not, in general, kidnapping. All the African slaves were **exchanged** for goods and commodities and many Africans profited in some way from this 'trade'. Slaves did not have to be captured by the British or other European nations first. It was much easier than that. Native Africans supplied the slaves and European slave traders simply collected them. These slaves could come from many sources: prisoners of war, convicts or outcasts from society.

The first Europeans to trade significantly in African slaves were the Portuguese, who established a trading post at Elmina in 1482. In fact, some say that the first person to transport slaves may have been Christopher Columbus on his voyages of discovery. Initially their main interest in Africa was not in slaves, but in gold. However, the **prevalence** of disease, especially malaria, did not encourage the mass exploration of Africa. The slave trade offered a relatively easy way for the Portuguese to make money with little expenditure or effort.

A contemporary illustration of early Portuguese slave trading.

A portrait of John Hawkins.

Britain's first venture into the slave trade probably came via John Hawkins – who is often identified as starting the Caribbean slave trade – in an attempt to take a slice of the profitable Spanish slave-trading network, which took slaves from Africa to South America and the Caribbean. The Spanish were particularly busy trading slaves in the early 16th century, with the slave trade to the West Indies in progress as early as 1518. Other countries that were engaged in the slave trade initially were the Netherlands and France, although many more would try to get involved.

Acceptable or unacceptable?

So why did many people believe that slave trading was acceptable as a way of life or a way of making money? Some slave traders actually believed that the slaves would have a better standard of life as a slave than they would have in their own country as a free person. If this is a question of morals, traders at the time simply did not have the same moral standards as many people have today. They saw nothing wrong with trading in people. In fact, being a slave trader was a 'respectable' occupation, not one that was looked down on. Very few people actually objected to the slave trade until it had been up and running for some time.

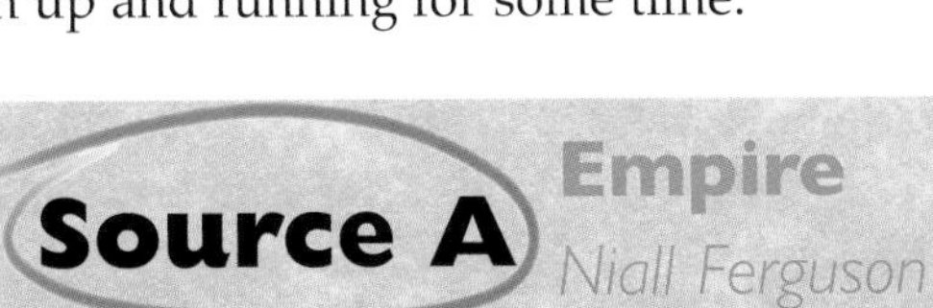

Empire
Niall Ferguson

"According to the Jamaican planter Edward Long, Africans were devoid of genius, and seem almost incapable of making any progress in civility or science. They have no plan or system of morality among them...they have no moral sensations."

To do task 2

Why do you think slave traders had little or no problem with trading in humans? Why did they not see that they were doing something wrong? Produce a spider diagram showing your views and thoughts.

Royal African Company

Slave-trading companies soon appeared, and one of the most well-known was the Royal African Company. It was established in 1660 by a group of rich businessmen and entrepreneurs who had a lot of money to invest. They were originally known as the Company of Royal Adventurers and had changed their name to the Royal African Company in 1672 when Charles II had been bold enough to declare that they would have a monopoly over British slave trading for the next 1000 years. In fact, their **monopoly** and the company itself was abolished in 1698, largely because there was such a potential for profit from selling slaves that others wanted to be part of it, and because the trade had become fiercely competitive.

The Gold Coast

The main slave-trading area of the West Coast of Africa was known as the Gold Coast, with the primary areas being Senegal, the Gambia and Guinea. Guinea even gave its name to a coin that was a product of the slave trade, which was equivalent to 21 shillings, or one old pound and one shilling. The influx of these coins onto the British market transformed the British economy.

5.3 Slave trading

Slave trading was very profitable and many people could gain from it. Here you will learn:

- What did it mean to be a slave trader?
- What were slaves traded for?

What were slaves traded for?

Slaves could be traded for an amazing range of different commodities such as guns, alcohol, horses, cowrie shells and even gunpowder.

Source A

Abolition Richard S. Reddie

"...newly enslaved Africans faced an excruciating march to the coast in shackles, coffles and other restraints. The walk could take months and substantial numbers succumbed to malnutrition, disease and ill-treatment. Slave raiders, however, had few cares for those who fell ill on the journey or could not keep pace and killed anyone who slowed their return to the coast. Once there, the deal was completed with the agent who would sometimes brand the enslaved Africans with the names of their new owners and house them in barracoons or holding cells, to await transfer to the slaver. (Slave ship.) Barracoons were little more than dimly lit dungeons...the favoured location for a barracoon was an island just off the coast from which it was hard for enslaved Africans to escape and which a rescue party would find it difficult to reach."

To do task 1

Comprehension

1. What types of goods could slaves be traded for?
2. Who wrote the hymn 'Amazing Grace'?
3. Name a disease common in the Caribbean.

Brutality

Many of you may have heard the hymn *'Amazing Grace'* but did you know that it was written by the slave trader John Newton?

> "Thro' many dangers, toils and snare,
>
> I have already come;
>
> 'Tis grace has brought me safe thus far,
>
> And grace will lead me home"
>
> *(Extract from 'Amazing Grace' by John Newton)*

Such a lovely hymn hides the reality of the slave trade behind soft words. While the slave traders could reasonably expect to make a huge profit on their investment, sometimes as much as 800%, life was not all rosy. By its very nature, the slave trade would have to be enforced using violence. It could not be a peaceful **venture**. Slaves did not want to be sold or taken away from their homes and their families. Keeping them 'hostage' for long enough to be able to sell them, or even alive long enough to get them to the plantations, meant that many brutal tactics had to be used. Violence was therefore a part of everyday life for these slave traders.

Many of the slave traders and the men who worked for them had no regard at all for the slaves and it was a tragically common aspect of slave trading that many female slaves would suffer sexual abuse before and after they were sold.

Dangers facing the slave traders

The slave traders faced difficulties in the places that they had to go to, and the people with whom they had to trade. Not all the Africans were keen or willing to trade with the Europeans and clashes were common, many becoming extremely violent. Slave traders had to accept that their lives might be at risk from the very people they were trading with.

To do task 2

Use the information on pages 116 and 117 to write the transcript for an interview with a slave trader. What questions would you ask, and what do you think the answers would be?

The trades also faced the permanent threat of disease: areas such as Africa and the Caribbean were rife with life-threatening diseases such as yellow fever, malaria and typhoid. These diseases struck men down quickly, usually without warning and there was little that could be done to save lives with the limited medical knowledge of the time. It would be a long time before travel vaccinations were introduced!

Traders also had to carefully navigate the often **treacherous** waters around Africa, the Caribbean and America, not to mention contend with the weather and the open seas. So you can see that as a business slave trading was hugely dangerous. Simply getting from Europe to Africa and then facing a return journey to America or the Caribbean was often perilous enough in itself. The crews on the boats, with their regular threat of mutiny, could also cause the slave traders some real trouble.

5.4 The Middle Passage

Slaves were transported on boats to where they were needed. Can you answer:

- What was the Middle Passage?
- What were slaves traded for?
- What were conditions like on the slave boats?

The Slave Trade Triangle

The 'Middle Passage' is a term describing the middle route of the **profitable** Slave Trade Triangle. This 'Triangular Trade' took its shape because it was dictated by the **dominant** and prevailing winds that would allow the ships to be carried relatively easily to the east coast of America and the Caribbean.

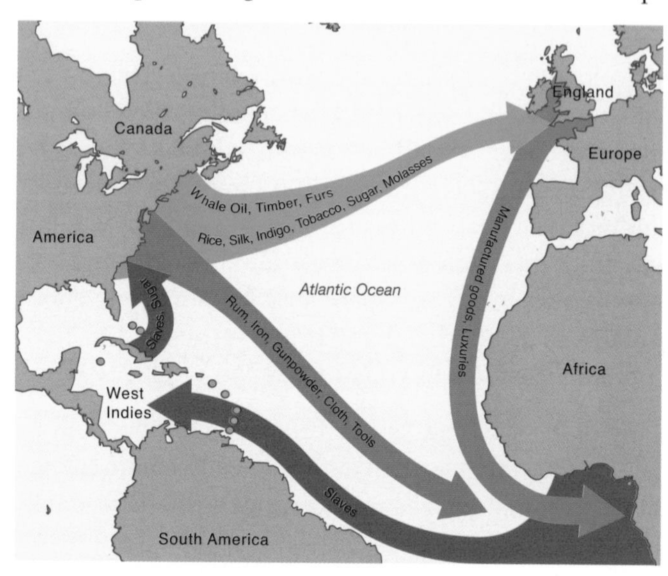

Source A

History: The definitive visual guide

Adam Hart Davies

"From the 16th–19th centuries, some 54,000 trade voyages were recorded. This peaked in the 1780s at 78,000 slaves a year, with half of them carried on British ships."

Source B

The birth of Industrial Britain

Kenneth Morgan

"The scale of the traffic in enslaved Africans was enormous. English vessels shipped some 2.7 million slaves across the Atlantic during the 18th century."

Each slaver (slave ship) could carry up to 600 slaves on each journey, and these people would have to endure, on average, 10 weeks of hardship on board the boat. In ideal conditions this journey may have been cut short to six weeks, but this was uncommon. The reason why the slaves were packed so tightly on board was that the owners earned profit according to the number of slaves that reached their destination. Many of the slaves had already been pre-purchased and so any loss was not the concern of the actual ship's Captain, who was often paid only to transport a cargo, not to look after the slaves.

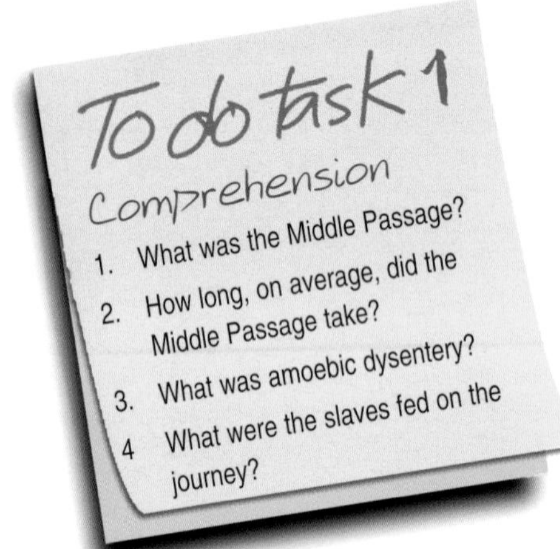

Conditions on board the slave ships

Life on a slave ship was quite often simply appalling. Restraints such as leg irons, chains and handcuffs were used to maintain control of the slaves, who were confined below deck and crammed as close together as was possible without actually killing them through suffocation.

To the traders, slaves were not people; they were simply regarded as cargo and were handled as such.

Below deck the air was stale and smelly. Without washing or toilet facilities the smells of sweat, excrement and vomit filled the air. Slave ships were so pungent that some people said that you could smell them coming into shore if the wind was blowing in the right direction. Female slaves were often not chained up like the men, but did also face the common threat of sexual assault.

Many slaves died from diseases during the Middle Passage. **Dysentery** and smallpox were widespread on board, and were easily spread through close physical contact and through the food and water supplies. Amoebic dysentery was known as the 'Bloody Flux' and many people died on board the boats from this disease.

The slaves weren't fed well on the journey, with food in general consisting of a sort of porridge or gruel served only once a day. They might occasionally get some variety which might be rice, plantain, yams or anything else that could be obtained cheaply whilst in port.

One of the most notorious and infamous slave ships was the Zong.

NB

Dysentery is intense diarrhoea, caused by an infection within the intestinal area. It can be fatal.

To do task 2

Read Source C. You are Luke Collingwood, Commander of the slave ship Zong. The insurance company has asked you for a report about what went on during the voyage. Produce a short statement explaining your actions. How much of the truth should you reveal?

Source C From the website www.hullwebs.co.uk

"The slave ship Zong was under the command of Luke Collingwood. The voyage from the African coast, from where they set sail on 6th September 1781, probably opened the eyes of the British public to the selfish cruelty of the slave-traders more than any other.

As was common practice, the crew packed on many more slaves than there was room for and, as a result, disease and malnutrition had claimed the lives of seven white men and sixty African slaves by 29th November. It was on that very day that Luke Collingwood decided that all remaining sick Africans should be thrown overboard to protect the crew and the remaining cargo of slaves. It is said that he assembled the crew and explained that throwing the slaves overboard whilst they were still alive, for the safety of the ship, would result in the ship's underwriters bearing the cost. Allowing the slaves to die a natural death on board would make the loss the crew's responsibility. European law, at this time, stated:

The insurer takes upon him the risk of the loss, capture, and death of slaves, or any other unavoidable accident to them: but natural death is always understood to be excepted: by natural death is meant, not only when it happens by disease or sickness, but also when the captive destroys himself through despair, which often happens: but when slaves are killed, or thrown into thrown into the sea in order to quell an insurrection on their part, then the insurers must answer.

When the owners attempted to claim the full value of the murdered slaves from the insurers, the company refused to settle. They discovered that the claim that the slaves had to be thrown overboard because of water depletion was untrue as it was later proven that the captain had an opportunity to take on water on 1st December and when the Zong landed in Jamaica on 22nd December, there was 420 gallons of water to spare."

BUZZ WORDZZ

dominant
dysentery
profitable

Restraints of the sort used on slaves: a leg shackle and lead ball, (top) a neck collar and chain, (bottom) actually depicted on a memorial to slaves in Stonetown, Zanzibar.

Another famous slave ship was the Brookes.

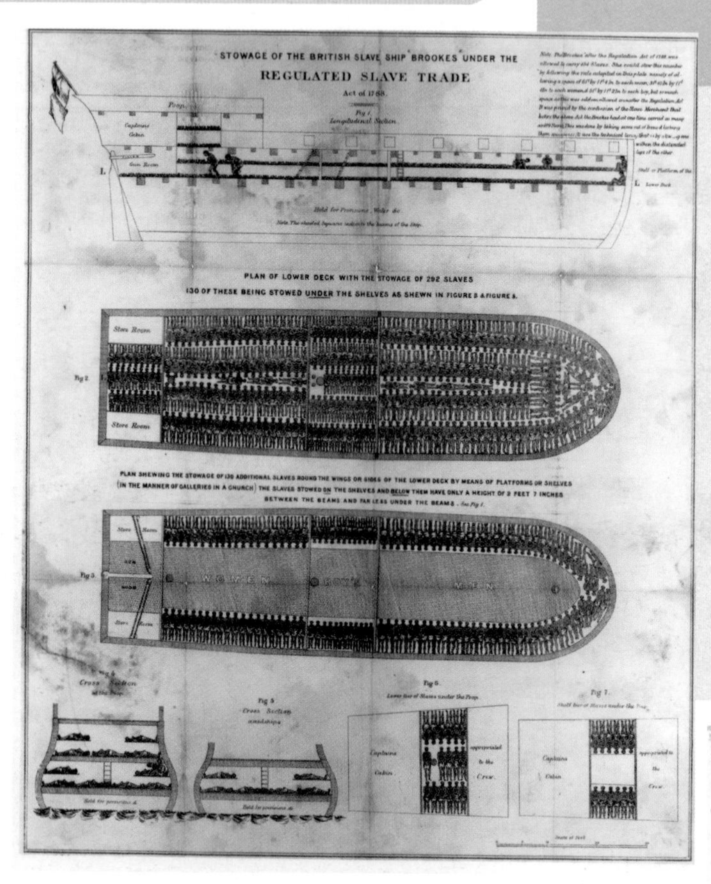

A diagram of the 'Brookes' slave ship, as mentioned in source D, showing the way slaves were packed on board.

Source D

From the website www.gloucestershire.gov.uk

"A diagram of the slave ship the "Brookes" was sent to the Society for the Abolition of the Slave Trade by an anti-slavery group in Plymouth. It was a graphic illustration of the inhumane way in which slaves were packed into slave ships to maximise profit.

The image had huge propaganda value and was re-worked by Thomas Clarkson and other members of the Society to show the ship carrying 482 slaves (this was erring on the side of caution since the ship had been known to carry over 600 slaves). In 1789, the Society printed 700 posters of the diagram which became one of the most shocking and enduring images associated with the trade."

Source E

The British Empire: Sunrise to Sunset

Philippa Levine

"Between 20% and 40% of those destined for slavery died during transport to the African coast for sale and shipping, another 3% to 10% died before they could be transported, and a further 15% or so died aboard the slave ships at more than twice the rate of un-enslaved paying shipboard passengers in this area."

Africa – a biography of a continent

John Reader

"Crowded vessels compounded the fear, cruelty and disease that sent more than a million slaves to their deaths on the "Middle Passage." They came to the ships weighed down with fetters and manacles, and fearing not only the pain of captivity but also the fate they believed they awaited them. Stories of white men from the ships eating their black captives were legend in the slave homelands. Huge copper kettles stood boiling on the foredecks, they had been told; African meat was salted, and fed to the crew; red wine was African blood; cheese was made from African brains; the victims' bones were burned and became gunpowder."

From a commercial viewpoint, traders knew that somehow slaves had to be kept relatively clean on the voyage. If not, disease would lead to death and every dead slave meant less profit. So traders and crew devised numerous ways of trying to keep the slaves clean, which were **brutal** in their own way. Being washed down with vinegar, limewater and salt water was painful, but each effectively cleaned the slaves and the sores that they had acquired on the journey.

As you might expect, slaves would feel incredibly scared about the prospects that lay ahead of them. Although they had no idea of their ultimate fate, they would surely have heard tales about the situation that they were being placed in.

It is no wonder that slave resistance was common in an effort to get off the slave ship. They would try almost anything to escape, even throwing themselves off the boat into the Atlantic Ocean, to face certain death.

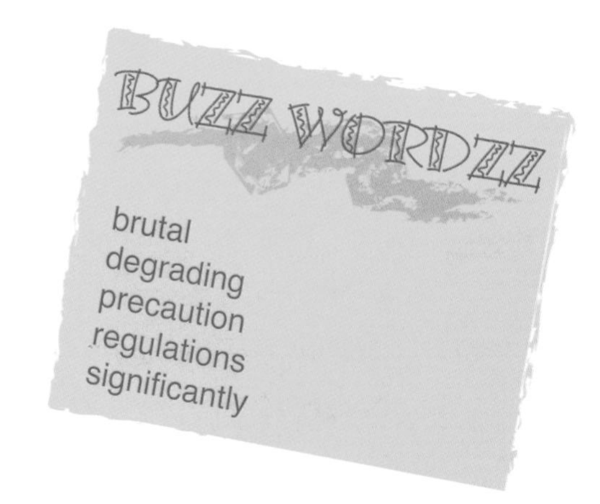

Overcrowding

As we have seen, the slave traders had very little regard for the slaves, and in the early years of the slave trade they simply tried to cram as many onto the boats as they possibly could. For instance, a ship weighing 200 tonnes should be able to hold at least 400 slaves, although at a push it could hold more. Any overcrowding, however, would impact **significantly** on the survival rate of the slaves.

The Brookes slave ship is infamous for the way that the slaves were packed into its hold like sardines in a tin can. Looking at the diagrams opposite, you have to wonder if it was possible to fit any more slaves in, other than perhaps on top!

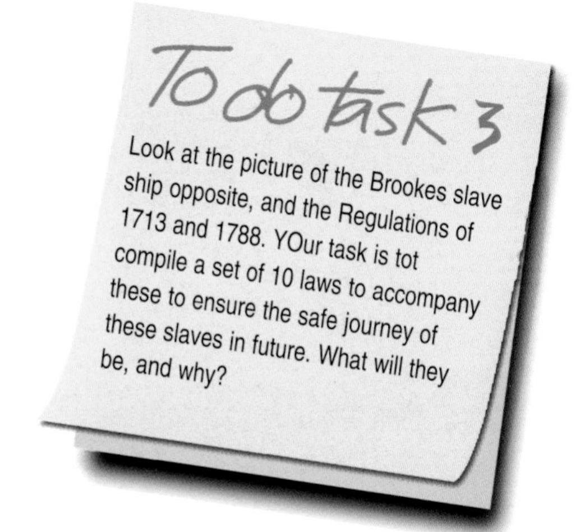

The Brookes was designed for a capacity of about 450 slaves, but the slave traders regularly crammed over 600 on board. This was fairly typical of what went on aboard the boats, and was not just confined to this one vessel.

Small improvements

Over time a number of laws and **regulations** were passed that were intended to improve the conditions for the slaves on board the boats. Two important ones were:

1713 – Minimum dimensions of space required per slave introduced by the Royal African Company.

1788 – Regulations issued that stipulated how many slaves could be accommodated on the slaving boats, determined by the tonnage of the boat – a slaver of 300 tonnes could carry no more than 425 slaves. Ships were also forced to carry surgeons to care for the welfare of the slaves.

Riots and uprisings were not uncommon on board slavers and they were difficult to suppress if they got going, largely due to the sheer number of slaves that could get involved. The crews had to be well armed and slaves were usually chained up as an extra **precaution**. Such riots rarely ended peacefully.

But the voyage, although torturous, dangerous and **degrading**, was actually nothing in comparison to what the slaves would have to endure for the rest of their natural lives – life on the plantations.

5.5 Slave auctions

When they reached their destination, slaves were often brought to slave auctions. Here you will find out:

- What was a slave auction?
- What were slaves traded for?
- Where did the slaves end up?

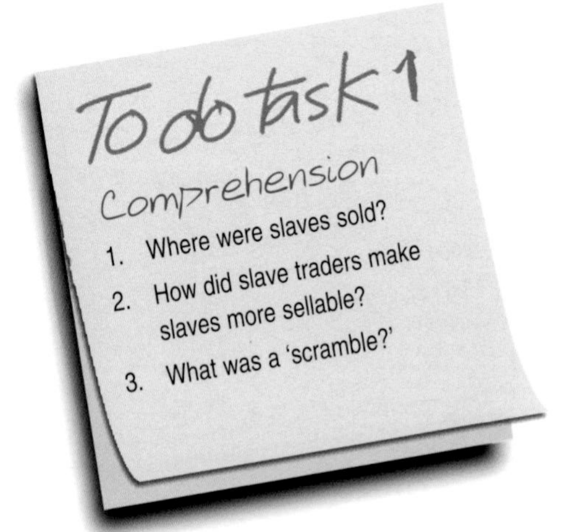

To do task 2

It is your job to design a poster advertising a slave sale. What would you put on it? How would you advertise the slaves?

Buying and selling

Slaves had to be sold and they were often sold in great numbers at the slave auctions. These were degrading spectacles where the slaves were treated no better than cattle. They were crammed into cages to await their turn to be callously marched out in front of the spectators and potential purchasers. Many people seemed to have a morbid curiosity and attended the sales even if they did not intend to buy a slave, much in the same way as people used to have a morbid fascination for public executions.

However, the slaves could not just be brought straight off the boats and placed under sale. They had to be prepared first so that they would be attractive purchases. After all, the slave traders wanted to get the maximum price for their goods. The effects of the long voyage had to be dealt with first. The slaves might have suffered injuries such as cuts, bruises or blisters whilst on the voyage, which would need medical treatment. Once these had been treated, the slave traders would move on to a slave's external appearance, working on removing any visible signs of defect that might reduce the price each could be sold for. Anything that could put off the buyers was rectified – even going as far as pulling out rotten teeth and cutting the hair of the slaves.

They were also often given a coating of oil that would make their skin shine and highlight muscles to make buyers think that the slave would be a hard worker. Slaves would also be branded so that they could be identified as the property of a certain trader and, at a later date, a certain owner.

The final indignity was the re-naming of the slaves. They lost their true identities and were given English names so that their new owners did not have to go to the trouble of learning foreign pronunciation.

Slave auctions sometimes took place on board the ship, and at other times in a local market square on the side of the docks. The sales did not always take an organised format, with many sellers offering the buyers the chance to rush in and grab the slaves that they wanted from among the crowd. This was known as a 'scramble'.

Posters advertising the sale of slaves were pasted up around the area where the sale would be held. They advertised the slaves that would be sold, highlighting specific details and the asking price. The auctioneer 'gabbled', the price and looked for the bidders positioned in the crowd. Many people also gathered to watch the spectacle and took a great amount of interest in the proceedings. Once they had been purchased, the slaves were paid for and their futures became more uncertain than ever, for nobody was entirely sure what they would face from that point onwards.

SALE OF

VALUABLE

SLAVES,

(On account of departure)

The Owner of the following named and valuable Slaves, being on the eve of departure for Europe, will cause the same to be offered for sale, at the NEW EXCHANGE, corner of St. Louis and Chartres streets, on *Saturday*, May 16, at Twelve o'Clock, *viz.*

1. **SARAH, a mulatress, aged 45 years, a good cook and accustomed to** house work in general, is an excellent and faithful nurse for sick persons, and in every respect a first rate character.

2. **DENNIS, her son, a mulatto, aged 24 years, a first rate cook and stew-**ard for a vessel, having been in that capacity for many years on board one of the Mobile packets; is strictly honest, temperate, and a first rate subject.

3. **CHOLE, a mulatress, aged 36 years, she is, without execption, one of** the most competent servants in the country, a first rate washer and ironer, does up lace, a good cook, and for a bachelor who wishes a house-keeper she would be invaluable; she is also a good ladies' maid, having travelled to the North in that capacity.

4. **FANNY, her daughter, a mulatress, aged 16 years, speaks French and** English, is a superior hair-dresser, (pupil of Guilliac,) a good seamstress and ladies' maid, is smart, intelligent, and a first rate character.

5. **DANDRIDGE, a mulatoo, aged 26 years, a first rate dining-room ser-**vant, a good painter and rough carpenter, and has but few equals for honesty and sobriety.

6. **NANCY, his wife, aged about 24 years, a confidential house servant,** good seamstress, mantuamaker and tailoress, a good cook, washer and ironer, etc.

7. **MARY ANN, her child, a creole, aged 7 years, speaks French and** English, is smart, active and intelligent.

8. **FANNY or FRANCES, a mulatress, aged 22 years, is a first rate** washer and ironer, good cook and house servant, and has an excellent character.

9. **EMMA, an orphan, aged 10 or 11 years, speaks French and English,** has been in the country 7 years, has been accustomed to waiting on table, sewing etc.; is intelligent and active.

10. **FRANK, a mulatto, aged about 32 years speaks French and English,** is a first rate hostler and coachman, understands perfectly well the management of horses, and is, in every respect, a first rate character, with the exception that he will occasionally drink, though not an habitual drunkard.

☞ All the above named Slaves are acclimated and excellent subjects; they were purchased by their present vendor many years ago, and will, therefore, be severally warranted against all vices and maladies prescribed by law, save and except FRANK, who is fully guaranteed in every other respect but the one above mentioned.

TERMS:—One-half Cash, and the other half in notes at Six months, drawn and endorsed to the satisfaction of the Vendor, with special mortgage on the Slaves until final payment. The Acts of Sale to be passed before WILLIAM BOSWELL, *Notary Public*, at the expense of the Purchaser.

***New-Orleans, May* 13, 1835.**

A poster announcing a slave sale.

Source A

From the Scottish Government website

www.scotland.gov.uk

"All...slaves...shall be held to be real estate. If any slave resist his master...correcting such slave, and shall happen to be killed on such correction...the master shall be free of all punishment."

"At length the auctioneer arrived and asked my mother which was the eldest. She pointed to me. He took me by the hand, and led me out into the middle of the street. I was soon surrounded by strange men, who examined and handled me like a butcher with a calf or a lamb he was about to purchase, and who talked about my shape and size as if I couldn't understand what they were saying. I was then put up to sale. The bidding commenced at a few pounds, and gradually rose to fifty-seven. People said that I'd fetched a great sum for so young a slave.

"I then saw my sisters sold to different owners. When the sale was over, my mother hugged and kissed us, and mourned over us, begging us to keep a good heart, and do our duty to our new masters. It was a sad parting; one went one way, one another, and our poor mammy went home with nothing."

5.6 Plantation life

Many slaves ended up working on plantations. Can you say:

- What was a plantation?
- What was life like for the slaves?
- Who else worked on the plantations?

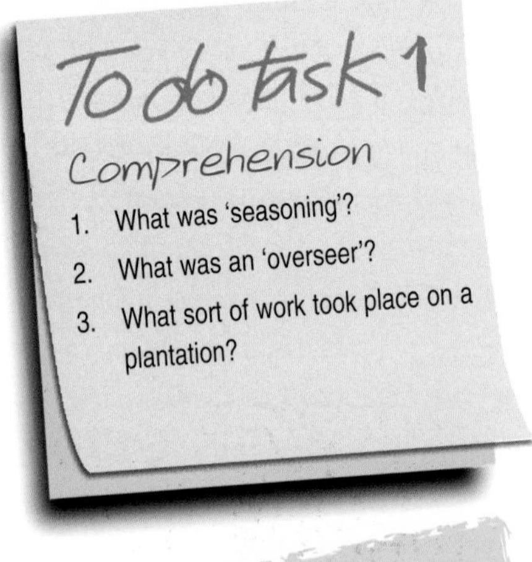

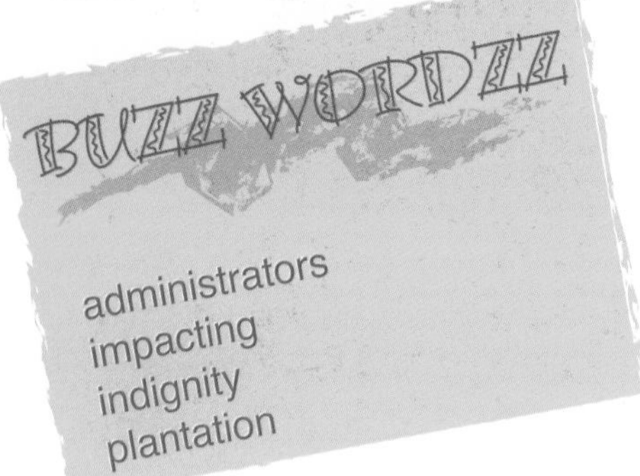

Working conditions

After the **indignity** of the slave auctions, the slaves had to face life on the **plantations**, whether in the Caribbean or America. Sugar plantations were harder to endure than the tobacco plantations because of the difficulty of sugar refining, so life was never easy on a sugar plantation. A slave's life there would be brutally short, far shorter than life would be on other types of plantation.

The slaves had no legal right to complain about their harsh treatment. The nature of slavery meant that they had no means of protest. In fact, they had no rights at all. They could be commanded to work whatever hours the plantation owner saw fit, and the slave-driver armed with a whip ensured that they did what was required of them at all times.

Life as a slave

There was no greater incentive to work hard than harsh physical punishment. Slaves would forever have to bear the scars of a flogging and the wounds were slow to heal. Harsh physical punishments left other slaves in no doubt as to what lay in store for them if they refused to do their work.

In order to fit into plantation life, the slaves were expected to speak English, not their native language. They also had to learn the necessary farming skills required to produce the crops. They were taught these through a process of 'seasoning', a form of unpaid apprenticeship under a more experienced slave.

Slave owners often liked to buy a number of female slaves as well as the more physically strong male slaves. This was because they knew that they would be able to 'self-populate' the plantations through the relationships between the male and females slaves, or through enforced sexual contact with either the plantation owners or the men who worked on the plantation. Mixed race children from such relationships were derogatorily referred to as 'Mulattoes'.

Many slaves died on the plantations through physical abuse, illness or through the sheer hardship of the work that they faced.

A 'white' workforce

The plantation also required a number of workers who would perform the administrative tasks, leading to jobs on the slave plantations such as a book-keeper – processing the income and expenditure of the plantations – or as a clerk to assist with this process. They might also be employed as a slave-driver or overseer who made the slaves work and punished them when it was deemed to be necessary.

Life on the plantations for these men was also difficult and few were willing to take on the roles. Pay was poor and hours were long. The only people who truly profited from the slave trade were the slave traders and the plantation owners, but actually not all the plantation owners grew fabulously rich. Many struggled to make ends meet against all the competition.

Slave resistance

Plantations were, in reality, little more than farms. The slaves were obliged to plant and harvest the crops, tend the soil and work the machinery. On a sugar plantation they would be expected to crush the sugar cane, extract the liquid sugar and boil it up to refine the mixture. All these jobs were back-breaking but the boiling and refining of the sugar was the most dangerous, often resulting in terrible burns and scalds.

Many of the early machines were powered by water, but eventually the steam engines of the Industrial Revolution sped up production. These led to the distinctive chimneys sprouting up amongst the tropical jungle. Slaves were also employed driving carts, moving the finished products and loading it onto the boats.

These are the preserved ruins of a sugar mill on a Caribbean plantation. The round building on the right is a common feature of all such plantation sites.

On the plantations there was a strict hierarchy, with the slaves right at the bottom, the white **administrators** just above the slaves and the plantation owners at the top. The slaves, when treated badly, were quite naturally prone to lash out at the overseers who had to enforce the strict regimes.

Making a profit

Although many of the slaves could not physically protest against the plantation owners, they found other ways of protesting against their treatment. One way was to deliberately work slowly to delay the processes, so **impacting** upon the profits. They might also pretend to be ill so that they couldn't work, once again impacting upon production, or cause harm to themselves with the same intention. Some female slaves would also go as far as to cause the abortion of their own baby so that it would not provide more slave labour.

Source A

From the website

www.mersey-gateway.org

"In the sugar plantations of the West Indies a gang system was operated. The First Gang had the most physically fit of adult male and female slaves, who were forced to carry out the hardest work. The Second Gang included slaves between twelve and eighteen years of age, the stronger older people and breastfeeding mothers or pregnant women. The work was still hard but slightly less physically demanding. The Third Gang included the very old or the very young, carrying out the most simple of tasks, but still being used to make sure that he slave owner got value from his slaves almost from the time they could walk to the time of serious physical decline.

All of these gangs were supervised by a slave-driver, a more favoured and trusted slave who had to ensure that the slaves were worked as hard as possible. The slave-driver would be under a white overseer and both would both punish those who they thought were not working hard enough."

To do task 2

You have to explain to a new worker what life on a plantation involves. Write a short guide to help them: what are the four main things you think they need to know?

5.7 The Caribbean

Many slaves ended up working in the Caribbean. Do you know:

- Where is the Caribbean?
- How did England use the Caribbean?
- What was life like in the Caribbean?

The Caribbean now

If you go on holidays to the Caribbean it is now possible to visit the site of a slave plantation, as many are preserved for visitors. This is possible because the history of the slave trade is inextricably linked to the Caribbean, with 40% of all the slaves that were shipped from Africa eventually finding themselves there.

The Caribbean before the Europeans

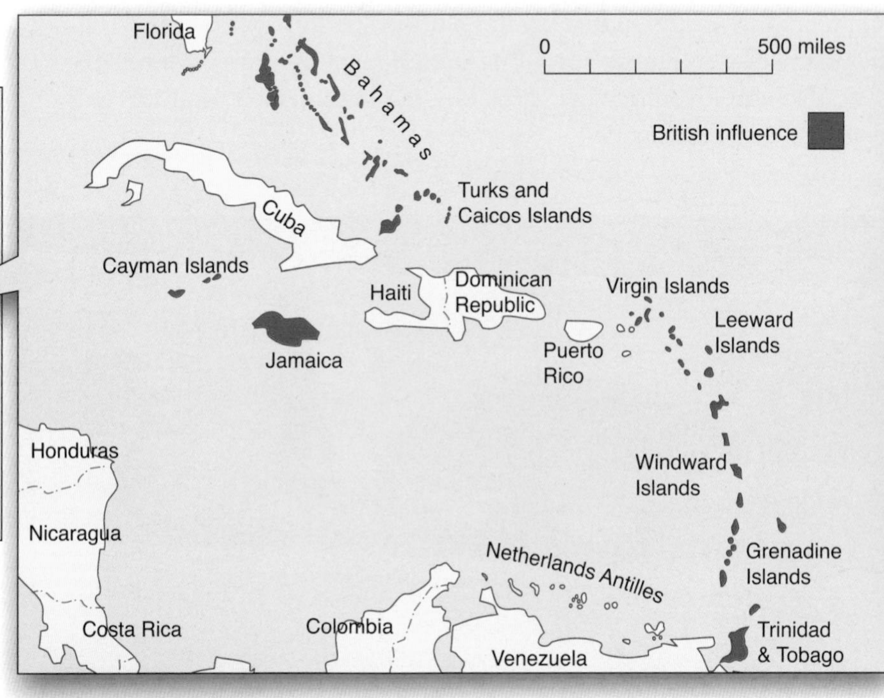

This map shows the location of the main Caribbean islands.

Modern-day Barbados.

When Christopher Columbus landed in the Caribbean in 1492, few people realised that this would be the start of hundreds of years of exploitation of these islands. They were populated by Native American Amerindians, Arawaks and Caribs. However their populations had been largely **obliterated** by the early Spanish settlers and invaders before the British arrived. The native population had been wrongly named 'Indians' along with the indigenous people of mainland America. This total lack of understanding about the people and their origins, and the European lack of regard for their well being, would create further torment among these populations.

The Caribbean, especially Barbados, was financially very important to the British. It was far more profitable to them than the mainland American colonies had ever been. This was partly because the British did not view Barbados as an area that could be settled. Instead, it was seen as an area that they could cultivate and make immense profits from. The fact that slave labour was cheap and plentiful meant that the plantation owners could work the slaves extremely hard for maximum return. If they died, but they had been productive, it was simply a loss that could be written off against the income that they had brought in. Slaves were 'tools', not people.

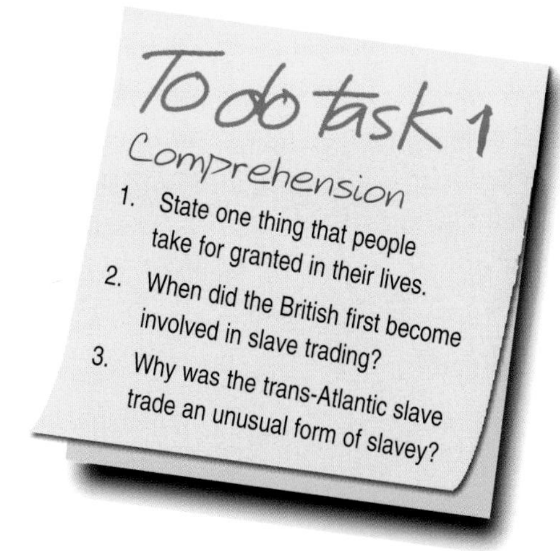

The plantation owners could also destroy potential competition through their ruthless use of these slaves. Unlike in America, where the 'indentured' servants could walk free and start a new life, Barbados and the other Caribbean islands simply did not offer this potential. Slaves could not become free and compete against the rich plantation owners who had a virtual monopoly over the sugar crops. The only way to a new life was to somehow leave Barbados, which for most would prove to be virtually impossible.

Native Arawaks.

Jamaica

Jamaica had previously been a Spanish colony, first exploited during the days of Christopher Columbus. The Spanish settlers had brought with them diseases that had proved deadly for the Arawaks who were indigenous to the area.

Source A

The Victorians A.N. Wilson

"The importance of Jamaica, the largest island in the British West Indies, was both emblematic and commercial. It had been a British colony since 1655, when the Cromwellian navy, led by Admirals Penn and Venables, had taken the island from the Spanish. Jamaica had a bloody history. Its peaceable native inhabitants, the Arawak Indians, had been systematically annihilated by the Conquistadors in 1509."

The British would profit tremendously from this acquisition, making good use of the opportunity to cultivate large crops of sugar.

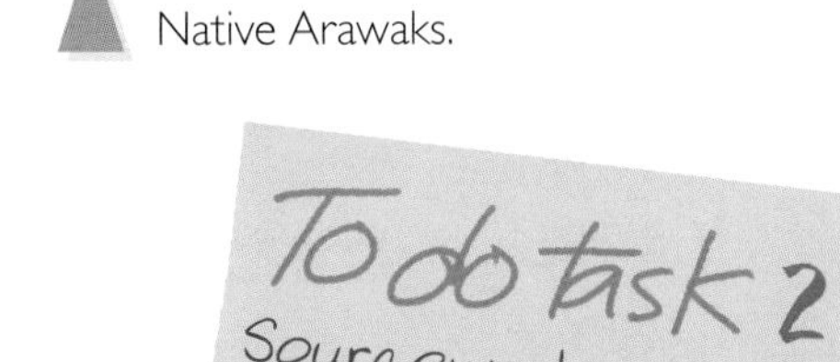

Look at the map on page 118. What other Caribbean islands can you locate? Produce a mini-guide to any island and its history, using whatever reference materials there are available to you.

Barbados

The island of Barbados had been acquired from the Spanish in 1625, and trade had taken off when a company known as the Barbados Company was established in 1627, with a charter granted by the monarch Charles I. By 1655 it was the biggest slave colony in the British Empire.

Source B From the website
www.barbados.org

"The first English ship touched the island on May 14th 1625...the island was therefore claimed on behalf of King James I. On February 17th 1627, Captain Henry Powell landed with a party of 80 settlers and 10 slaves to occupy and settle the island. People with good financial backgrounds and social connections with England were allocated land. Within a few years much of the land had been deforested to make way for tobacco and cotton plantations. The production of sugar, tobacco and cotton was heavily reliant on the indenture of servants. To meet the labour demands, servants were also derived from kidnapping, and convicted criminals were shipped to Barbados. Descendants of the white slaves and indentured labour (referred to as Red Legs) still live in Barbados... "

Some companies built their own sugar processing factories close to a port in Britain, preferring to ship raw unprocessed sugar beet from the Caribbean. This one was built near Southampton in 1851.

The Caribbean crops

After initial attempts at farming tobacco and cotton, settlers soon switched to the crop that will be forever identified with the Caribbean – sugar. Sugar was an important crop mainly because of the insatiable desire of the British for its sweet taste. It was essential for sweetening drinks like tea and coffee, and was also later used in the production of chocolate. The fashion for these drinks meant that people simply could not get enough sugar.

Without this **profitable** home market for sugar, the Caribbean islands may well not have prospered in the way that they did. As well as refined cane sugar, the islands also exported molasses (made from the sugar) and rum.

Source C

The birth of Industrial Britain

Kenneth Morgan

"In 1776 the valuation of sugar estates in Jamaica alone amounted to £18 million sterling (about £9 billion in today's money) which accounted for half of British investment in the Caribbean."

These are the cocoa beans, which form the base for producing chocolate.

Why slaves?

The plantation owners needed slaves because they required a labour force that could withstand the harsh working and living conditions. Work could be incredibly intense and there was no escaping the tropical diseases that were prevalent on the islands – specifically, malaria and yellow fever. Many people also suffered from dysentery. The plantation owners had initially used Irish labour but this had proven to be unsuccessful. These **indentured** labourers were known as 'redlegs' because of the effect that the climate had on their legs, as they suffered terribly from sunburn.

Although Barbados was not a prison colony in the same way as America was, some British prisoners were still sent there to serve their sentence. It was even more difficult for them to survive for any length of time in the Caribbean islands, due to the intense heat and the incapacitating illnesses.

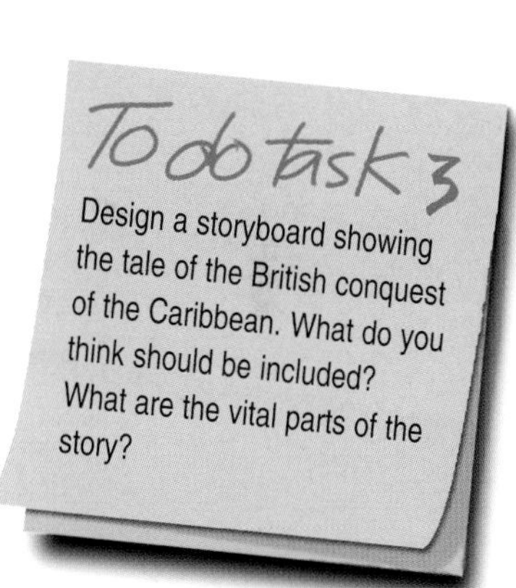

What were 'white slaves'?

Indentured servants also found life in the Caribbean extremely difficult, and any children born while they were serving out their terms were 'bound' to work for the owner of the plantation, despite the fact they did not have a contract in the same way as their parents. The life of the indentured servant in the Caribbean meant hardship, disease and endless sunburn. They were, in every sense of the term, White Slaves. Servants often had their length of service purposely extended when they broke the rules of the plantation.

The sheer amount of people needed to keep the sugar trade going in the Caribbean meant that it was simply not possible to rely on indentured labour, as people were not keen to go to the Caribbean. They would much rather travel to mainland America. There was, therefore, a continual need for slaves, and they had to be constantly replaced due to high death rates. A low birth rate meant that the population was not self-renewing. As the slave trade started to decline, the plantation owners then began to import 'coolie' labour from India to supplement the workforce.

'Coolie' labour photographed on a plantation in Jamaica.

Slave rebellions

Quite naturally the slaves often tried to escape from the **torment** of the sugar plantations, and in fact the islands of the Caribbean were the perfect places to hide out amongst the thick jungle vegetation. However it was difficult for the slaves to 'disappear' as they were instantly recognisable by the colour of their skin.

Nevertheless communities of escaped slaves soon formed in the islands and those living in them were known as 'Maroons'. They were so skilled at hiding out and living in the Caribbean landscape that they were able to cause real problems for the British, even requiring the army to put down revolts led by the Maroons.

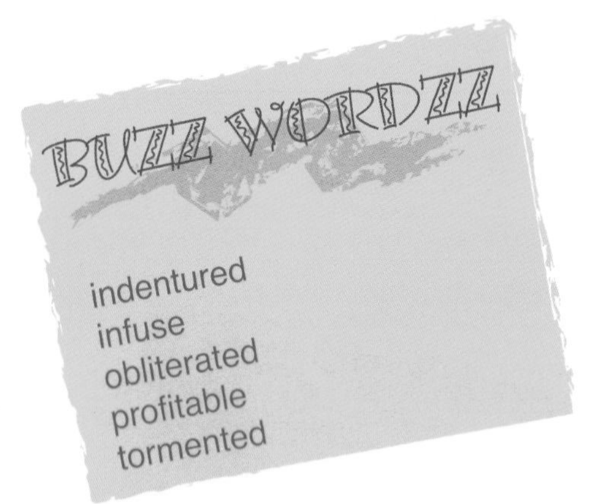

Tacky's revolt

One of the most spectacular instances of slave revolution that did not come from the Maroons was known as 'Tacky's revolt'.

To do task 4

Read Source D. This information must form the basis for a story on Tacky's Revolt. The story is for a primary school history book: with that audience in mind, what do you think the key parts of the story should be, and can you write it in less than 200 words?

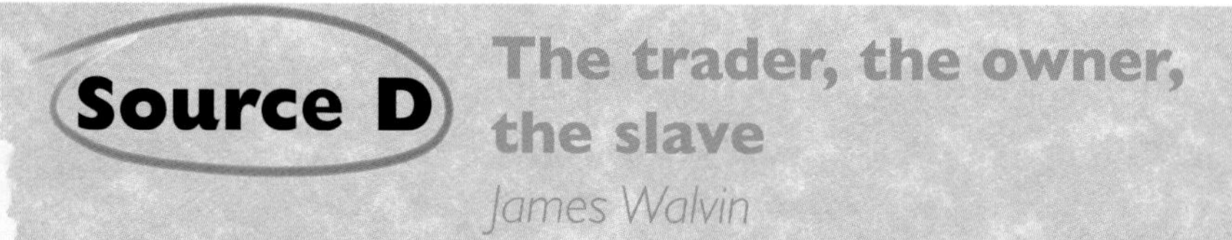

"The Jamaica slave rebellion – known as Tacky's Revolt – threatened to bring down the whole edifice of plantation slavery. On 7th April 1760, Easter Day, more than 100 slaves, under the leadership of Tacky, a handsome young African slave, swept down from their estates to Port Maria on the coast, where they raided the gun store. Then they moved rapidly south-east, burning and killing and gathering recruits until they were four hundred strong. Local militia did what they could to stall the rebellious slaves until trained soldiers rushed from the other side of the island, but even their arrival did little to quell the revolt. Rebellion now flared like bushfire on other parts of the island, in the far east of Jamaica and in the central valleys. "

Other nations that had colonised the Caribbean also had difficulties with slaves. One of the most spectacular occurred on the island of St Dominique (modern day Haiti). The most famous participant in this rebellion was a slave named 'Toussant L'Ouverture'.

Source E

From the anti-slavery website

"In 1789, the French Revolution led to tensions among the island's various white, black and mulatto (mixed race) populations, which on 22 August 1791, erupted into revolt. What began as a revolt against slavery and French plantation owners became a struggle that lasted for 13 years resulting in revolution and independence from France. By early 1792, Toussaint had joined the rebellion. The various populations on the island were increasingly divided as a result of a series of conflicting decrees issued by the French Government to its colony. These included first granting and then withdrawing freedom and political rights to the island's mulatto and black populations. Toussaint successfully organised the slaves into a revolutionary army and rapidly began his ascent to power, aided by his ability to play the region's European powers – France , Spain and Britain – off against each other. Throughout the 1790s, he skilfully switched allegiances among the powers to achieve his goals of an end to slavery and independence. Toussaint briefly formed an alliance with the Spanish…gaining him arms and money. It was during this time that he adopted the name "L'Ouverture", meaning opening. A year later, he allied himself with the French. But Toussaint's rotating alliances were expedient measures to achieve his ends: "...I want liberty and equality to reign throughout St. Domingue. I am working towards that end. Come and join me, brothers, and combat by our side for the same cause."

5.8 The impact of the slave trade on Britain

Although this was all happening far from Britain, it did have an effect on life at home. You should be able to answer:

- How did the slave trade impact upon Britain?
- Which ports and cities benefitted from it most?

To do task 1

Comprehension

1. Name two British slave trade ports.
2. What jobs connected to the slave trade did these ports provide?
3. What was much of the revenue from the slave trade used for?

The economy

The sheer scale of the slave trade meant that many nations made a huge amount of money from it. The slave trade was so profitable that it was a considerable source of revenue towards the financing of the Industrial Revolution in Britain. Many people relied on the slave trade for their way of life.

Source A

The birth of Industrial Britain

Kenneth Morgan

"Profits earned in the Atlantic trades were undoubtedly put into ship building, snuff mills, sugar refineries, glassworks, ironworks, textiles, leather manufactories, coalmines and other industrial enterprises in the major British ports and their hinterlands."

The slave trade ports

Certain areas in Britain profited more from the slave trade than others, specifically the ports and docks which grew rapidly, resulting in the growth of individual 'port communities'. The most famous of the slave trading ports in Britain were Glasgow, Liverpool and Bristol. Bristol and Liverpool did not rely just on shipping slaves – they also had large tobacco-processing industries, which means even more jobs were available. As a result people flocked to the slave trading ports to seek their fortune.

Bristol dock and quay c.1760.

Bristol

Bristol took advantage of the early slave trade when slave ships were smaller because it was a shallow water port. However it had been a thriving port and dock long before the beginning of the slave trade, with merchants sailing out of Bristol since the 14th century. Bristol's good luck was that it was able to capitalise on a growing industry.

Source B

From the BBC website www.bbc.co.uk

"Bristol merchants were granted the right to trade in slaves in 1698...and to the end of the Slave Trade in Britain in 1807, just over 2,100 Bristol ships set sail on slaving voyages. According to Richardson (The Bristol Slave Traders: A Collective Portrait Bristol: Historical Association, Bristol Branch, 1984) this amounted to around 500,000 Africans who were carried into slavery, representing just under one fifth of the British trade in slaves of this period.

During this time an average of 20 slaving voyages set sail from Bristol each year, sometimes with 'ordinary' people providing a quantity of cash or trade goods to be bartered for captured Africans at the end of the outward passage. Later voyages seem to have relied on one or two wealthy investors, perhaps with an eye to not diluting the profit!"

The slave trade provided jobs for many people in many different industries.

The crowded docks in Liverpool photographed in 1875.

Source C

Abolition Richard S. Reddie

"The Transatlantic slave trade needed men and women with a range of skills to service the industry and newly arrived aspirant workers found jobs on Bristol's docks as labourers involved in the building, equipping and repairing of vessels. Others found work in industries that provisioned ships or in the production of items used to barter for enslaved Africans such as copper, brass, pottery, pots and pans, clothing and any other items that could be exchanged. In addition, work could be found for the more skilled individual as a clerk, book keeper or administrator."

Liverpool

Liverpool soon overtook Bristol as the leading slave trading port because it had deeper water and so could accommodate larger ships. It was also closer to the relevant processing industries.

Source D From the website www.liverpoolmuseums.org.uk

"Liverpool was a major slaving port and its ships and merchants dominated the transatlantic slave trade in the second half of the 18th century. The growth of the trade was slow but solid. By the 1730s about 15 ships a year were leaving for Africa and this grew to about 50 a year in the 1750s. Numbers declined during the American War of Independence (1775–83), but rose to a new peak of 120–130 ships annually in the period 1787–1807. Overall, Liverpool ships transported half of the 3 million Africans carried across the Atlantic by British slavers."

Historians have debated the reasons for Liverpool's dominance of the trade. Some think it was because Liverpool traders were finding other trades such as sugar or tobacco too competitive. However an important reason was that Liverpool was well-connected to a network of rivers and canals transporting the goods made in Britain that were being traded for slaves: textiles from Lancashire and Yorkshire, or firearms from Birmingham. The wealth acquired by the town was substantial and it gave a real boost to industrial development in Britain.

It is important to remember this huge amount of income, allied to the large numbers of jobs that came from the slave trade and its associated industries, when considering the impact of the slave trade. Britain relied on this revenue at a time when vast sums were needed to sustain the growth of the country and the further growth of the Empire. Just how much the slave trade actually financed the Industrial Revolution will always be debated. What is beyond doubt is that cities like Liverpool and Bristol definitely profited and grew because of it.

5.9 The impact of the slave trade on Africa

The slave trade undoubtedly had a large impact on Africa. Although the trade itself did not move very far inland into the **continent**, the effects were wide ranging.

- How did the slave trade affect how African chiefs made money?
- How did it affect where African communities were being established?

To do task 1

Comprehension

1. Why were some African chiefs willing to sell people into slavery?
2. What effects did the slave trade have on Africa?

continents
industries
migrated

What happened?

Source A Atlas of World History
Patrick K. O'Brien

"The period 1500–1800 saw an enormous increase in the scale of the American, Mediterranean and Asian purchase of slaves. In some areas, such as Angola, the consequence was a demographic haemorrhage as thousands of people were sold abroad each year, thereby undermining the capacity of communities to renew themselves. In the Niger Basin whole communities were devastated by raids which caused death, famine and disease on a spiralling scale. In contrast to this, some successful broker kingdoms built up their agrarian economies with new crops and preserved their population by refusing to sell young women captives abroad. In the long term, however, the effects of the slave trade were to entrench violence as a way of life and create a damaging intellectual climate which presumed that white people were superior to black people."

Some African chiefs were very willing to supply slaves and the financial potential of the slave trade was such that many African societies **migrated** away from their traditional means of income and began to rely on the money that they could gain from selling slaves to the Europeans. Wars may even have been started between African tribes purely to make money from the slave trade. Any captured individuals could then be sold to the slave traders. There is certainly evidence to suggest that traditional **industries** such as farming, fishing and craft work were put aside and skills were lost.

The Africans moved important centres away from the coast and re-established them further inland so that they were not impacted upon by the Europeans.

African slaves are brought to East African coastal ports for sale to European slave traders.

Source B

From the website of *The Liverpool Echo* newspaper www.liverpoolecho.co.uk

"A staggering two-thirds of enslaved people were young men aged between 15 and 25. They were in huge demand to work the booming plantations producing ever-growing quantities of crops. Arms brought to Africa by traders helped perpetrate conflict and political instability. Robbing the workforce of healthy individuals caused industrial and economic stagnation. Displays at the International Slavery Museum, in the Merseyside Maritime Museum, focus on the consequences of the trade on Africa. Trade routes that existed before European intervention were disrupted. The development of African communities and cultures was severely stunted. The labour and inventiveness of enslaved peoples shaped the Americas and enriched Western European, rather than their African homelands."

Courtesy of Liverpool Echo

There is no doubt that the removal of so many people from a nation will have a massive impact on a community. Africa must have suffered massively. Exactly how much the continent suffered will never be known. It is for people to debate. Nobody can turn back the clock. The fact that Africa had a number of powerful, well-developed empires and nations, but today is one of the most under-developed continents in the world, may sway your thinking. But once again, the decision is up to you.

The only way to understand the impact of the slave trade on Africa is to do extensive social and economic research. This is almost impossible to do because of a lack of original documents from the nation during this period. Perhaps an easier way would be to consider the effects such events would have had on our own nation. What would have been the effects on Britain of millions of vital men and women being kidnapped and removed from our nation. Imagine the effects that it would have on our infrastructure today. Many parts of our society would simply cease to function, and Britain's ability to compete in an increasingly ruthless and competitive world would be seriously impaired. That is what happened to Africa.

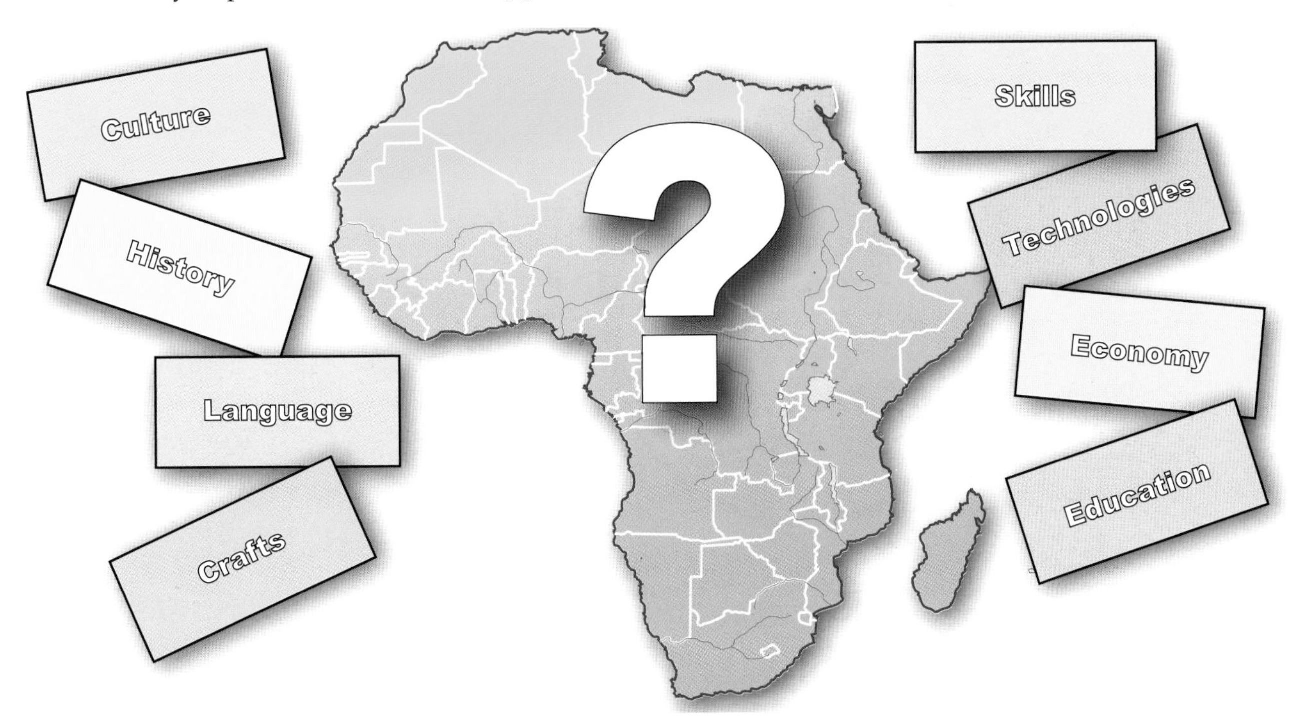

5.10 Abolition

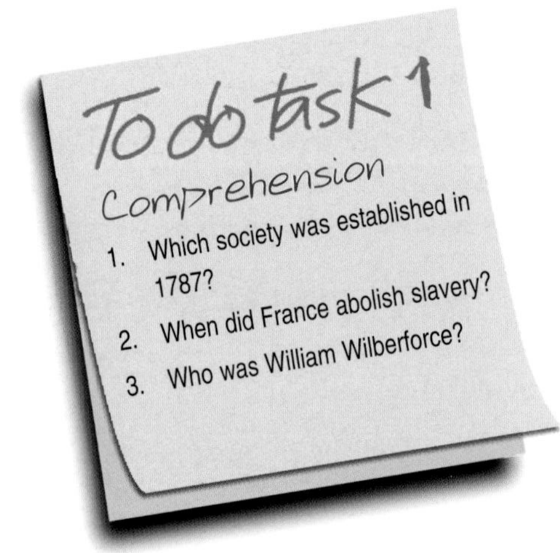

The slave trade did eventually end, with different effects on those involved. Can you answer:

- How did the slave trade come to be abolished?
- Who were the main activists?
- What did it mean for the British Empire?

To do task 1

Comprehension

1. Which society was established in 1787?
2. When did France abolish slavery?
3. Who was William Wilberforce?

How does it end?

The effects of the slave trade on Africa and the people who were forcibly removed from their homes and families cannot be questioned. However, the people who were trading in slaves did not seem to have any moral qualms about what they were doing. The sheer number of slaves available meant that slave owners did not have to look after them and their treatment was **brutal** to say the least. They only began to see the error of their ways at the end of the 18th century, when, in 1787, the Society for the Abolition of the Slave Trade was established. The real question in their minds that needed to be answered was how could such a brutal and cruel industry possibly continue in a modern world? This was definitely an enlightened way of thinking because the British Government of the time had not yet come up with a suitable solution for looking after many of the people who lived in Britain, never mind people from other nations.

A number of countries **abolished** their own slave trade within a relatively short period of time:

Denmark 1803

Britain 1807

USA 1808

Netherlands 1814

France 1818

Portugal and Brazil 1830

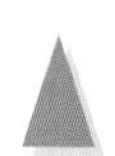

The seal of the English Committee for the Abolition of the Slave Trade, from 1787.

In 1833 slavery was abolished throughout the whole of the British Empire. So how did this come about and who were the main people behind the campaign for the abolition of the slave trade?

Slave trade abolitionists

Many individuals campaigned for the abolition of the slave trade. This book is not long enough to be able to talk about them all in the detail that their stories deserve. This section, however, should give you a glimpse of the people who made a major change possible and helped to spare the lives of many potential slaves.

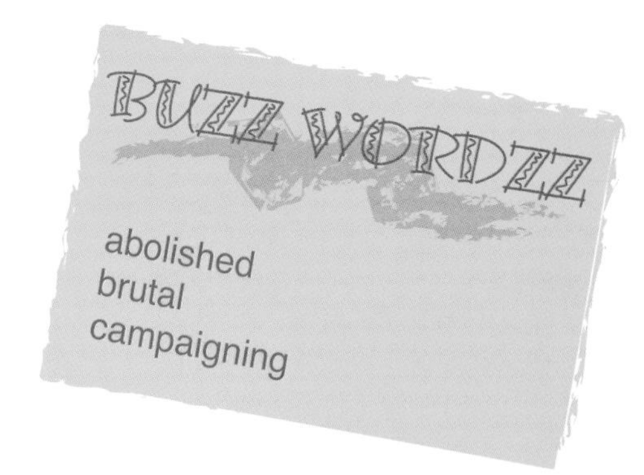

Thomas Clarkson

Thomas Clarkson was able to interview many victims of the slave trade and compiled a lot of evidence that could be used to push through the necessary laws to get the slave trade banned. He had two books published detailing what he found: 'Summary View of the Slave Trade and of the Probable Consequences of Its Abolition' and the 'History of the Abolition of the African Slave Trade'.

William Wilberforce

One of the most famous slave trade abolitionists, William Wilberforce spent a long time **campaigning** for the abolition of the slave trade. Wilberforce's working life was spent as an MP, and he was able to use his influence within Parliament to exert some pressure to get legislation passed.

Erasmus Darwin

Erasmus Darwin was the grandfather of Charles Darwin. He was a man of many talents, skilled as a writer, poet, doctor and inventor, amongst other things. His interest in, and writings on, the slave trade possibly came out of his friendship with fellow slave trade abolitionist Josiah Wedgwood.

Sons of Africa

One particular group that campaigned fiercely for the abolition of the slave trade was known as the Sons of Africa. One of the main activists was Olaudah Equiano.

NB

Lord Mansfield's edict
In 1772 Lord Mansfield made a historic decision that prevented a slave known as James Somerset from being taken back into service by the owner, in Britain.

Source A

From *The Independent* newspaper website

"For decades before the passing of the Slave Trade Act in 1807, Africans had been successfully agitating for their freedom. That culminated in Lord Mansfield's edict of 1772 which acted as a green light for Africans to come to Britain to campaign against the slave trade. They called themselves the 'Sons of Africa'."

Robert Nurden, 25 March 2007, © www.independent.co.uk

Among them were Olaudah Equiano (pictured left) and Ottobah Cugoano, who were just as important as the British abolitionists. Equiano travelled the country for five years reading from his autobiography in which he described the terrible conditions on slave ships and in the plantations. His speeches in Birmingham directly inspired local anti-slavers such as Joseph Sturge, Josiah Wedgwood and Erasmus Darwin. And Birmingham had much to address: it made the leg irons and guns that fed the trade.

Cugoano, also an ex-slave, was set free in 1772 and later published his 'Thoughts and Sentiments on the Evil and Wicked Traffic of the Slavery and Commerce of the Human Species'. In it he destroyed the defence of slavery. He was the first writer in English to declare that enslaved blacks had not only the moral right but also the moral duty to resist.

To do task 2

Write a short speech campaigning for the end of the slave trade. Use the information from this chapter so far to provide the evidence that you will need to put your point across.

Source B

From the UK Government information website

www.direct.gov.uk

"The Government regrets and strongly condemns the evils of the transatlantic slave trade. The 1807 Act marked an important point in this country's development towards the nation it is today – a critical step into the modern world and into a new, and more just, moral universe. Its bicentenary offers a unique chance for the people of Britain to reflect on the wider story of translatlantic slavery and its abolition, and on the roles of ordinary people and politicians, alongside other Britons, Africans and West Indians, in helping to bring an end to slavery."

The heroic British navy

Many slaves were still transported after the slave trade had been outlawed in Britain. The end of British slave trading was not the end of slave trading throughout the world. The British now took on the role of ensuring that much of the remaining slave trading was unsuccessful. To do this they used their powerful navy to run down and overtake slaving vessels.

In an attempt to reduce the number of slaves that were being shipped illegally, the British navy employed squadrons of boats that would sail around the West Coast of Africa, keeping a look-out for any vessels that were engaged in slaving. The main base for these boats was in the Gambia.

Freetown

An area that was transformed in some ways by the end of the slave trade was Sierra Leone. The capital of Sierra Leone was Freetown, a reference to the number of freed slaves who made it their home. Many of these slaves were freed from the slave boats that had continued to trade even after the British ban. The freed slave community of Freetown grew rapidly under this British policy.

In testament to this history, an arch was built in Freetown that reads 'Freed from slavery by British valour and philanthropy'. This arch is known as the Freedom Arch.

The story of the abolition of the slave trade is an interesting and complex one, that cannot be covered in detail here. In summary, however, an Act was finally passed that outlawed the slave trade in Britain and within its colonies forever.

Today many people, including the Government, still regret the part that was played by Britain in the slave trade.

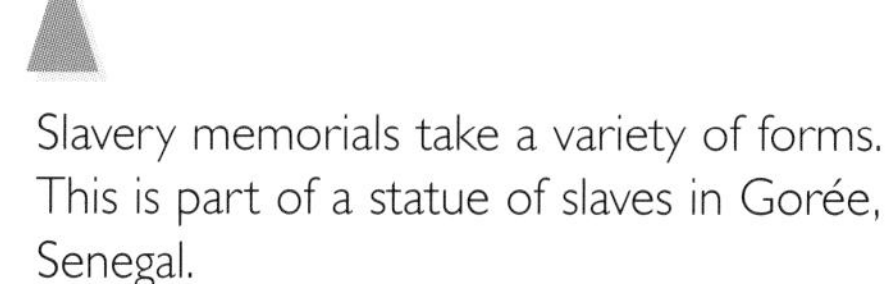

Slavery memorials take a variety of forms. This is part of a statue of slaves in Gorée, Senegal.

Source C

From the History Channel website www.history.co.uk

"The campaign to abolish slavery gathered force in 1823 with the formation of the Anti-Slavery Society. In 1833 an act was passed abolishing slavery throughout the British Empire."

5.11 The scramble for Africa

There was a lot of interest in the continent of Africa. Here you will find out:

- What was the 'scramble for Africa'?
- Who were the explorers who uncovered Africa's hidden secrets?
- Why was there so much interest in the continent?

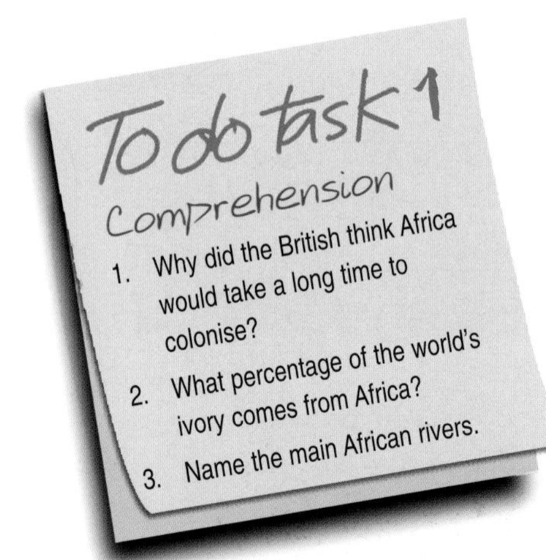

So much to explore

With the abolition of the slave trade, a new source of revenue was required and a continent that was still largely available was Africa. The sheer size of Africa meant that to **colonise** it, or conquer it, would take a very long time, and there was a significant amount of danger and inconvenience attached to the venture.

Source A

Africa – A biography of the continent

John Reade

"Africa is only the second largest continent, but it contains 22% of the Earth's land surface. The Sahara desert is as large as the continental United States. In fact, the United States, China, India and New Zealand could all fit within the African coastline, together with Europe from the Atlantic to Moscow and much of South America. But Africa is much less densely populated, with less than $1/4$ of the population of the other regions. Indeed there are more people living in India (with 1/10th of the land area) than in all of Africa."

Prior to the abolition of the slave trade, the Europeans had been discouraged from any conquest of Africa away from the coastline because of the threat of disease, especially **malaria**, and also because the slave trade was so lucrative that they simply did not need to venture any further inland. Africa, to the Europeans, was essentially a blank canvas, if they ignored the significant African cultures that existed inland. Africa also had a tremendous potential for exploitation, with many valuable natural resources to be found there; 85% of the world's ivory, for example, has come from Africa.

Source B

Atlas of world history

Patrick K. O'Brian

"With the formal abolition by Britain of the slave trade in 1807, ivory, rubber, palm oil, cloth, gold and agricultural products assumed ever greater importance as trading commodities."

The threat of malaria was quickly reduced by the introduction of **quinine** and the whole continent was rapidly overtaken by Europeans.

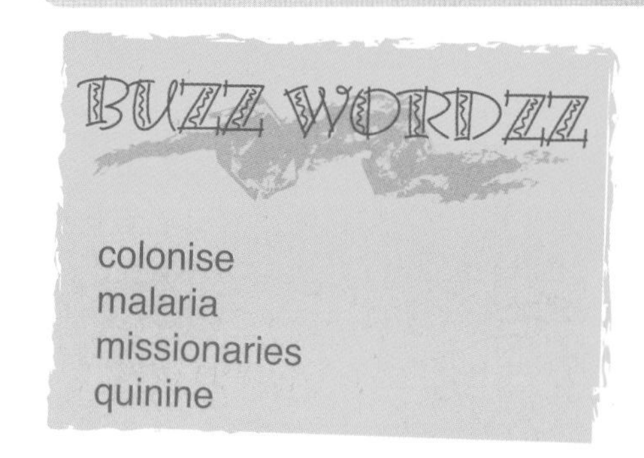

The explorers

As with earlier ventures, Africa needed to be explored to discover its true potential. These explorers would be able to open up the continent by charting the courses of the main African rivers – the Nile, the Congo, the Zambezi and the Niger. They looked for habitable land and natural resources that could be exploited. **Missionaries** also looked to convert the predominantly Muslim continent. Africa was in fact often known as the 'Dark Continent' and the role of the missionaries was to 'enlighten' it. Many famous explorers left their mark, such as Richard Burton, John Hanning Speke and James Grant, but the most famous of them all was David Livingstone.

A statue commemorating the life of David Livingstone.

Livingstone

The most famous of all the explorers was Scottish-born David Livingstone, who managed to cross Africa in 1853. Being an explorer, however, was not his first chosen career path as he began as a missionary, but he became an explorer in 1848, while working in Africa. Born in 1813 in Lanarkshire, Livingstone was a man of many talents, showing a flair for learning languages, which helped him translate the Bible into some of the many languages of Africa.

He also often entertained the Africans with his 'magic lantern', an early light projector that showed moving images, that he carried with him on his travels.

Sources C and D tell us about the famous meeting between David Livingstone and Henry Morton Stanley.

Source C

Who was David Livingstone?

Amanda Mitchison

"The journalist Henry Morton Stanley was a fierce little man who liked to do things in style. So when his editor told him to go into the heart of Africa to find the long lost explorer David Livingstone, and to spare no expense in doing so, Stanley took his boss at his word. He set out with 193 porters and six tons of luggage including 20 miles of cloth, a million beads, two collapsible boats and a number of giant kettles to warm the water for his baths."

Source D

Who was David Livingstone?

Amanda Mitchison

"But, oh how different Livingstone looked now! Stanley had expected a stern, vigorous man with a firm handshake and upright bearing. But this Livingstone was a pathetic-looking figure: a haunched, trembling old man with a pale, lined face and a walking stick. Livingstone's tunic was frayed and bleached, his eyes had that starved, sunken look of the very ill, and he had lost nearly all his teeth. He was only 58. The crowd fell silent in expectation. Stanley marched forward, raised his hat and said, with a slight tremor in his voice, "Dr Livingstone, I presume?"

Livingstone's most famous discovery was Victoria Falls.

Source E

The life and African explorations of David Livingstone *Dr David Livingstone*

"It had never been seen before by European eyes; but scenes so lovely must have been gazed upon by angels in their flight. The falls are bounded on three sides by ridges three hundred or four hundred feet in height, which are covered with forest, with the red soil appearing among the trees. I believe that no one could perceive where the vast body of water went: it seemed to lose itself in the earth, the opposite lip of the ***fissure*** *into which it disappeared being only eighty feet distant. At least I did not comprehend it until, creeping with awe to the verge, I peered down into a large rent which had been made from bank to bank of the broad Zambezi, and saw that a stream of a thousand yards broad leaped down a hundred feet and then became suddenly compressed into a space of twenty yards. In looking down into the fissure on the right of the island, one sees nothing but a dense white cloud, which, at the time we visited the spot had two bright rainbows on it. From this cloud rushed up a great jet of vapour exactly like steam, and it mounted two hundred or three hundred feet high."*

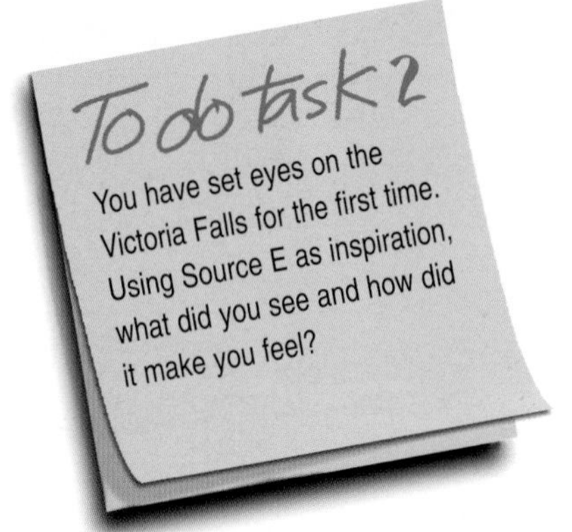

Livingstone believed that the land surrounding the falls might be suitable for British colonisation.

Source F

Empire *Niall Ferguson*

"Right beside the Victoria falls was precisely the kind of place where British settlers could establish themselves: the Bakota plateau, a landscape of open undulating lawns covered with short herbage, where wheat of superior quality and ***abundant*** *yield also flourished, along with other cereals and excellent roots in great variety. It was here in the Zambian highlands that Livingstone believed his countrymen – ideally poor but hardy Scots like himself – would be able to establish a new British colony. Like so many explorers before and since, he believed he had found the Promised Land. But this was to be a cultural as well as an economic El Dorado. Once settled by white men, the Bakota Plateua would radiate civilizing waves until the whole continent had been cleansed of superstition and slavery."*

The land alongside the Zambezi: fertile land that Livingstone believed could be farmed and colonised.

The trading companies

With the knowledge gained from the explorations absorbed and assessed, many new trading companies were established to take advantage of Africa:

- Royal Niger Company in West Africa (1886)
- British East Africa Company (1888)
- British South Africa Company (1889).

The Berlin Conference

In the Berlin Conference of 1884–1885, the European nations, led by Otto Bismarck of Prussia, took it upon themselves to divide up Africa amongst the nations of Europe. They gave little respect to the needs of the African people, but paid a lot of attention to their own needs.

A contemporary illustration by an artist imagining the proceedings at the Berlin Conference.

Transforming Africa

To allow an effective means of communication and transport in Africa, one of the first steps was to lay a railway.

Source G

From the website www.britishempire.co.uk

"In Africa, railways were built to provide an infrastructure that would lure white colonists into an area in order to farm the area and turn it into a profitable colony. South Africa, Rhodesia and Kenya all wanted to increase their white population and increase the economic activity of their lands and all spent copious amounts of money and effort into building railways in what were very often inhospitable areas to European settlers. They all had varying degrees of success, but were built nonetheless. Indeed, one of the burning issues of late nineteenth century was Cecil Rhodes' burning ambition to build a Cape to Cairo railway line that passed through British territory all the way. And this dream, although not realised by a train network, certainly influenced a great deal of Central African colonisation during the period."

South Africa

One of the most interesting regions of Africa was the South, around the Cape of Good Hope. This area had long been an important trade route, principally as a passage to India and the East. The area also provided potential for the British to **exploit** the natural resources of gold and diamonds that were to be found in South Africa. Another country that had a great interest was one of the British Empire's rivals – Holland, whose **descendants** are known as 'Afrikaners' and many of them arrived during what was known as the 'Great Trek' of 1835–6.

Map of the Suez Canal.

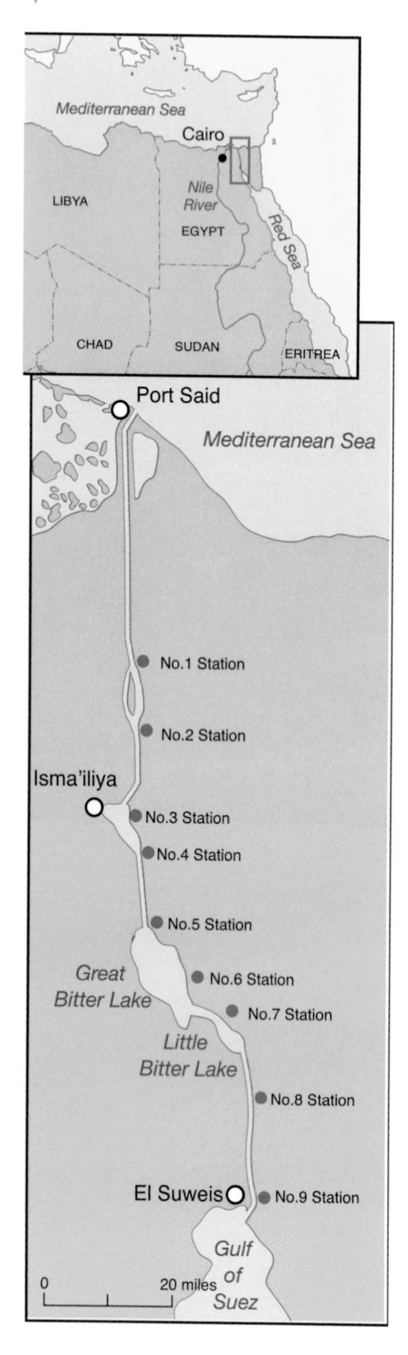

Egypt and the importance of the Suez Canal

A very important part of the conquest of Africa was the Suez Canal which was opened in 1869 and would have been a hive of activity for British shipping, providing a more direct route from Europe to Asia. The Suez Canal was constructed in Egypt.

The Suez Canal carries about 7.5% of all the world's seaborne trade, and it takes between 11 and 16 hours to sail along it. This is a local ferry crossing in between major container ships. The inset shows the construction of the Suez Canal underway.

Source H From the History Channel website www.history.co.uk

"Artificial waterway from Port Said to Suez, linking the Mediterranean and Red Seas; 160 km/100 mi long and with a minimum width of 60 m/197 ft. The canal was built at sea level, with no locks, and can accommodate vessels of up to 150,000 tons. It separates Africa from Asia and provides the shortest eastwards sea route from Europe."

Africa had been exploited once again by Europe, with little overall consideration for the lives of the people who lived there. It was not just Britain, however, that had done the exploiting. As so often in the quest for Empire, the people of Europe, had collectively been responsible for what had gone on in Africa. Once again, the fate of a nation had been decided by an external power, rather than by the nation's own people. How might the history of Africa have been different if the slave trade had not pre-occupied the European for so long?

BUZZ WORDZZ

descendants
exploiting

To do task 3

Read Source H and look at the map of the Suez Canal opposite. What benefits – if any – did the opening of the Canal in 1869 bring, and to whom?

Africa today

Even today, Africa is a land of contrasts, with some parts more developed than others and many areas currently in turmoil. After the segregation of Africa, many new lands and nations came into existence. The most troubled in recent years have been South Africa and Zimbabwe, with clashes between white and black Africans, and struggles over democratic rights. Ethiopia, once a proud and strong nation, has been struck by famine and disaster. Africa cannot, it seems, escape its troubles. What would it be like today, if Europeans had not intervened in its natural progression over the course of many hundreds of years?

Africa in the 21st century.

Chapter 6
Australia

6.1 Captain Cook

This chapter is about Australia. Here you will learn:

- Who was Abel Tasman and why is he important to Australian history?
- How did Captain Cook discover Australia, and what did he find there?

Finding Australia

It is very difficult to get any further away from Britain than Australia. Some of you may never go there. This is simply because of the sheer distance and time that it takes to get there, and the expense that goes with it. The first colonists who travelled to Australia knew very little about it.

Strange though it may seem, for a long time there had been much debate as to whether Australia existed at all. From around 150 AD in the time of Ptolemy, people were speculating about a land known as 'Terra Australis Incognita'. The great minds of the period believed that, in order for the landmasses of the globe to be in balance, there must be a great landmass in the Southern Hemisphere. But without any way to reach it there was no way to prove or disprove its existence.

Many people set out to find it and failed, but the most famous name connected to the discovery and exploration of Australia is Captain James Cook. He reached Australia on his ship, the Endeavour, in 1786 during his exploration of the Pacific. However he was not the first European to reach its shores. Its discovery in 1642 is credited to a Dutchman called Abel Tasman, (pictured alongside in his monument at Hobart, Tasmania) who gave his name to the islands of Tasmania. He originally named it Van Diemen's Land, after the man who had sponsored his voyage.

NB

Tasmania is a group of islands situated off the south-east coast of Australia. They are a part of Australia although they are separated from the mai-land.

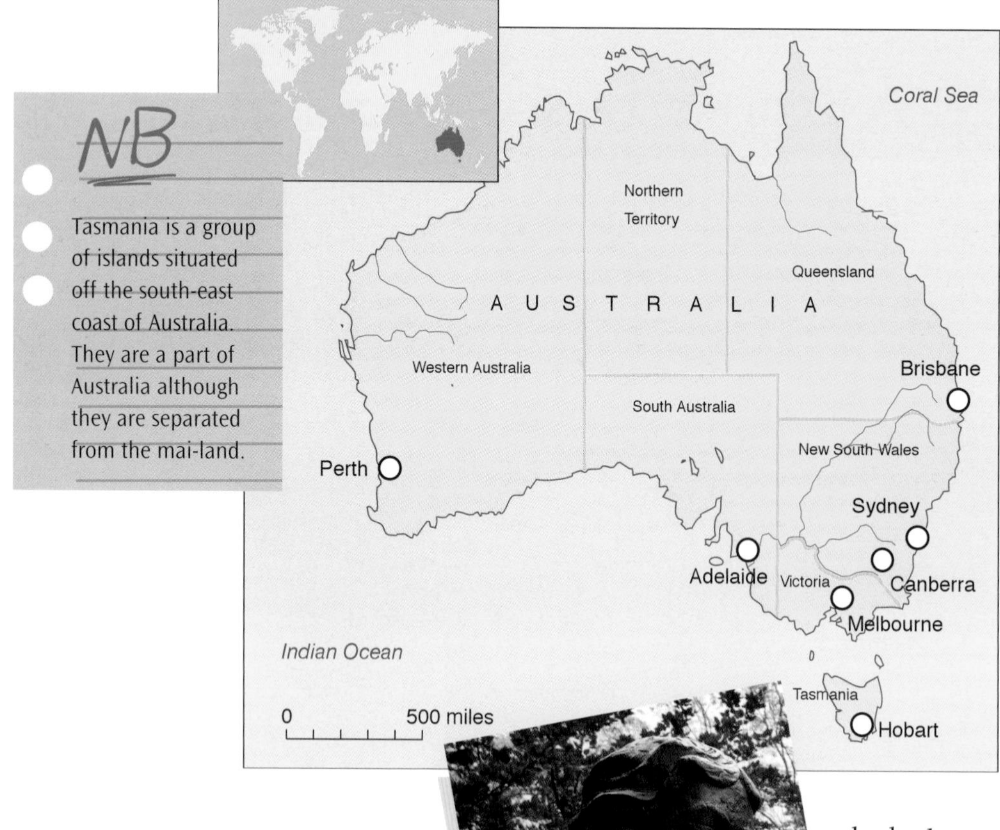

Source A The Explorations of Captain James Cook in the Pacific

A. Greenfell Price

"Cook probably sailed for Australia with two great geographical problems in his mind. First, how far did New Holland, the lands skirted by Tasman, Van Nuyts and others, stretch towards New Zealand. Second, were these lands one great continent of which Van Diemen's land, New Guinea and de Queiros' Espiritu Santo were all parts, or were they only island groups? To answer these questions, which had puzzled Europe for over a century, Cook sailed in the Endeavour on 1st April 1770, to discover the east coast of Australia."

An illustration from after the event, depicting Captain Cook's landfall in 1770.

The area that James Cook had visited and chosen as a potential area for settlement was 'Botany Bay'. The area had been given this name because of the unusual and varied plants that could be found in the area. He had originally decided to call it 'Stingray Bay' because of a number of stingrays that had been observed. However it was later changed to 'Botanist Bay' and finally abbreviated to 'Botany Bay'.

Source B

Captain Cook Vanessa Collingridge

"As they approached, women and children on the beach slid away into the trees; just two men were left who attempted to repel these strange white men seemingly intent on invading their coast. By now the men on the shoreline were turning angry. Cook fired a warning musket between the two men but this merely drove them back to where they had laid their spears. Cook fired again with small shot. Some pellets struck one of the warriors but he merely picked up a shield to defend himself and retreated towards the trees. The water grew shallow, Cook's boat had beached....Cook knew the significance of what was to follow; he turned to Isaac Smith, the cousin of his Elizabeth, and quietly gave his order, "Isaac, you shall land first". The mystery of that great South Land was about to be demolished."

To do task 1

Comprehesion

1. What hemisphere is Australia in?
2. In which Ocean does Australian lie?
3. On which ship did Captain Cook reach Australia?

To do task 2

Read Source B. Imagine that you were a member of the party that landed in Australia. Write a continuation of Source B, detailing the meeting between Cook and the Aborigines.

6.2 Why Australia?

Exploring a new continent is a challenging experience. Here you will learn:

- What was so attractive about Australia?
- What was transportation and how did it provide a workforce for Australia?
- Where were the settlements made, and how did the population expand?

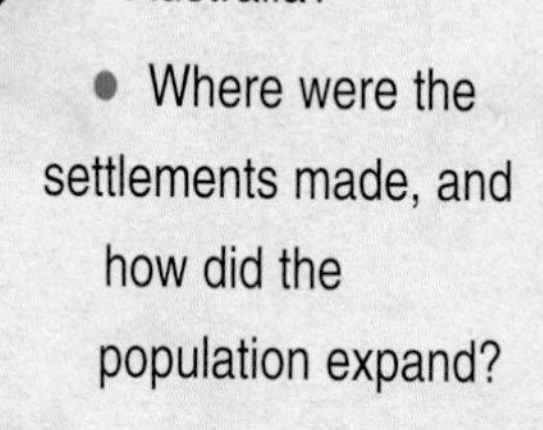

Starting out

As an area for encouraging exploration and colonisation, the Pacific Ocean was never as attractive as the Americas or the Caribbean. This was largely because it was far more difficult to get to than it had been to reach America. The Pacific was at first little more than an area through which trade with the East could be conducted. Only from the voyages of Captain Cook did the British realise that the area could be colonised and profits be made.

Just as America had promised great things and an opportunity to grow valuable crops, it was hoped that Australia would allow the settlers to grow all the crops that had been cultivated in other parts of the Empire. In this way it would be like an America and an India combined.

The labour force required for colonisation would come either from the prisons of Britain, in the same way as America had been partly colonised, or through slave labour. In reality the main way to make money in Australia proved not to be crops as in the Americas or the Caribbean. Sheep (and their wool) and cattle would become the main 'crop' of Australia. Whaling and sealing industries would also grow in this island nation where settlement was mainly on the coastline.

To do task 1

Comprehension

1. What would the main 'crop' of Australia be?
2. when did the Australian Gold Rush take place?
3. When did Australia cease to be a prison colony?

Australians shearing sheep, photographed in the late 19th century.

Gold

The colonists also exploited Australia's natural resources in precious metals such as gold and silver, as well as large copper reserves. The Gold Rush of the 1850s encouraged many people to make the long journey to Australia to seek their fortunes.

An Australian prospector photographed in the late 19th century

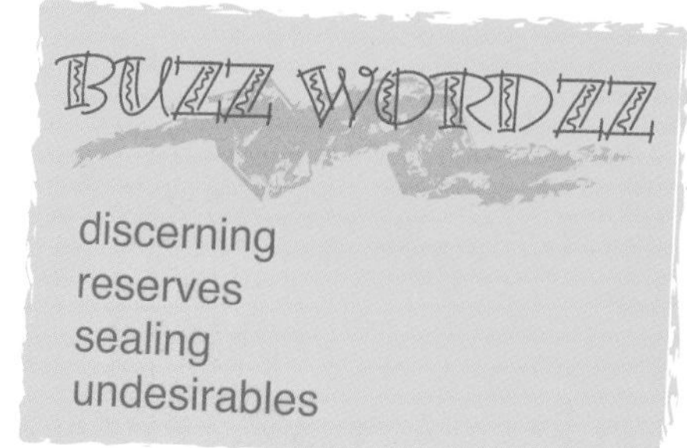

BUZZ WORDZZ

discerning
reserves
sealing
undesirables

A prison colony

In little more than 100 years from Cook's first footsteps upon the continent, Australia had a population of over four million people. So how did Australia end up being home to so many immigrants? A very large proportion of the initial colonists were transported there in the same way as people had previously been transported to America. The difference was that Australia was primarily a prison colony. Initially there was little desire to colonise Australia, but simply to use it as a sort of dumping ground for undesirables. Australia only really came into the British consciousness when America was lost in 1776; it was used as their next prison colony by the British until 1857.

To do task 2

Think about the British Government's policy of transportation. What were the advantages and disadvantages of adopting such a policy?

The British Government did not think Australia had as much potential in terms of large scale migration as America. They did, however, recognise its potential as an immediate solution for the social problem caused by a rising prison population. The harsh conditions that were found there, combined with its huge distance from Britain, meant that it would be the best, most inhospitable prison that could be built, without having to do any building work at all. The journey to Australia was far longer than the one to America, taking up to eight months on a prison ship.

The British Government was not discerning as to whom it transported either, sending anybody they could. Even some freed slaves who had committed a minor crime could end up on a boat to Australia to spend even more years in hardship.

A contemporary illustration showing convicts and guards transported to Australia.

Transportation

Transportation had been a way for the British Government to rid itself of criminals who might ordinarily have been sentenced to death under a more hostile regime. It was also a solution to the poor state of the prisons in Britain. Transportation was when prisoners were sent away to another country for a period of 7 years, 14 years or life. When they arrived at the destination they would be forced to do hard labour and work off their debt to society. Once their time had been served, they would be allowed their freedom, and if possible return home. After the American War of Independence in 1775, the policy of transportation to America was suspended. A new destination was needed and finally a solution was reached – send them to Australia.

To do task 3

You have been asked to vote for or against the policy of transportation. Read sources A, B and C to help you decide. Make a list of the positive and negative points about transportation.

Source A

Empire *Niall Ferguson*

"On 13th May 1787 a fleet of eleven ships set sail from Portsmouth, crammed with 548 male and 188 female convicts, ranging from a nine year old chimney sweep, John Hudson, who had stolen some clothes and a pistol, to an 82 year old rag dealer named Dorothy Handland, who had been guilty of perjury. They arrived at Botany Bay, just beyond what is now Sydney Harbour, on 19th January 1788, after more than eight months at sea."

Source B From The National Archives

"Australia had been mapped and claimed as British territory in 1770, so convicts began to be sent there. From 1787 to 1857, 162,000 British convicts were transported to Australia. Seven out of eight of these were males; some were as young as nine or ten; some were over eighty. Many political prisoners were transported, including Luddites, Chartists, the Tolpuddle Martyrs and Irish Nationalists.

They were sent first to the "hulks" - disused warships. Conditions on these rotting vessels were often terrible, with death rates of one in three. The long voyage to Australia could take six months. Many lives were lost among the convicts, locked in iron cages below decks in insanitary conditions, although by the end of the transportation era more care was taken and loss of life on the voyage was minimised.

Once in Australia, convicts lived in barracks and worked in gangs, building roads and bridges or working on farms or quarries. Some were sent out to work for farmers. If they behaved themselves, their sentence could be reduced by a "ticket of leave." The majority of convicts decided to stay in Australia at the end of their sentences, recognising that they could make a better life there than returning to Britain and, probably, poverty and crime."

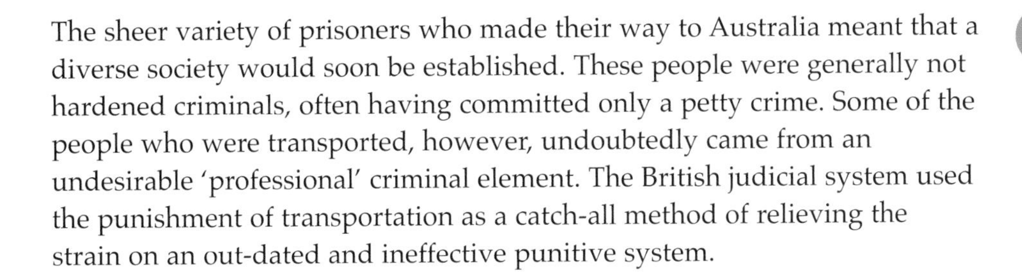

The sheer variety of prisoners who made their way to Australia meant that a diverse society would soon be established. These people were generally not hardened criminals, often having committed only a petty crime. Some of the people who were transported, however, undoubtedly came from an undesirable 'professional' criminal element. The British judicial system used the punishment of transportation as a catch-all method of relieving the strain on an out-dated and ineffective punitive system.

NB

Punitive
This means to do with punishment or punishing

Source C

The Commonwealth of Thieves *Tom Keneally*

"The offences for which a prisoner could be transported under the accumulated Transportation Acts of Britain made up an exotic catalogue. Quakers could be transported for denying any oath to be lawful, or assembling themselves together under pretence of joining in religious worship.

Notorious thieves and takers of spoil in the borderlands of Northumberland and Cumberland, commonly called "moss troopers" were also subject to penalties of transportation; similarly, persons convicted of wilfully burning ricks of corn, hay or barns in the night time; persons convicted of larceny and other offences; persons imprisoned for exporting wool and not paying the excise on it; persons convicted of entering into any park and killing or wounding any deer without the consent of the owner; persons convicted of assaulting others with offensive weapons with the design to rob; vagrants or vagabonds escaping from a house of correction or from service in the army or navy; persons convicted of stealing any linen laid to be printed or bleached...and many more."

To do task 4

Read Source C. What types of crimes were punished by transportation? Was this a fair or equitable system?

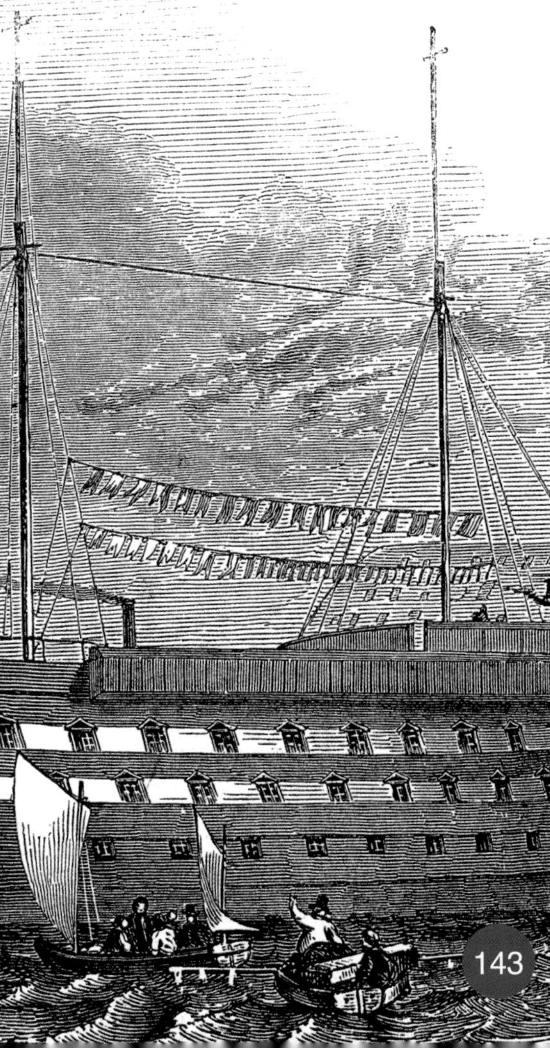

The prison hulk Warrior, berthed at Woolwich, London.

Not all the prisoners who were transported actually made it to Australia. The journey was long and the conditions were generally harsh, although some enterprising souls did manage to make the whole ordeal less harrowing.

Source D Australia – A biography of a nation

Phillip Knightley

"The convicts on the better transport ships were issued with sturdy clothing and a pair of shoes. Laundry was done on deck and bedding aired regularly. In balmy climes the convicts were encouraged to sing and dance. They were served one substantial meal a day (which included meat and sometimes a glass or two of wine) and two snacks. There was a daily dose of lemon juice to avoid scurvy. To alleviate boredom some transport ships had lectures given by the ship's officers or better educated convicts."

To do task 5

What do you think was the worst aspect of the punishment illustrated on this page? Why do you think it was so feared by prisoners?

Due to the harsh nature of the climate and landscape these convicts found themselves thrown into, the labour provided by the convicts was vital in setting up the colony quickly. This meant that instead of being strictly punished they became integrated into everyday life if their specific skills and talents were valuable. Prisoners who could read and write were much sought-after in the new towns.

Some convicts were less fortunate and when they were punished this was often brutal. Many were punished harshly, receiving hundreds of lashes. The wounds from these these whippings would be then be treated by having stinging salt water poured on them to try to prevent infection.

The convicts would often be shackled in ill-fitting leg irons. Perhaps the most extreme punishment – besides death – was to be chained up and placed in an underground chamber almost filled with water, where they would have to stay for two days at a time.

Botany Bay

The destination for the first prison ship was Botany Bay, as recommended by Captain James Cook. The coastline in the area was called New South Wales because of its resemblance to the coast of South Wales.

Source E

The Fatal Shore *Robert Hughes*

"Never had a colony been founded so far from its parent state, or in such ignorance of the land it occupied. There had been no reconnaissance. In 1770 Captain James Cook had made landfall on the unexplored east coast of this utterly enigmatic continent, stopped for a short while at a place called Botany Bay and gone north again. Since then, no ship had called: not a word, not an observation, for seventeen years."

Modern-day Aborigines still use traditional hunting methods to live off the land.

Naively, settlers and Government officials in Britain simply assumed that this area would provide for the people who settled there. However the Bay did not live up to its potential. Terribly isolated, with little chance of large-scale cultivation and shelter, the colonists must have felt terribly alone in a strange land. The typical pattern of European settlement was to establish a base and stay there, building a community. However, the only people who had previously lived in Botany Bay had been nomadic, living off the land by hunting aand gathering, and moviong around according to the seasons.

The expected pasture land and vital water supplies were just not there to be found. As the picture above shows, the landscape around Botany Bay was harsh and so there was little chance of being able to establish a colony successfully. Expeditions were therefore sent out to look for a more suitable site for a settlement. This was found at what is now called Sydney, then named Port Jackson.

Source F

The original Australians

Josephine Flood

"On 26th January 1788 (now Australia day), the British flag was raised at Sydney Cove, and the land became a "settled colony" and a dominion of the crown."

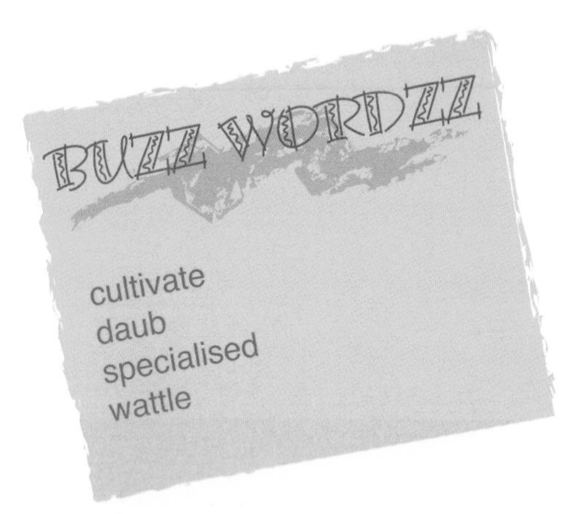

cultivate
daub
specialised
wattle

To do task 6

If you were a modern-day transportee, what would be the most difficult thing to leave behind and why? Write a letter home, imagining that you have been transported and describing the hardships you are facing.

Survival

Because of all these initial problems the settlers had to take full advantage of any supplies that they could bring with them from Britain. The first boats brought supplies for two years, long enough for the settlers to establish themselves properly and begin to produce their own crops. In essence they had to bring 'England' with them, transporting everything that they needed to survive. It was like living in a piece of England that had been uprooted and placed into a foreign landscape. Animals struggled with the conditions too and low survival rates meant that they had to be constantly exported from Britain to Australia at high expense.

Although it proved to be difficult to settle in Australia, people were still given the customary land grants that settlers had also been given in America. By the end of 1789 the new colony was beginning to look much more permanent, despite many early attempts to **cultivate** crops failing: wheat seemed to be the only crop that would grow. Houses were being built, albeit somewhat slowly due to the lack of adequate tools.

One of the more sophisticated houses built by the settlers. Compare it to the primitive shacks or huts that were their first houses (below)

Settling in

Everybody had trouble adapting to life in this new place, partly because the people who travelled to Australia did not represent a true cross-section of society. In normal life there is an opportunity for tradesmen to be employed or skilled craftsmen to take over where people are lacking in their own ability. Natural resources – such as might be needed to build houses for instance – are easily available, along with a plentiful supply of **specialised** tools. None of these were available to the colonists. They had to start from scratch, in a society based solely on the skills of whoever had been transported.

The result was houses that looked as if they had been plucked from a forgotten, Medieval Age. They were made primarily from **wattle** and **daub**, and later they were fashioned from irregular shaped bricks that were crafted by hand. The bricks were held together by mortar that had been made from crushed oyster shells. So you can see that early settlers had to be very adaptable just to get by.

Initially people even had to buy or swap fish, maintaining a supply from the indigenous people, who were much more adept at catching them in their nets than the new settlers. The settlers found the land very difficult to cultivate, being far removed from what they were used to back home. Many of the animals that they had transported with them quickly died or had to be eaten.

The settlers had to get used to eating strange foods like kangaroo, but a lot of their diet was seafood, making use of the best natural resource that they had – the sea. Bizarrely, the effect of all this was that for many people their previous homes and lives in Britain seemed suddenly very desirable. Such problems led to people looking for better sites for new settlements. One was formed at a location known as Norfolk Island, where the people survived by eating a strange bird known as the Mutton Bird, or Bird of Providence. But like many others, this colony was abandoned by 1813 and its materials were recycled and re-used elsewhere.

Convicts and guards on Norfolk Island.

Overall, the venture to Australia was costly. People really did struggle to make it work. Those who managed to survive the initial period became known as 'Yeomen', who could then cultivate land of their own and truly begin their own new lives.

Norfolk Island remains a remote and hostile land today.

The expansion of Australia

The population of Australia soon began to grow at a steady rate, with the original settlers multiplying naturally, and new settlers arriving regularly. Voluntary settlers also began to see the potential of Australia as a site for settlement.

To do task 7

Read Sources G, H and I. What factors brought new settlers to Australia and why?

Source G

The British Empire *Philippa Levine*

"By 1820 there were 32,000 colonists in New South Wales and Van Diemen's land, and by 1850 the white population had grown to 400,000. In addition to a constant flow of migrants, both voluntary and convict, the dramatic growth in population was also a result of natural increase. The settler population was mostly a youthful one, and the growth in the number of children was striking."

Source H

From the BBC website www.bbc.co.uk

"The image of early Australia as a convict society obscures the fact that not everyone was a felon. Both felons and freeholders created the successful longer term story of the colony: the 1850s gold rush, wooden ship-building in Tasmania, iron ore from Broken Hill, prairies of wheat and the big wool industry. The pace set by the original settlers was faster than any other colonial experiment in the history of the British Empire.

By the time that the policy of transportation to Australia was abandoned, the foundations for a successful colony had been laid, and the potential for serious expansion was there. Australia would soon detach itself from the British Government, although it would retain the British Monarch as its Head of State."

Lord Bathurst was Secretary for the Colonies. In 1817 he said the experiment to settle Australia as a convict colony was failing, because of the cost of transportation and the fact that crime in Britain wasn't falling.

The Ross Bridge in Tasmania is one of the oldest in Australia, and was built by the transported convicts in 1863.

Australia's history will always be inextricably linked with the notion of a prison colony, but that is only part of the story: there was more to it than that. If you look beyond the period of transportation and look at the people who chose to settle there, as well as the people who had been there a lot longer than the European settlers – the Aborigines – Australia's history is interesting and diverse. Australia was never as valuable to the British Empire as America, but it is no less worthy of mention. Many people did, after all, make their own way to Australia.

Source I

From the website www.iexplore.co.uk

"The discovery of gold in 1851 by Edward Hargraves, fresh from the California fields, had a dramatic bearing on Australia's future. The first major strikes in New South Wales and Victoria brought an immediate rush of hopeful miners from Sydney and Melbourne and, once the news spread overseas, from the USA and Britain. The British government, realizing the absurdity of spending taxes on shipping criminals to a land of gold when there were plenty of people willing to pay for their passage, finally ended transportation in 1853. Gold also opened up Australia's interior far more thoroughly than explorers had done; as returns petered out in one area, prospectors moved on into uncharted regions to find more. Western Australia and Queensland (which was saved from bankruptcy by the discovery of gold in 1867) experienced booms up until 1900 and, although mining initially followed in the path of pastoral expansion, the rushes began to attract settlements and markets into previously uncultivated regions."

6.3 The Native Australians

Europeans did not arrive in Australia and find a totally empty continent. There were people already living there who had been there for some time. Here you will learn:

- Who lived in Australia prior to the arrival of the Europeans?
- What are the characteristic features of Native Australian life?
- How did the settlers and the Native Australians interact?

Who are the Native Australians?

Native Australians are usually known as **Aborigines**, which is a reference to the fact that early settlers believed these people were primitive examples of early man. Current research suggest that Aborigines are most likely descended from Indonesians who arrived in Australia at least 50,000 years before the Europeans arrived.

Aborigines were nomadic, moving with the seasons to take advantage of the natural resources in new areas. They moved around through necessity but in time this meant they tended to group together in areas which had good potential food supplies through fishing or hunting. If those areas were not visited by the settlers, then each group might remain ignorant of the other for a long time.

Initially settlers thought that Australia was barely populated because they had expected to see towns and villages. All they actually saw were small amounts of smoke as evidence of some sort of settlement based slightly further inland, and occasionally small groups of people who met their vessels as they came ashore. The first Native Australians who were encountered by the by the settlers were called the Lora people, from the area around Sydney.

Source A

From the website www.cityofsydney.nsw.gov.au

"The traditional owners of the Sydney City region are the Cadigal band. Their land south of Port Jackson stretches from South Head to Petersham. The "Eora people" was the name given to the coastal Aborigines around Sydney. The word Eora simply means "here" or "from this place". Local Aboriginal people used the word to describe to the British where they came from and so the word was then used to define the Aboriginal people themselves. The name Eora is proudly used today by the descendants of those very same people. Central Sydney is therefore often referred to as "Eora Country"."

The Lora People

Unlike the Native Americans, who had grouped together into tribes with names, Aborigines had no such organisation. They spoke a huge number of languages and dialects perhaps as many as 250 in total. However they were unlike any European style languages as they had totally different ways of **pronouncing** words and expression of dialect, with a much larger range of sounds. In fact, there were probably about 750,000 Aborigines in Australia when the first settlers arrived. They were just so scattered around the huge country that the settlers hardly ever met them.

As they were forced to live off the land, the Aboriginal people were skilled hunters and trappers. The main tool that they used was the boomerang.

BUZZ WORDZZ

Aborigine
dialect
nomadic
pronouncing

Source B — The original Australians

Josephine Flood

"A boomerang is a bent or curved thin hardwood missile. Returning boomerangs sweep in a near circular arc of up to 50m (160ft) radius and were used to kill birds or drive them into nets across flightways. Straight flight, non-returning boomerangs were used for hunting and fighting. Hunting boomerangs have a range of up to 200m (650ft) and were thrown at possums, gliders, bandicoots, flocks of pigeons, ducks or cockatoos, and even soaring wedge-tailed eagles, whose feathers were prized for ceremonial decoration. Fighting boomerangs were heavier and longer with a shallow curve and sharper edges. They were thrown through the air, ricocheted from the ground or used as clubs or "swords"."

Different types of boomerang, including a fighting boomerang (left).

Relationships with the Aborigines

Relationships between the Aborigines and the early settlers were strained, mainly because of the lack of understanding between the two groups. The settlers did not understand the way Aborigines led their lives without any real signs of civilisation.

NB

The word aborigine is commonly used to describe the native people of Australia. However it can also be used to decribe indiginous peoples in general in any country.

Because of the major language differences, the settlers found it very difficult to negotiate or converse with the Aborigines, and they often required **mediators** or **translators** to help the process along.

One of the main problems was that the Europeans and the Native Australians had different concepts of land ownership and use. The Europeans saw the land as 'Terra Nullius' or 'Nobody's Land'. They therefore saw no problem with taking that land as their own. This was contrary to what the Aborigines believed, who felt that the land was 'common land' and should be shared by everybody. Where they would naturally have migrated to areas during certain times of the year, they were forced out by the new settlers. In the eyes of the Europeans, who just viewed the whole of Australia as up for grabs, land was there for the taking. In their view the Native Australians were not using the land to its full potential.

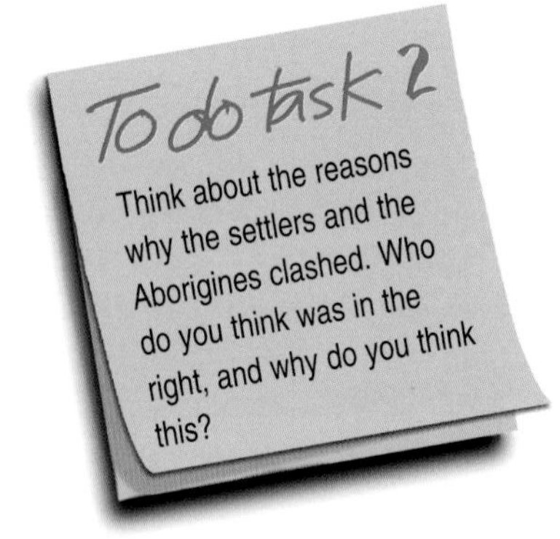

Source C **The British Empire**
Philippa Levine

"Outside the cities, on farms and sheep and cattle stations, Aboriginal labour was crucial to success, for settlers relied upon indigenous knowledge of a harsh land where water was sparse and dangerous storms could blow up in minutes. Trackers assisted surveyors, settlers and others to navigate and pass through the hinterlands, yet despite their importance in helping settlers, Aboriginal workers were often poorly treated."

The impact of the settlers on the Native Australians

Unfortunately one of the main impacts was disease. In the same way that disease had impacted heavily upon the Native Americans, the Aborigines were devastated by new diseases to which they had no resistance. By the 1920s their population had fallen as low as 60,000 people. The diseases were typical ailments such as smallpox, cholera and influenza; sexually transmitted diseases had a severe impact on their fertility. One of the major epidemics came early on, when smallpox ripped through the Aboriginal population in 1789.

Source D

The commonwealth of thieves

Tom Keneally

"Though it could be lethal, smallpox was a disease most of the residents of Sydney Cove were used to. Many British people of all classes carried the pitted faces of survivors of the illness."

The effects of guns

The arrival of firearms in Australia, like in America, had a significant and deadly impact upon the Native Australians, who were defenceless against them.

Australia – A biography of a nation

Phillip Knightley

"Aboriginals held their own in the first campaigns, but the arrival of the repeating rifle made their cause a hopeless one, and they were eventually defeated, although clashes continued until the 1920s."

And so in many ways the relationship between the British and the Native Australians is very similar to that experienced by Native Americans. Circumstances repeated themselves and lessons about the value of integrating with indigenous peoples were not learned. Do you think that one reason why you study history is to try and learn lessons from the mistakes of the past?

The Winchester rifle, the firearm most commonly used in Australia by settlers.

Chapter 7

Diversity in modern Britain

7.1 Making a home in Britain

Today, Britain is home to people from many different nations and incorporates many religions and beliefs. In this section you will learn:

- Where have people come from to make Britain their home?
- Are they made to feel welcome in Britain?
- What problems could immigants have living in Britain?

People will come...

Modern Britain is truly a diverse nation and some of this diversity is a direct result of the legacy of the British Empire. Diversity brings many benefits to Britain, including varied cultures and languages. However one unfortunate side-effect has been to provoke racist attitudes and actions within some people who fear or cannot understand people, ideas, cultures or beliefs that are new to them. Despite the best efforts of many people over several decades, prejudice because of skin colour, accent, culture or religious beliefs still hinder attempts to totally integrate the different communities.

This is not, however, solely a British problem, and it would be wrong to say that it is. In fact, Britain is a far more tolerant place for different peoples to live together than you may be aware of. Why some people believe that Britain should be kept only for the 'British' is nonsensical; indeed, it is almost impossible to actually say what 'British' is.

One definition of being British today is that you either were born in Britain, or that you have become a British citizen. There are many different routes that can be taken to reach Britain, both legal and illegal.

Source A

From *The Independent* newspaper website www.independent.co.uk

"Our history as a nation is fundamentally entwined with migration. Yet whereas the United States and Canada have grasped that reality and celebrate it as part of their history, there is no equivalent in Britain. We talk about dates and battles, kings and queens, but rarely does immigration through the ages merit a mention in our popular history."

Barbara Roche, © www.independent.co.uk

There are those who live in Britain who believe that there is no longer any reason to allow immigration and that people who try to come to live in Britain should either be banned, punished in some way, and if necessary forcibly removed. Many people across a range of political and social classes object strongly to this view, and in doing so they make a very good point: those doing the banning forget their own individual ancestry, which often reflects the effects of migration of people to and from another country.

And so the history of Britain is full of tales of the migration of different people from wide and varied parts of the globe. The history of 'Britain' is actually the history of England, Wales, Scotland and Northern Ireland, and of all the different people who have made Britain their home.

Source B

From the *Daily Mail* website

www.dailymail.co.uk/news/

"If there were to be a British Statue of Liberty, it should be erected at Victoria coach station in London. For it is here that most of the tired, poor, huddled masses of Eastern Europeans have arrived seeking what Michael Howard once called the 'British dream'. The influx of the past ten years has been the largest in Britain's history, changing the country for ever. Immigrants now make up a ninth of our population, produce a fifth of our babies and fill (or create) most of our new jobs."

Britain is also now part of the European Union, and membership has brought down some more of the economic, social and cultural barriers to immigration that had previously been raised to prevent people coming into Britain. One of the key revolutions that the EU has created is the right for citizens of member states to travel and work freely throughout European Union countries.

Source C

From the Foreign & Commonwealth Office website, a branch of the civil service
www.fco.gov.uk

"12 member countries have decided to share a single currency (the Euro). EU member countries are working together to create an area of freedom, security and justice across Europe. All of the member countries, except the UK and Ireland, have agreed to scrap their border controls with each other. These are the "Schengen" arrangements – named after the village in Luxembourg where they were first agreed. They allow citizens to travel freely without checks at the internal borders. The UK and Ireland have a right to choose whether to sign up to EU laws on border controls, immigration and asylum. However, the UK and Ireland play a proactive role with other member states in working to tackle illegal immigration and abuse of the asylum system."

As British people, we should really feel flattered that those from other nations view Britain so positively that they want to come and live here. After all, people have been travelling to Britain for as long as records have existed. One of the earliest examples of legal **immigration** to Britain is highlighted through the example of what is known as a 'Patent of Denization'.

A major complaint made by some citizens of the UK today is that it is now too easy to make a home in Britain, either through seeking asylum, being smuggled into the country via people-traffickers, or other forms of illegal entry. The reality is, however, that most of the people who attempt to enter the country by these means are discovered by the relevant officials, although some do get through the net.

Source D

From the BBC news website

"Serious questions have been raised over Britain's border security after a BBC journalist entered the UK twice on fake and stolen passports.

Shahida Tulaganova obtained 20 illegal passports – each from an EU country, including the UK – within months. Those in the trade told her to travel via sea or bus, saying port security was less stringent than airports. The Home Office said it works closely with the EU to tackle the crime, taking the issue of false documents seriously. In 2004, 8,285 fraudulent documents were detected at UK ports of entry, according to Home Office figures."

It is vital that the border authorities in Britain prevent illegal immigration into the country, Britain, because there is a maximum number of people that any country can justifiably sustain. Also, in a society that requires people to pay taxes and contribute to the upkeep and administration of the country, any people who do not contribute to this become an additional burden. Of course, everybody who legally holds British nationality pays their taxes. Plenty of people take out of the system without paying into it!

How tight should border controls be?

Source E

From the *Daily Telegraph* website

www.telegraph.co.uk/news/newstopics/politics/lawandorder

"A UK Border Agency spokesman said: "We are committed to responding to every police request where they arrest people who have been smuggled into the UK in lorries. We work closely with the police, through new Immigration Crime Partnerships, to target together the harm caused to Britain by illegal immigration. We have one of the toughest border crossings in the world at Calais. Over the past five years we've stopped 88,500 attempts by illegal migrants to cross the channel, and searched nearly three million lorries." Hauliers can face fines of up to £2,000 for each illegal immigrant found in their vehicles."

NB

In 2007, UK customs officials caught 12,00 people hiding on trains, ferries or lorries. Each one was trying to enter Britain illegally.

Despite all the stories of illegal immigration and the fact that certain sections of the modern media often only give one side of the story, you must not assume that most of the people who have come to this country must have done so illegally. This is unfair to the majority of people who have settled legally in this country. There is absolutely no reason why somebody cannot legally settle in Britain provided that they fit the necessary criteria.

The Government has made a conscious effort to encourage people to settle in the UK, especially those people from the former countries of the British Empire who would fulfil useful roles within the workforce and the community. That decision was susequently revised partly due to hostility from certain sections of the press and public, making entry to the UK limited to those who were British citizens.

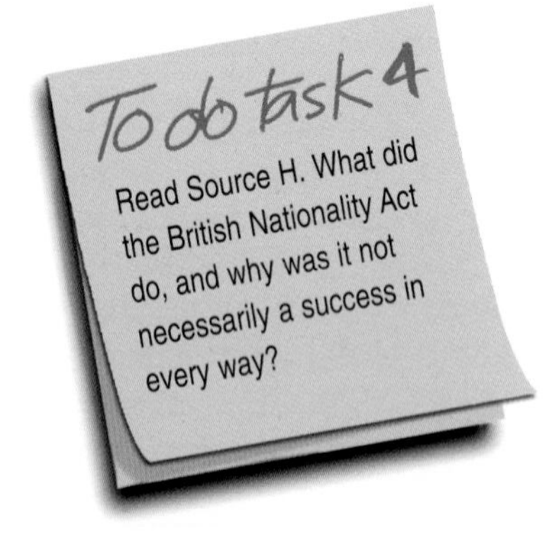

Source F

From the National Archives

"At the beginning of the century, if you could prove you were born within the British empire you could claim full nationality rights in Britain. The British Nationality Act of 1948 conferred the status of British citizen on all Commonwealth subjects and recognised their right to work and settle in the UK and to bring their families with them. However, Commonwealth immigration generated hostility out of all proportion to its size, especially during times of economic downturn.

Consequently, the right to reside in the UK was restricted by the 1971 Immigration Act. From 1971, 'right of abode' was limited to those with a prior link to the UK, such as a parent or grandparent who was born here – which had the effect of virtually ending 'primary' immigration.

The British Nationality Act of 1981 abolished the 1948 definition of British citizenship and replaced it with three categories: British citizenship, citizenship of British dependent territories, and British overseas citizenship. Of these, only British citizenship provides the right to live in the UK."

BUZZ WORDZZ

immigration
rigour

Laws today are tighter than ever, with those people who enter the Britain having to meet strict criteria before they are allowed into the country, leading to a reduction in the number of people who can enter the country legally .

Source G

Part of this increased **rigour** is that people are now being asked to take a test to prove that they are capable of becoming a part of the nation. Some of the questions that they are asked are quite tough. Would you be able to answer them? Look at Source J and see what you think.

Source H Part of the Life in the United Kingdom test

Migration to Britain

- *Where have migrants come from in the past and why? What sort of work have they done?*

The changing role of women

- *Do women have equal rights in voting, education and work, and has this always been the case?*

Children, family and young people

- *Do many children live in single parent families or step-families?*
- *When do children take tests at school? How many go on to higher education?*
- *What are the minimum ages for buying alcohol and tobacco? What drugs are illegal?"*

To do task 5

Read Source J. Have a go at answering the questions. How easy are they? What do you think of them as a measure of someone's potential as a British citizen?

Reverse migration

Since the late 1990s Britain has experienced significant immigration from countries within the European Union. Much of this has been so-called economic migration, and one of the major contributing nations has been Poland. Poland became a member of the European Union in 2004, prompting a **surge** in Poles leaving their homes to make their way to Britain to find work.

Far from the media portrayal of the Poles providing cheap labour for the building trades, they have also provided key workers in areas such as the NHS. They have also contributed key staff to agriculture and many other sectors that previously could not draw in sufficient numbers of British workers. Their reputation is one of hard workers who get the job done quickly and to a high standard. The British economy has found them invaluable in many ways and in many sectors.

This Tesco supermarket in West London recognised that there was a demand from Polish immigrants for their foods from home. Will displays like these continue as reverse migration increases?

However, the global recession and the credit crunch of 2008 and 2009 has meant that the situation has been reversed. Many economic migrants have now returned to their home nations in search of work.

One of the questions that some British citizens and some parts of the media have been asking concerns the impact of these migrants: for instance, have they placed too much strain on social services, such as the NHS? They have also questioned whether the amount of British currency leaving the country has been beneficial or detrimental to the British economy. The British Government's stance states that the migrants have not placed an unnecessary burden on these essential services. Instead, they have offered a solution to many employment issues that simply would not have been possible had they not arrived in the UK looking for work.

The statement that these migrant workers make life increasingly difficult for British citizens is generally incorrect. They have simply filled a gap within the British labour force that would not have been filled otherwise. The importance of this cannot be denied.

Source L

From *The Times* newspaper website www.timesonline.co.uk

"Hard statistics on the number of Poles leaving Britain do not exist. There are no embarkation controls on EU members so they are not counted out. But Polish officials, British employment agencies and the Polish media all believe that the tide of immigration has turned. Since Poland joined the EU in 2004, 274,065 Poles have signed up for work permits. They make up 66 per cent of all applications from Eastern European countries. But a combination of tightening economic conditions in this country, a comparatively weak pound and an unprecendented surge in the Polish economy has made it unattractive for Poles to remain. Jan Mokrzycki, president of the Federation of Poles in Great Britain, said: "The first thing that's been hit is the builders. There's no doubt about it. Many aren't prepared to wait for the construction boom that's going to happen for the Olympics in 2012. "Also, the Polish economy is experiencing an upturn."

Alexi Mostrous and Christine Seib, 16 February 2008.

With cheap air travel and the desire to extend horizons, it is no surprise that people are looking further afield, and making their homes away from the countries that they were born in. Generations of families are being born in countries different from where their ancestors were born. This is true of Britains as well as other nationalities.

Only time will tell wether these trends will contiue or reverse..

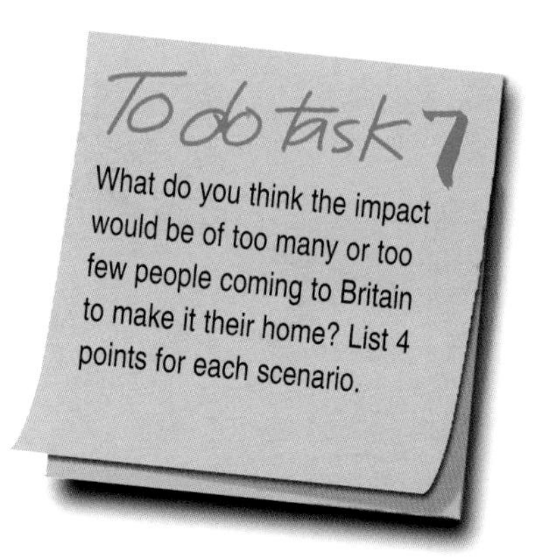

Source I

From *The Guardian* newspaper website www.guardian.co.uk

Romania, which enjoyed 8 per cent economic growth in the first half of this year, is suffering from acute labour shortages caused by an exodus of workers following its accession to the European Union in 2007.

Next month the Romanian embassy will stage a conference for Romanian students in London at which it will promote the benefits of returning home after their studies. It has 50,000 workers in this country, among them many doctors, nurses and construction workers whose skills are now in high demand at home.

7.2 Diverse communities in Britain

Britain is truly diverse, with a wide range of people settling here. Here you will learn:

- Where have they come from?
- What prompted them to settle in Britain?
- How diverse is Britain today?

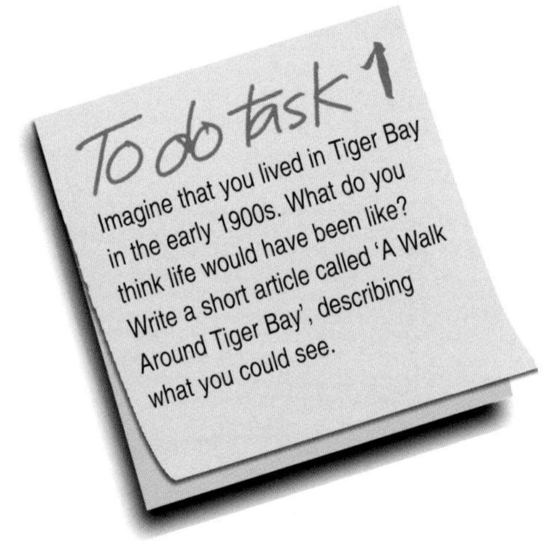

Children of all cultures and nationalities mixing during a religious celebration in the 1960s Tiger Bay.

Who lives here?

One of the most interesting aspects of living in Britain today is the wide range of diverse communities that are found in this country. Many towns and cities in Britain have areas that are **uniquely** different from other parts, usually because of the community that lives within them. One of the most common examples of this is what is known as a 'China Town', with such areas flourishing in London, Manchester and Liverpool amongst others. Other, more diverse communities, have grown up around the ports and docks.

The dock communities

One of the ways in which the British Empire has historically promoted the move to England is through 'docks' and ports, on the boats that brought goods into and out of the country. Quite naturally the people who sailed, or worked on the boats, would be keen to live in the places that they visited, even if only for a short period of time.

One of the most famous examples of this work-related immigration, which has had a big impact on Britain, was the immigration of Chinese workers to Britain on the Blue Funnel Line. (See Source A).

The sheer variety of countries that shipping and trading lines visited meant that many different **nationalities** came to, and settled in, Britain. Many of these people settled in close proximity to the docks that the ships moored in. Dock communities therefore often contained a wide variety of people from around the world, many from Asia and India. These foreign 'seamen' were known collectively as **Lascars** and their heritage can be seen in many parts of Britain. One of the most famous port cities is Tiger Bay in Cardiff.

Source A

From the website www.liverpoolmuseums.org.uk

"Alfred and Philip Holt established the Blue Funnel Line in 1865 to run steamers, equipped with Alfred's own design of compound engines, from Liverpool to Asia. The Suez Canal reduced the long voyage and gave Blue Funnel steamships an advantage over their sailing contemporaries, to which the Suez Canal was not accessible. In the 1870s the Holts developed the service further with the assistance of Butterfield and Swire, agents in Shanghai, and were instrumental in establishing the Far Eastern Conference in 1879. Blue Funnel continued to expand, for example, into Sumatra and the tobacco trade, and later a Dutch subsidiary was established to run a direct service from Amsterdam to Indonesia. By 1901 a direct UK to Australia service commenced."

Source B

From the website www.channel4.com

"Tiger Bay was an area of racial and cultural diversity. This was because of the port, which attracted people from all over the world, such as Norwegians, Chinese and Japanese. In the area of Tiger Bay they lived alongside each other with no problems. The children would go to different religious festivals. Christians and Muslim are mentioned and would be given sweets. One's own background did not matter. Within Tiger Bay there was a strong sense of community. Outside the Bay, they could expect to find racist attitudes."

From the Caribbean studies Black and Asian History website www.casbah.ac.uk

"The growth of Cardiff docklands also attracted a kaleidoscope of immigrants to build the docks, to work aboard the tramp-steamers, and to otherwise service the new industrial and maritime city. More docks had to be built to keep pace with the constantly expanding trade, culminating in 1907 with the opening of the 52 acre Queen Alexandra Dock. Containerisation and the decline of the coal trade - a mere 229,105 tons were exported in 1964 - brought Cardiff's days as a major port to an end.

But by then, Cardiff docklands, especially the famed community known as Tiger Bay, was a cosmopolitan island. In addition to people from the Welsh valleys, mid-Wales, Ireland, the West Country and Scotland, the area was a magnet for people from at least 50 other nations including:

Greeks, Spanish, Portuguese, Cape Verdeans, Italians, Germans, French, Maltese, Turks, Cypriots, Caribbean islanders, Chinese, Malays, Indians, Somalis, Arabs, Jews, Poles, Russians, Baltic peoples, Ukrainians, Scandinavians, Mauritians, West Africans, South Africans, North Americans, South Americans, Central Americans and a few others, including one Maori and at least one Fijian."

Irish communities in Britain

The docks, and the trade in and out of them, were not the only reason why people came to Britain. It is not surprising, given the proximity of Ireland to the British mainland that many Irish men, women and children have come to settle here. The historical relationship between England and Ireland was mentioned in Chapter 3, and ever since the Tudors claimed the throne of Ireland for themselves, there has been movement between the two islands. There has also long been a degree of political tension over the independent status of Ireland.

Discussion point – Should we encourage multi-racial or single-race communities in Britain?

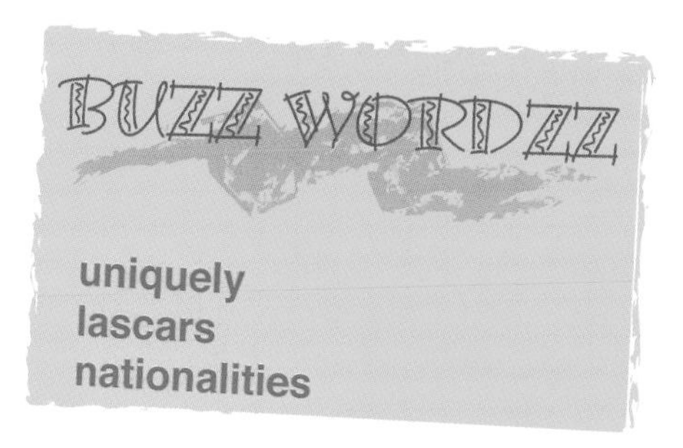

uniquely
lascars
nationalities

To do task 2

What do you think is better for Britain? Mixed race communities or areas where communities and ethnic groups are isolated? Put across your point of view in no more than 100 words, or 5 bullet points.

This Irish pub is evidence of the links between Britain and Ireland and in this case shows the strong link with the port of Liverpool. The pub is opposite the site of the Cavern Club, a famous nightclub in Liverpool where The Beatles perfomed in the 1960s.

Source D

From *The Mersey Reporter* newspaper website

"The Irish Potato Famine touched Ireland by the mid-1840s. Millions of desperate Irish people crossed the Irish Sea on dodgy vessels called 'coffin ships'. Very often these overloaded ships reached Liverpool after losing a third of their passengers to disease, hunger and other causes. Liverpool was for a lot of them only a stage before emmigrating to North America. In 1846 280,000 people entered Liverpool from Ireland of whom 106,000 moved abroad."

Source E

Bloody foreigners

Robert Winder

"As the Imperial administration grew, returning families uprooted Indian maids and servants to look after the children during the voyage, only to abandon them upon arrival. In 1857 the Strangers' Home for Asiatics, Africans and South Sea Islanders was set up on West India Dock Road, and it was soon full of sacked Indian ayahs, who could do little but tout despairingly for domestic jobs with families heading east."

One of the main reasons why Irish immigrants came to Britain was because of the 'potato famine' that hit Ireland in the 1840s. This catastrophic event may have killed as many as a million people, due to a condition known as Potato Blight, that destroyed the staple crop of the people – the potato. One advantage of the close history shared by England and Ireland was that the Irish could make their way to another nation in this troubled period.

Due to the close ties between Britain and Ireland, and the troubled historical relationship that arose from the Plantations [see page 33], the subject of British rule in Ireland has long been a controversial question for some groups. The most famous of these who have campaigned for Irish independence has been the IRA, whose terrorist actions have brought horror and despair to many people and many nations. The Irish Republican Army conducted a long campaign over the division of Ireland, and fought for the cause of home rule for the whole of the country.

This resulted in a prolonged armed struggle with the IRA and other paramilitary groups. The issues led to many acts of terrorism in Ireland and on the British mainland, with one of the most devastating examples seen in the bombing of Manchester city centre in 1996. Today, the issues in Ireland have been mainly resolved, crucially following a decision in the 1990s to 'abandon the bomb for the ballot box', and continue the cause of a united Ireland through peaceful, democratic means. Northern Ireland still remains part of the UK, not part of an independent Ireland.

Indian communities in Britain

As India was the 'Jewel in the Crown' of the British Empire, you might have expected that the Indian community would make their way to Britain as well. This was not always an entirely voluntary migration however...

Source F

A history of Modern Britain Andrew Marr

"In the thirties the Indian community numbered perhaps 8,000 at most – a tenth of them doctors, intriguingly – and there were a few Indian restaurants and grocery stores in the biggest cities. There had been a tiny West Indian presence. No detailed surveys were done, but there were at most a few thousand, many of them students."

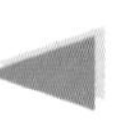

Road sign in East London with a Bangladeshi translation underneath: evidence of how far Indian communities are part of 21st-century Britain.

Many Asian communities have chosen to settle in Britain – in fact the catch-all term 'Asian' itself is not strictly accurate, as it lumps together numerous separate communities under one label. Citizens of India, Pakistan, Bangladesh, along with people from China, are often wrongly labelled as 'Asian'.

The impact of these societies and cultures can be seen right across British modern day life. Muslim and Hindu religious festivals are observed by many in Britain, and the British have adopted numerous dishes from these countries into the national identity – none more famous than curry, which has replaced fish and chips as Britain's favourite takeaway.

These communities, however, have far more to offer than just culinary diversity. Indian communities have carved out a niche in society that is as valuable as any other. Members of their communities fill important roles in medicine, the legal system and the education system. Aspects of Indian culture that would once have been considered on the sidelines of British society – such as Bollywood films – have become mainstream.

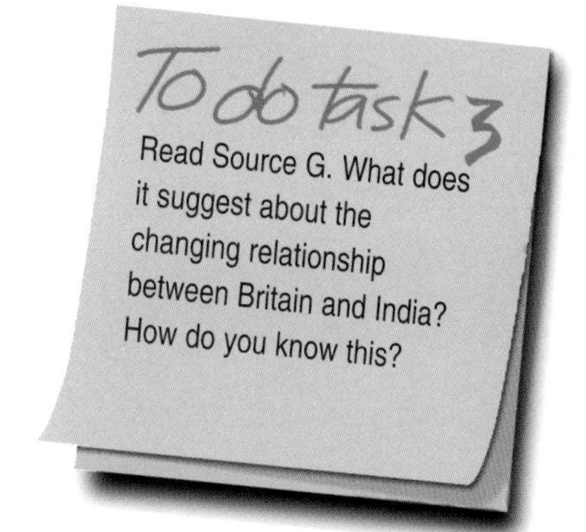

Source G

From the website of The Mayor of London 2007

www.london.gov.uk

"The Mayor Ken Livingstone said: "India is a rising economic superpower. It has a growth rate of over nine per cent a year, 1.2 billion people and it already accounts for the second highest number of inward investment projects into London after the US. Last year, India was one of the three countries accounting for the majority of world economic growth. "The Indian community is already the largest minority ethnic community in London and London's strength as the most globalised city is helped immensely by its Indian community - there are already 10,000 Indian-owned businesses in the capital. "The aim of this visit is to continue to build on and reinforce these links to strengthen a deep rooted and special relationship between London and India."

Film stars Shah Rukh Khan and Deepika Padukoneat at a Bollywood premiere in London. The Indian film industry was worth about £8bn in 2007, in part fuelled by demand in the UK Indian communities.

Black communities in Britain

Black communities have existed in Britain for hundreds of years. So how much has the British Empire contributed to this migration, and how much has come about since the end of the British Empire?

By the 18th century, African communities were based in the cities of London and Liverpool, although often not entirely legally and in houses that were not fit for purpose. Many black women who found themselves in England, like other women of that age, turned to prostitution to survive.

Source H

Dr Johnson's London *Liza Picard*

"Whatever their legal status, by 1764 there were perhaps 20,000 negro servants in London, mostly young men. Whether they were slaves or not when they arrived here, they realised soon that their fellow servants were being paid as employees, and they asked for the same terms, and left if they did not get them, sinking into the anonymity of London, whence their masters would find it difficult to retrieve them."

Source I

Bloody Foreigners

Robert Winder

"Black servants soon became an elegant (and cheap) way of complimenting and setting off the pale skin of their owners. A duchess could hardly afford to be seen in public without a dashing black companion, lavishly dressed in brocade and a turban, and given a heroic name like Pompey or Caesar, Scipio or Socrates. They were fashion accessories, more or less: they brought a touch of tamed jungle to the Georgian living room."

At the time an insulting name for a black person living in England was a 'Hottentot'. The most famous woman of her times was Saartje Baartman, who was given the name of the 'Hottentot Venus' (pictured right.)

Some 'wealthy' British people also chose to bring black servants to work in their own homes and many ex-slaves came to Britain.

One of the most famous ex-slaves who made their way to England was Olaudah Equiano. Equiano had been born in Nigeria in 1745. He was captured as a slave at the age of 11 and was sold into a life of slavery, where he was given the name Gustavus Vassa after the then King of Sweden. His life as a slave covered periods in both Barbados and Virginia. His autobiography – 'The interesting narrative of the life of Olaudah Equiano, or Gustavus Vassa, the African' is a fascinating account of his life and an insight into the period. It was published to great acclaim in 1789. Equiano eventually settled in England.

Source J

The trader, the owner, the slave

James Walvin

"Unlike slavery in the Americas, there was no real economic need for African labour in England. Instead, Africans settled in the company of returning masters and owners, arriving as slaves to sailors on the home-bound slave ships, as enslaved servants of ex-planters and military, or merely as exotic personal attendants to those who were keen to cut a swagger in fashionable circles. "

Source K

Form the website 100greatblackbritons.com

"He travelled throughout England promoting the book. It became a bestseller and was also published in Germany (1790), America (1791) and Holland (1791). He also spent over eight months in Ireland where he made several speeches on the evils of the slave trade. While he was there he sold over 1,900 copies of his book. In Equiano's lifetime, his narrative went through eight British editions; six more followed in the 22 years following his death. He had won widespread recognition as principal spokesman of Britain's black community. "

The number of black people that had moved to England decreased rapidly after the end of the slave trade, leaving Britain, once again, as a predominantly white country.

Although many black people have made their way to Britain because of the British Empire, many have also made the journey to this country after the Empire had declined. One particular cause of the migration to Britain was the 'British Nationality Act' of 1948. (See page 168)

A famous example of black migration in British history was the arrival of the SS Windrush in 1948.

Jamaicans on board the Empire Windrush as they arrive in England in 1948

Source L

From the website understandingslavery.com

"The SS Empire Windrush docked at Tilbury in June 1948. The ship had sailed to Britain from Jamaica. During the Second World War, thousands of Caribbean men and women had been recruited to serve in the British armed forces. The ship was sent to the Caribbean to bring back servicemen and women who had been given temporary home leave to visit their families. Extra berths were offered to anyone who wanted to emigrate to Britain and could pay the fare of £28. No papers or visas were needed, since at that time people from British colonies in the Caribbean had British passports. Very few of the 600 or so people on board the SS Empire Windrush had planned to stay in Britain for more than a few years. "

Many black people came to Britain from areas such as the Caribbean and Africa, and over successive generations have made Britain their home.

Race Riots

One of the key indicators that all is not well within an increasingly diverse society is racism. A proportion of the British population are unwilling to accept the changing nature of the national community. Instead they choose to voice their opinions on what they believe is an injustice – the settling of different races in the British isles – through racist views and attitudes.

On some occasions this has led to the minority communities standing up against this racsism. An early example of a disturbance within and between communities came in Notting Hill in 1957. Acts of violence and abuse by the white community of Notting Hill directed at the black community had caused widespread aggravation and ill-feeling. This finally resulted in violent clashes on the streets. (see source M)

Source M

From *The Independent* newspaper website

"After three days of constant rioting, though, the tide finally turned. A group of mostly Jamaicans retaliated by throwing home-made Molotov cocktails on to the baying mob outside their base, the Totobags Café at 9 Blenheim Crescent. As the white crowd backed away, a few of the West Indians gave chase waving machetes and meat cleavers.

Before the West Indian fightback, the police, despite mounting one of the biggest operations of the decade, had struggled to contain the crowds. But now the white gangs had effectively been broken, and within 48 hours an uneasy calm at last settled on Notting Hill. In total, 108 people were arrested, and despite numerous injuries, almost miraculously, nobody was killed."

Mark Olden, 29 August 2008 © The Independent

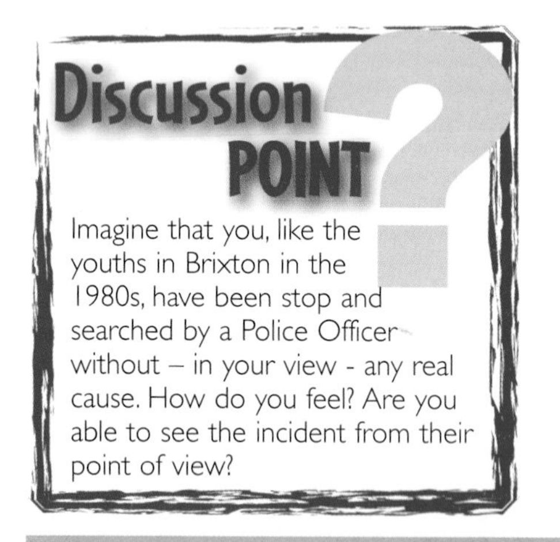

Discussion POINT

Imagine that you, like the youths in Brixton in the 1980s, have been stop and searched by a Police Officer without – in your view - any real cause. How do you feel? Are you able to see the incident from their point of view?

Violence like that – fuelled by ignorance and prejudice, should not be a part of a truly integrated and diverse society. The Notting Hill riots led to much discussion about the state of British society at this time.

Racial tensions continued to rise during the 1970s and 1980s, with more outbreaks of race-motivated rioting such as in Brixton (London), Toxteth (Liverpool) and Moss Side (Manchester). The incidents in Brixton came about because of a Police operation known as "Operation Swamp." This was an attempt by the Metropolitan Police to use their powers of "Stop and Search" as a method of control and to prevent crime.

Their enquiries, however, had been largely focussed on the black community, which was seen to be unfair and as a suggestion that the majority of crime was being committed by black youths. The rioting that followed was some of the fiercest ever seen in Britain.

Source N

From the BBC news website

"The rioting which began in Brixton, in the south London borough of Lambeth, in April 1981 shocked the nation. For three days, rioters – predominately young, black men – fought police, attacked buildings and set fire to vehicles. More than 300 people were injured and the damage caused came to an estimated value of £7.5m. What was most shocking to many people was the unexpectedness of events. On the surface it seemed that black people were well-integrated into the fabric of UK society. "

The rioting led to a thorough investigation led by Lord Scarman, with the findings published in 1981 in the Scarman Report. This report denied that the Police were "Institutionally Racist" but did say that there was a divide between the mainly white Police Force and the ethnic minority communities. Resentment and ill-feeling over the policies and the attitudes of the Police Force had led to such violent clashes.

A key recommendation was that racist actions should be punished severely and categorised as a criminal offence. Scarman also suggested that the Police recruit a wide variety of ethnic groups. Finally, a Police Complaints Commission should be established to allow formal investigation into actions by the Police that could be seen to be unfair or discriminatory.

The Brixton riots: April 1981

Source O

From the website ThisisLondon.co.uk

The police should no longer be accused of "institutional racism", the head of Britain's equalities watchdog said today.

On the 10th anniversary of the report into the murder of black teenager Stephen Lawrence, Trevor Phillips said the term had been hijacked by "guilt-tripping white folks" who refuse to acknowledge that Britain has become "by far the best place in Europe to live if you are not white". Lord Macpherson's report into the bungled investigation of the 1993 Lawrence killing in Eltham labelled the police "institutionally racist".

The incident referred to in Source P that re-opened the question of racism within the Police was the murder of Stephen Lawrence in 1993. Lawrence was stabbed to death in a racist attack by a group of white youths. A 'bungled' investigation into the killing led to another report being published – named the MacPherson report. This report stated that the Metropolitan Police was still 'institutionally racist '.

The important aspect of the inquiry was that if said institutional racism played a part in the flawed investigation by the Metropolitan Police Service (MPS) of Stephen's murder. Investigating officers failed to recognise the murder as a `racially motivated crime', and as a result there was a lack of urgency and commitment in some areas of the investigation. The Campaign for Racial Equality also strongly suggested that racism existed in other police services as well, and also in other everyday organisations.

Since then the Police and the Government have made real efforts to work at eradicating racism and racist attitudes within public services, institutions and society. Programmes within schools that target racism have had an impact, as have increased sentences for those convicted of racist crimes. But have these methods been successful enough?

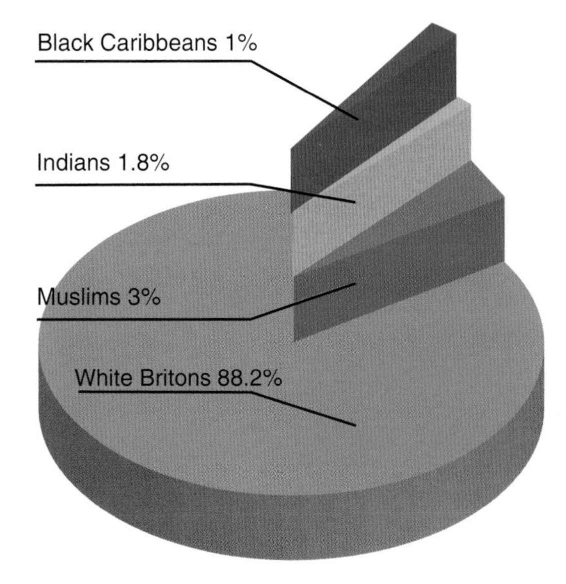

White Britons make up 88.2 per cent of the population.
Muslims make up three per cent of the population.
The Indian population is the largest non-white ethnic group, accounting for 1.8 per cent.
Pakistani Muslims are the biggest non-white ethno-religious grou
Black Caribbeans account for one per cent of the population.
One in three Black Africans was born in Britain.

So just how diverse is Britain today?

The communities that have been mentioned are just some examples of previous migration to Britain. It would be wrong to believe that migration has been limited just to people from Africa, the Caribbean, India and Pakistan. While it is correct to say that most migrants have come from countries that were once part of the British Empire, many other races and nationalities have also come to settle in Britain. For example Britain has very large Polish and Italian communities. How many people from different nationalities live in your area or go to school with you?

The days of the British Empire and its rule over large parts of the globe are over. The UK Government and the people of Britain must adapt and provide a truly multi-cultural and multi-ethnic society, with equality for all. The true test will be to ensure that certain sections of society do not prosper at the expense of others. Only then will the legacy of the intolerances of the British Empire be left behind.

Source P

Percentage of people by ethnic origin in Britain 2001 and 2007:

	2001	2007
White	93	90
Mixed	1	1
Asian or Asian British of which	4	5
Indian	2	2
Pakistani or Bangladeshi	2	2
Other Asian	0	1
Black or Black British of which	2	3
Black Caribbean	1	1
Black non-Caribbean	1	1
Chinese or Other	1	2

(Note figures are rounded up, so the totals add up to more than 100%)

Buzz Wordzz

Abolished – Got rid of / ended

Aborigine – Native Australian

Abundant – Plentiful

Acquisition – Something that has been acquired / gained

Acute – Serious

Administered – Dealt with / GIven

Administrator – Organiser

Agricultural – To do with farming

Algonquian – Native American tribe

Brackish – Mixture of salt and fresh water

Brutal – Nasty / Vicious

Campaigning – Mounting a campaign

Caribbean – Chain of island in the Atlantic

Climate – Generalised weather condition

Colony – Overseas possession of an Empire

Commodities – Goods

Compromised – Exposed / Agreed through negotiation

Confederacy – Group or band of states

Congress – Group concerned with legislation

Continent – Land mass – ie: America

Cultivate – Grow

Daub – Paint / put on

Declaration _ statement

Degrading _ embarassing

Descendants – people related to

Devastating – terrible

Dialect – language

Dignity – pride

Dispute – argument

Dominant – more powerful than others

Dysentery – Bowel infection

Economically – To do with money

Emperor – Head of an Empire

Enhanced – increased

Exchanged – swapped

Expansionism – to do with expanding and empire or business

Expenditure – cost

Exploit – Take advantage of

Fissure – Crack

Floundering – Struggling

Free Trade – Trade that is unregulated

Generations – Successive branches of a family

Geographical – Linked to Geography

Idyllic – Beautiful

Immigrants – People who have moved to another country

Immigration – The process of moving to another nation

Impacting – effecting

Indentured – contracted

Independence – freedom

Indigenous – native to

Industrialisation – to do with industry

Industry – manufacturing

Influenza – flu

Influx – surge of

Infuse – insert / put in

Isolated – lonely

Lascars – Overseas sailor

Lifeblood – essence

Malaria – disease carried by mosquito

Massacred – murdered

Mediators – negotiators

Migrated – moved to

Missionaries – religious messengers

Monopoly – total control over

Mughal – Muslim ruler of India

Nationalities – Where people come from

Nawab – Indian Prince

Nomadic – No settled place of residence

Obliterated – Destroyed

Oppression – Keeping down through force

Persecuted – victimised

Pioneers – People who lead the way

Pilgrim – traveller

Plantation – Farm

Plentiful – plenty of

Plundering – stealing

Precaution – cautionary action

Presidency – British part of India

Prevalence – plentiful

Profitable – making profit

Pronouncing – saying

Prosperity – wealth

Proximity – closeness

Quinine – Drug used in treatment of malaria

Regulation – rule

Representation – presentation

Rigour – Strict

Sanctuary – Shelter

Sanitation – hygiene

Scurvy – disease caused by lack of Vitamin C

Self-sustaining – Needing no outside influences

Shareholders – People with shares in a company

Significantly – Importantly

Solution – Remedy

Specialise – Concentrate on something

Subservient – Lesser than

Surge – Rush

Tolerance – respect for other beliefs / ideas

Tormented – tortured

Translators – people who translate a language

Transportation – punishment where people are sent to another country

Transposed – Placed on top of

Treacherous – Dangerous

Uniquely – Individually

Venture – Go forwards into

Virginia – American state

Wattle – Twigs

Acknowledgements

Chapter 1

7: Source A: A.C. Benson; Robert Harding Picture Library Ltd / Alamy (Upper) Albo / Shutterstock (lower); 8: Stuwdamdorp / Alamy, 10: (left) XtravaganT / Fotolia (top middle) Shariff Che'Lah / Fotolia (bottom middle) cashcb / Fololia (right) CraterValley Photo / Fotolia; 11: James Steidl / Fotalia;
12: Vladimir Khirman / Fotolia 13: Daria Miroshnikova / Fotolia 14: (upper) Sharpshot – Fotolia (middle) World Pictures/Photoshot (lower) UPPA/Photoshot; 15: Source A www.thesurvivalexpert.com; 16: (upper) World Illustrated/Photoshot (lower) Irochka / Fotolia; 17: Source B bbc.co.uk website (upper) Vtls / Fotolia, Source C The Science Museum Website, (lower) Roman H. – Fotolia

Chapter 2

20: Pictorial Press Ltd / Alamy Source A www.historic-uk.com; 21: Source B www.nationalarchives.gov.uk (upper) Fotolia VI (lower) Sammy / Fotolia; (lower) Raxxillion/Fotolia; 23: World Illustrated/Photoshot; 26: (left) Alan J Jones / Alamy; Source A An Utterly Impartial History of Britain, John O Farrell; 27 Source B The British Empire Frank McDounough; (lower) The Print Collector / Alamy; 28: Justin Kase zelevenz / Alamy; 29: Pictorial Press Ltd / Alamy

Chapter 3

32: Mary Evans Picture Library; 33: The Print Collector/Heritage Images; 35: The Art Archive/Corbis; 38: J Lycke/Fotolia; 40: MPI/Getty; 41: (both) Shutterstock; 42: (upper)Don Smetzer/Alamy (lower) Shutterstock; 44 (both) Shutterstock; 46: Shutterstock; 47: Shutterstock; 48: Fotolia; 50: Fotolia; 52: Burstein Collection/Corbis; 53: Bettman/Corbis; 54: Timothy Millett Collection/Bridgeman; 55: Michael Ventura/Alamy; 56: North Wind Picture Archives / Alamy; 57: The Granger Collection, New York/ Topfoto; 58: North Wind Picture Archives / Alamy; 59: North Wind Picture Archives / Alamy; 60: (left) Eight Arts Photography / Alamy, (right) Medical-on-Line / Alamy; 61: Morgan Hill / Alamy; 62: (top) M Waits/Shutterstock, (middle) Kateryna Potrokhova /Shutterstock, (bottom) Reb/Fotolia; 65: Photos 12 / Alamy; 66: INTERFOTO / Alamy; 67: Source C www.learningcurve.gov.uk/empire/pdf/g3cslbkgd.pdf;

Chapter 4

68: Source A, © The Independent; 70: Mary Evans Picture Library; 71: modest life/Fotolia; 73: World Illustrated/Photoshot; 74: UPPA/Photoshot; 76: (top)The Print Collector / Alamy; (bottom) The National Trust Photolibrary / Alamy; 77: (top) North Wind Picture Archives / Alamy; (middle) UPPA/Photoshot; 78: VWPics/Photoshot; 79: Source C Peter Popham, © The Independent; 80: Uros Petrovic; 82: (left) INTERFOTO / Alamy; (right) Alan King Etching 07 / Alamy; 83: Mary Evans Picture Library; 84 Source C The National Army Museum website (www.national-army-museum.ac.uk/exhibitions/indiaRising/page11.shtml; Source D www.bbc.co.uk/history/british/victorians/indian_rebellion_05.html; (main spread image) Classic Image / Alamy; 86: Photoshot; Source A www.bl.uk/learning/langlit/texts/empire/delhi/1903.html; 87: Scott Latham/Fotolia; 88: Kettle, Tilly (1735-86) / Yale Center for British Art, Paul Mellon Collection, USA / The Bridgeman Art Library; 89: The Print Collector / Alamy; 90: Sydney Alvares/Fotolia; 91: Source E www.telegraph.co.uk/travel/destinations/asia/india/738715/Shimla-Indias-mountain-retreat.html; IMAGEPAST / Alamy; 92: HIP / The British Library
TopFoto.co.uk; 94: National Railway Museum/ Science & Society Picture Library; 95: The Granger Collection / TopFoto.co.uk; Source D www.nls.uk/indiapapers/plague.html; 97: Source C www.thehistorychannel.co.uk/site/encyclopedia/article_show/Salt-March_/m0028805.html; Sid Viswakumar/Fotolia; 98: (left) Trinity Mirror / Mirrorpix / Alamy; (right) Dinodia Images / Alamy; Source D www.thehistorychannel.co.uk/site/encyclopedia

Chapter 5

101: North Wind Picture Archives / Alamy; 105: Vladimir Wrangel/Fotolia; 106: (left) North Wind Picture Archives / Alamy; (right) Pictorial Press Ltd / Alamy; 107: The Trustees of the British Museum; 111: (upper) Sergey Kishan/iStock; (lower) Erik Kolstad/iStock; Source C www.hullwebs.co.uk; 112: The London Art Archive / Alamy; 115: Photos 12 / Alamy; 117: George Burba / Shutterstock; 118: graham tomlin/fotolia; 119: The Granger Collection / TopFoto.co.uk; 121: (top) Howard Sandler/Shutterstock (bottom)The Print Collector / Heritage-Images; 123: Source E www.antislavery.org; The Granger Collection / TopFoto.co.uk; 124: Bristol City Museum and Art Gallery, UK/ Bridgeman Art Library; 125: UPPA/Photoshot; 126: North Wind Picture Archives / Alamy; 127: Source B www.liverpoolecho.co.uk/views/liverpool-columnists/echo-columnists/2008/11/22/huge-impact-of-the-slave-trade-100252-22313095; 128: Lordprice Collection / Alamy; 129: (upper) The Granger Collection / TopFoto.co.uk; (lower) Wilberforce House, Hull City Museums and Art Galleries, UK/ Bridgeman Art Library; 130: UPPA/Photoshot; Source A Robert Nurden © The Independent; 131: Sean Wallace-Jones/fotolia; Source C www.thehistorychannel.co.uk/site/microsites/Abolition/index_microsite.php; 133: Reisbegeleider.com/fotolia; 134: (upper) Natasha Owen/fotolia; (lower) Dmitry Pichugin/fotolia; 135: Mary Evans Picture Library / Alamy; 136: Adrian Beesley/iStock; (inset) iStock; 137: Source H www.thehistorychannel.co.uk/site/encyclopedia/article_show/Suez_Canal/m0015494.html

Chapter 6

138: deadlyphoto.com / Alamy; 140: Balean / TopFoto.co.uk; 141: (upper) The Print Collector / Alamy; (lower) Mary Evans Picture Library / Alamy; 143: The Print Collector / Alamy; 145: (left) Steffen Hauser / botanikfoto / Alamy; (right) PCL / Alamy; 146: (left) Clearviewstock/Fotolia; (right) Mary Evans Picture Library / Alamy; 147: (upper) Mary Evans Picture Library / Alamy; (lower) Haur Sen Yew/Fotolia; 148: 19th Era / Alamy; 149: Fotolia X; 151: Shutterstock/Westbury & Gualtiero Boffi; 153: H. ARMSTRONG ROBERTS / ClassicStock / TopFoto.co.uk

Chapter 7

154: Fotolia; 155: Carsten Reisinger/Fotolia; Source B http://www.dailymail.co.uk/news/article-1068169/The-great-lie-How-immigration-actually-costs-Britain-money-cause-huge-social-problems.html; Source C www.fco.gov.uk/en/fco-in-action/institutions; 156/7: Robert Wilson/Fotolia; Source F www.telegraph.co.uk/news/newstopics/politics/lawandorder; 160: Gregory Wrona / Alamy; Source K http://www.guardian.co.uk/world/2008/sep/21/poland.nhs; http://www.timesonline.co.uk/tol/news/uk/article3378877.ece; 162: Trinity Mirror / Mirrorpix / Alamy; 163: UPPA/Photoshot;

Source A www.liverpoolmuseums.org.uk/maritime/archive/displayGuide.aspx; Source B http://www.channel4learning.com/support/programmenotes/netnotes/program/printyes/programid1070_printyes.htm; Source C http://www.casbah.ac.uk//surveys/archivereportGLAM.stm; 164: Beren Patterson / Alamy; 165: Entertainment Press; 166: Mary Evans Picture Library / Alamy; 167: UPPA/Photoshot; Source N http://www.independent.co.uk/news/uk/home-news/white-riot-the-week-notting-hill-exploded-912105.html; 168: David Hoffman Photo Library / Alamy